International Yearbook
for Research in Arts Education
Volume 2 (2014)

Waxmann Verlag GmbH
Steinfurter Straße 555, 48159 Münster
info@waxmann.com

# International Yearbook for Research in Arts Education

## Volume 2 (2014)

edited by
Larry O'Farrell, Shifra Schonmann and Ernst Wagner

Waxmann 2014
Münster • New York

"The World Summit on Arts Education 2013"
has been supported by the Stiftung Mercator.

**Bibliographic information published by die Deutsche Nationalbibliothek**
Die Deutsche Nationalbibliothek lists this publication in the
Deutsche Nationalbibliographie; detailed bibliographic
data is available in the Internet at http://dnb.d-nb.de

Print-ISBN     978-3-8309-3003-7
E-Book-ISBN    978-3-8309-8003-2

© Waxmann Verlag GmbH, 2014
www.waxmann.com
info@waxmann.com

Cover: Anne Breitenbach, Tübingen
Typesetting: Stoddart Satz- und Layoutservice, Münster
Print: Express Printing Service, Hong Kong

All rights reserved. No part of this publication may be reproduced, stored in
a retrieval system or transmitted in any form or by any means, electronic,
electrostatic, magnetic tape, mechanical, photocopying, recording or
otherwise without permission in writing from the copyright holder.

# Contents

Introduction ............................................................................................................9

Samuel Leong
Polylogue II World Summit on Arts Education 2013: An Overview .....................12

Christian Manhart
UNESCO's Present Position towards Arts Education ...........................................18

## Evaluation and Monitoring

Shifra Schonmann
On Evaluation .......................................................................................................23

Lode Vermeersch
The Evaluation of Public Policies on Arts Education:
Not just 'this-leads-to-that' ....................................................................................29

Michael Wimmer
Let us be brave! – Towards a Political Contextualisation
of Arts Education ..................................................................................................36

Susanne Keuchel
Arts Education Development Index (AEDI) –
A Comparative International Empirical Research
Approach in Arts Education ..................................................................................42

Tatiana Fedorova and Liubava Moreva
Arts Education in the CIS Countries: National Reports and Regional
Observatory on Promoting Creative Capacities in the XXI Century ....................52

Jan Jaap Knol
On the Mapping of Cultural Education in Europe and More ...............................57

Benedicte Helvad
Monitoring ...........................................................................................................63

Fianne Konings and Barend van Heusden
Evaluating Partnership, or how to Evaluate the Contribution of Cultural Institutions
to an Integrated Curriculum for Culture Education in Primary Schools .............66

Jessy Siongers, Dries Vanherwegen and John Lievens
The Multiple Layers of Arts Education in School .................................................79

## Competencies and Assessment

Ernst Wagner
The Concept of Competencies in Formal and Non-Formal Arts Education –
The Perspective of Research .................................................................................89

Eckart Liebau
Limitations of the Competence-Approach ............................................................93

*Ellen Winner, Thalia R. Goldstein and Stéphan Vincent-Lancrin*
Does Arts Education Foster Creativity? The Evidence so far ................................... 95

*Robin Pascoe*
Arts Assessment: A Need for Critical Engagement .............................................. 101

*Diederik W. Schönau*
Self-Assessment for Learning in Visual Arts Education ....................................... 107

## Arts Education and Education for Sustainable Development

*Samuel Leong and Ernst Wagner*
UNESCO & Arts Education for Sustainable Development –
An Introduction.................................................................................................. 113

*Yeon-hee Jung*
Expanding Sustainable Thinking through Arts Education ................................... 116

*Gerd Michelsen*
Education for Sustainable Development:
Status Quo and Perspectives ............................................................................... 121

*Ernst Wagner*
Arts Education and Education for Sustainable Development ............................... 130

## Arts Education and Peace Education

*Cynthia Cohen*
Linking Arts Education with the Field of
Peacebuilding and the Arts ................................................................................. 141

*Eugène van Erven*
Exploring the Peace Building Potential of Community Arts ................................ 146

*Wolfgang Dietrich*
Education for the Arts and the Peace"s" ............................................................. 149

*Anne Bamford and Matt Qvortrup*
Politics of the Soul: The Contribution of the Arts to Social Cohesion and Peace ........... 152

*Peter Harris*
'Playing' with 'Others' in a 'Neutral Zone':
*Intergroup Contact in the Aesthetic Space* ......................................................... 160

*Vedat Özsoy*
Arts Education and Violence in Schools ............................................................. 164

*Mousumi De*
Rethinking UNESCO's Commitment to Education for Peace and International
Understanding through Art: From the Bristol Seminar to the Seoul Agenda ............ 172

*Shifra Schonmann*
Arts for Peace Education:
False Reflections or a Real Chance for a Change? ............................................... 183

## Presentations given at The World Summit on Arts Education, Polylogue II, Wildbad Kreuth/Munich, Germany, May 2013

*Nicole Pereira and Ralph Buck*
Building Community Well-Being: Global and Local Policy Intersections ......................... 191

*Nicholas Rowe*
What Challenges face Students, Teachers and Researchers of Community Dance, within Cross-Cultural and Cross-Educational Contexts? A Sino-Kiwi Experience ......... 193

*Naomi Faik-Simet*
Undertaking Research for Dance Education ....................................................................... 196

*Lily Chen-Hafteck*
Educating the Creative Mind Project: Bringing Arts-Based Education
to Every Child ........................................................................................................................ 198

*Andrea Creech*
Community Opera in a Centre of Excellence: An Instrumental Case Study ..................... 200

*Ann Kipling Brown, Susan R. Koff, Jeff Meiners and Charlotte Svendler Nielsen*
Dance Learning in Motion: Global Dance Education ......................................................... 203

*Susan A. O'Neill*
Engagement in the Arts ......................................................................................................... 204

*Patricia A. González Moreno*
Creating and Fostering Partnerships to enhance Arts Education:
Challenges and Opportunities .............................................................................................. 208

*Sergio Figueiredo*
Why Advocacy? Music and Arts Education in the Brazilian Context ................................ 210

*Samia ElSheikh and Mai Nour*
Curriculum Development and Change are a Need to the Community in Egypt ............... 214

*Galyna P. Shevchenko*
Improving the Quality of Artistic Education through Interaction of Different
Kinds of Art: The Experience of Ukraine ............................................................................. 216

*Teresa Torres de Eça*
Comparangoleiros: A Transnational Arts Education Project ............................................. 219

## An Artist Reflects

*Judith Marcuse*
An Artist's Odyssey: Adventures in Art and Education ...................................................... 225

Contributors ........................................................................................................................... 233

# Introduction

The editors are pleased to introduce the 2014 INRAE Yearbook following the inaugural edition of last year. INRAE (The International Network for Research in Arts Education) was established through a collaboration of UNESCO Chairs and Observatories in the field. The current edition focuses on a number of important issues and opportunities that are becoming increasingly important to arts education.

Many of the articles in this publication originated in presentations that were given at The World Summit on Arts Education, Polylogue II, a conference involving 134 participants from around the world. This event was held at the Wildbad Kreuth conference centre near Munich Germany between May 13 and 17, 2013. It was organized by the World Alliance for Arts Education (WAAE) together with INRAE and the European Network of civil servants working in the field of Arts and Cultural Education (ACEnet). It was hosted by the German Federation for Arts Education and Cultural Learning (BKJ) and the UNESCO Chair in Arts and Culture in Education, Friedrich-Alexander University Erlangen-Nuremberg. This event was generously supported by the German Ministry for Family Affairs, Senior Citizens, Women and Youth, the Hanns Seidel Foundation, the City of Munich and the Mercator Foundation.

The World Summit was organized around three central topics: Evaluating, Mapping/Monitoring and Competencies. The evaluation theme examined the question of quality in curricula, non-formal programs and student achievement with a particular reference to the three goals of the *Seoul Agenda* (access, quality, social dimension). The mapping/monitoring theme provided a transnational perspective on the *Seoul Agenda* with respect to the potential for monitoring the application of this action plan in every country. The theme of artistic and cultural competencies in formal and non-formal arts education was concerned with the shaping and implementation of this concept in curricula in formal education as well as in methods and programs outside of school in non-formal education. These themes are reflected in two of the major divisions of this volume, one of which is Evaluation and Monitoring while another is Competencies and Assessment. A commitment to monitoring implementation of arts education globally is central to the mission of INRAE. Following the World Summit, the organizers collaborated with the UNESCO Institute for Statistics (UIS) in Montreal, Canada in the preparation of a workshop on monitoring held in March of 2014 at UIS headquarters and for a subsequent planning meeting hosted by the UNESCO Chair in Arts and Learning at Queen's University in Kingston, Canada.

Participants at the World Summit took the opportunity to discuss current issues that were of increasing importance to the field of arts education. A result of this dialogue was a decision to explore ways in which the work of INRAE could be more closely integrated into the major programs of UNESCO, notably Education for All, Education for Sustainable Development and Peace Education. With this recommendation in mind, the editors have introduced two other broad divisions in the Yearbook – Education for Sustainable Development and Peace Education. In this context two contributions by UNESCO chairs from these respective fields must be highlighted, the one of the German UNESCO Chair "Higher Education for Sustainable Development" and the other of the Austrian UNESCO Chair for Peace Studies. The theme of Peace Education was extended beyond the World Summit with the development of plans to inaugurate the International Arts for Peace Festival in Hong Kong in May of 2014. Collaborating organizers of this event include the UNESCO Observatory for Local Cultures and Creativity in Education, UNESCO-Hong Kong, UNESCO Chairs in Canada and Germany, the World Alliance for Arts Education and INRAE.

Yet another aspect of the World Summit to affect the structure of this Yearbook was a section of the Summit program entitled Pecha Kucha. It provided an opportunity for participants to present brief overviews of their current work. Several of these presentations were later developed into papers for inclusion in the book. The origin of these contributions, in the Pecha Kucha format, explains why some of the papers in this edition are relatively short. The editors have included these summaries to reflect the diversity of work being done in the field.

The members of INRAE continue to collaborate on advancing the major themes of this Yearbook. The monitoring workshop in Montreal and the launching of the Arts for Peace Festival in Hong Kong are excellent examples of this kind of cooperation. In addition, we are already making plans for the next INRAE Yearbook which will be edited by Dr. Shifra Schonmann, following a unique anthology approach that was pioneered in the preparation of her 2010 publication, *Key concepts in Theatre/Drama Education* and announced in the last chapter of the yearbook's volume 1.

## Editorial Board

Skye Burn, Executive Director, the Flow Project, Bellingham, Washington USA

Andrea Creech, Senior Lecturer in Education, the Institute of Education, London

Samuel Leong, Professor and Associate Dean (Quality Assurance & Enhancement) of the Faculty of Liberal Arts and Social Sciences, The Hong Kong Institute of Education. Director, UNESCO Observatory for Research in Local Cultures and Creativity in Education

Eckart Liebau, Professor and holder of the UNESCO Chair in Arts and Culture in Education at Friedrich-Alexander University Erlangen-Nuremberg, Germany

Laura McCammon, Professor, Teacher Certification Program Coordinator, School of Theatre, Film & Television, University of Arizona in Tucson

Larry O'Farrell, Professor Emeritus and holder of the UNESCO Chair in Arts and Learning, Queen's University, Canada

Aud Berggraf Saebo, Professor in drama, the University of Stavanger, Norway

Shifra Schonmann, Professor ha'ver, Hanan Bar-Netzer Endowed Chair, Education, Society and Theatre for Young People at the University of Haifa, Israel

Ernst Wagner, UNESCO Chair in Arts and Culture in Education at Friedrich-Alexander University Erlangen-Nuremberg, Germany

Max Wyman, Cultural critic, policy advisor, former President, Canadian Commission for UNESCO

Samuel Leong

# Polylogue II World Summit on Arts Education 2013: An Overview

## Introduction

The Polylogue II World Summit on Arts Education saw over 130 arts and culture leaders, researchers and practitioners from 40 countries gathered at Munich and Wildbad Kreuth, Germany, May 13-17, 2013[1].

The rich programme kicked off with an evening reception at the historic Town Hall of Munich, followed by visits to arts education institutions and projects in Munich that showcase a great variety of real-world examples of education *in* the arts and education *through* the arts. The gathering moved from Munich to Wildbad Kreuth, where all academic activities were held including opportunities for delegates to share information through Roundtables[2] and Pecha Kucha[3] presentations.

## Main Themes

Three main themes were focussed during this world event:
- **Evaluating** what is quality in curricula, non-formal programmes, student's achievement in respect to the three goals of UNESCO's *Seoul Agenda* (access, quality, social dimension).
- **Artistic and Cultural Competencies** in formal and non-formal arts education.
- **Mapping/Monitoring** arts education in a transnational perspective concerning the three goals of UNESCO's *Seoul Agenda* (access, quality, social dimension).

Each theme was addressed by three keynote speakers and the main discussion points of roundtables are summarised below:

## Theme 1: Issues Relevant to Evaluating Quality

Use of terminology: Different understandings of terminology can lead to confusion, e.g. assessment and evaluation are sometimes used interchangeably, sometimes understood as distinctly different concepts.
Purpose: Goals, aims and objectives of the programme need to be clear so that they can be evaluated.

- Why are we carrying out the evaluation? reflective practice through feedback, change practice, influence policy, accountability for parents and other stakeholders. Major part of evaluation purpose could be to feed back to teacher training and artists in the community
- What is being evaluated? E.g. classroom effectiveness (behaviour, attainment etc.), should take account of school ethos, quality, space. Evaluation is dependent on many variables so the purpose needs to be clear. Evaluation should also be relevant and useful, contributing to sustainability.

Methods for evaluation: Evaluation tools need to be aligned with purpose and be rigorous.
- Criteria should allow for evaluation of creativity and evaluation needs to be flexible enough to capture unintended learning outcomes.
- Qualitative and quantitative research approaches need to inform criteria for assessment in the arts.
- Multiple approaches are needed and they should consider such as process versus product, different arts disciplines and regions, and the embodied nature of arts learning.
- Who does the evaluation? Students, teachers, researchers, civil servants, community members, internal versus external, peer evaluation, school senior leadership having major stake in the evaluation. Partnership approaches to evaluation and self evaluation are important.

Contextual issues: Transnational evaluation should consider different contexts including socioeconomic factors. A useful approach is to use the global criteria from the *Seoul Agenda* to different countries, regions, and contexts.
- Considerations for teacher education should include: Why arts education is important, what teachers value, and what are the philosophical frameworks?
- For the evaluation of arts education outside formal contexts, considerations should include its purpose, who evaluates what and why.


**Recommended Actions to take:**

- Evaluation tools should be designed so as to convince a range of government departments of the value of arts education.
- Models of best practice in evaluation should be disseminated more widely, e.g. OECD
- Existing networks such as WAAE should facilitate the sharing of evaluation approaches and comparative studies, development of internationally understood criteria.
- Start to define quality criteria from a transnational perspective, avoiding eurocentric approaches.
- Networks should collaborate to find common ground, speaking with one voice as advocates.

## Theme 2: Artistic and Cultural Competencies

<u>Need for new competencies</u>: There was some scepticism, even resentment regarding the need to discuss competencies and what would be gained by such discussions. On the other hand, there is a general consensus on the urgency and necessity for a global change that recognises how the nature of learning and teaching has changed radically under the influence of our globalized, diversified, and digitalized society.

<u>Key issues</u>:
- <u>Notion of competency</u>: A "too Western" approach, the term has been questioned and has its limits. Would be better to focus on the "aims" as a starting point: what children/individuals need to *learn* (curriculum) versus what they need to be *capable of* doing (learning outcomes). Challenge of translating "competencies" to "what a student can do" and relationships and expectations between teachers and students should be considered. To clarify who these competencies are for, we should consider:
    – learners: children/pupils, youngsters/students, adults etc.
    – teachers: teachers in general, specific arts teachers; cultural/artist educators in non-formal settings; artists in general.

Often these categories are interlinked.

- <u>Notion of the new "learner"</u>: Invests in own education by bringing in own interests, i.e. creating own educational path and self-discovery of identity through the arts, with own culture ultimately leading to diversity and understanding of other cultures.

- <u>Notion of "school"</u>: This has to evolve with adjusted curricula to cater for the emerging student/learner so as to bridge the gap between school and everyday life. It should start from common values/principles: inclusiveness, diversity, quality, arts and culture as a universal right for all. Noted evolutions in educational systems all over the world that include the traditional formal curriculum inside school with non-formal outside school and the newer integration of informal within the formal curriculum inside schools/during school time. Would the latter approach require different competencies? How to implement this? Should there be a combination of both, a so-called "third way"?

- <u>Notion of "artistic & cultural competencies"</u>
    – Difficulties in defining and describing them.
    – "Artistic" competencies are "cultural" by definition.
    – All the arts hold social, cultural and embodied ways of knowing.
    – Competencies ≠ *skills*; competency includes skills, knowledge, ability, attitude etc.
    – *Attitude* may include creativity and imagination, "being open to unknown" etc.
    – May be both domain- and context-specific (formal vs. non-formal), although there can be overlaps or similarities.
    – Artistic or cultural competencies can entail or produce other skills.

- Should consider differences at the global scale: holistic view vs. a demarcation of disciplines or art systems. Do these entail a separation of competencies or integration and separate treatment?

**Recommended Actions to take:**

- Undertake research of teaching and learning methods/approaches in formal, non-formal and informal settings
- "How to measure the immeasurable": The arts are another way of producing knowledge and should not try to conform to scientific methodologies but develop our own appropriate research methodology – interdisciplinary, transnational etc.
- Create means for sharing research – criteria for publication, synthesis, identify existing resources for publishing, use new media etc.
- Identify indicators for arts and cultural competencies, and recognize criteria for competencies
- Provide space for dialogue regarding social responsibility of research given interdisciplinary and transnational nature of cultural, arts education and cultural education research
- Mapping what overlap and arts systems/disciplines
- Teacher training: general and cultural or arts specific
- Transfer of competencies, e.g. through partnerships: artists in residence, cultural exchanges, arts in business (design, architecture etc.) – channelled by invested parties (i.e., government, UNESCO, ministries)
- Undertake project on individual learning paths: learner determines own trajectory of education; invests self and decides on chosen path
- Experiment: provide space for exploring arts as spiritual practice
- Teach/show/establish advantages of seeing the world through the eyes of art
- Evaluating: gather examples of different ways of evaluating; undertake integrated projects; evaluation tools should be developed by communities that implement them
- Identify goals: influence legislation; financial support; community support.

## Theme 3: Monitoring/Mapping Arts Education

- <u>All monitoring projects should have clear</u>:
  - Aims and scope (size, depth, breadth).
  - Definitions and consistent use of terms.
  - Relevance and significance in different cultural contexts.
  - Relevance to specific audiences.
  - Review of literature and existing data.
  - Methodology – including consideration of the most suitable methods in respect to who the research target is, e.g., young persons, teachers, artists.
  - Transparent analysis and conclusions.
  - Monitoring must respect practitioners and value their voice.

- Methodologies can close the gaps between theory and practice, academics and grass roots practitioners.
- Reflect on the dominant paradigms defining the research ethics, methods, findings, and consider implications for the teacher, communities, and children in diverse contexts.
- Diverse monitoring projects with diverse methods are equally valuable, e.g., longitudinal, case study narratives, practice based/led projects.
- Do current monitoring infrastructures and systems exist? E.g., do UNESCO Observatories have a role and value in facilitating monitoring? Similarly does ACEnet and other organizations have a role?
- Advocacy is best when it is based on evidence based research. (Noting that evidence comes in diverse forms). Research needs to include local and global projects that accept 'inconvenient truths' or findings.
- A standard taxonomy of terms needs to be developed (definitions made clear and used consistently).

- <u>How does monitoring support relationships between children and</u>: arts education, teachers, families, institutions/systems, cultural traditions and children and learning (on-line, in classroom, in community)?
- Arguments for arts education should positively articulate the role of the arts across society, especially in economic terms; remembering, however, that data are never enough and stories also have power.
- International mapping can be used as a tool to get information about what is going on and to find out about shared beliefs and differences.
- <u>Risks of mapping and monitoring</u>:
  - Data can be interpreted in many ways.
  - Difficult to compare different systems etc.
  - It can lead to the creation of "mono-culture".
- Why make rankings? Can be used to bring more funding to education.

**Recommended Actions to take:**

- Rankings should be made based on both quantitative and qualitative data:
  - Aims and goals should define what we should do in arts education and how we should map what is going on?
  - Are there global values of arts education?
    ~ Yes, but there is the risk of creating a "mono-culture"
    ~ Respect for diversity, philosophies etc.
- Consider how to make a global database of information but which is not presented in an interpreted form:
  - Solutions to language issues should be considered.
  - What kinds of document should be in there?

## Notes

1. Polylogue II was co-organized by the International Net for Research in Arts Education (INRAE), the World Alliance for Arts Education (WAAE), the European Arts and Cultural Education Network (ACEnet), supported by the German Federation for Arts Education and Cultural Learning (Bundesvereinigung Kulturelle Kinder- und Jugendbildung), the UNESCO Chair in Arts and Culture in Education at Friedrich-Alexander University Erlangen-Nuremberg, the German Commission for UNESCO, German Ministry for Family Affairs, Senior Citizens, Women and Youth, the City of Munich, Stiftung Mercator Foundation, and Hanns Seidel Foundation.
2. Participants were to come with issues and ideas relevant to the theme, and be willing to share these. They were invited to provide perspectives and offer information from around the table including contrasting views, issues from diverse cultures and contexts, existing projects or activity that demonstrate good practice, discussion that deepens insight into specific issues. The round table discussions were meant to:
   - deepen and widen participants understanding of diverse issues.
   - give participants of the different groups the opportunity to discuss the themes further, and start 'translating' the themes to their own working domain.
   - develop networks of persons who have experience or insights that may be helpful beyond the summit.
   - produce recommendations that will assist (WAAE, INRAE, ACEnet) carry out strategic planning and action.
   - possibly identify 'leaders' who want to activate projects within the organisations.
3. Summit delegates were also treated to a unique sharing of 22 Pecha Kucha presenters featured in "Windows to the Diverse World of Arts Education". Each of the session was limited to six minutes, and they provided a succinct overview of key messages of a range of projects from different parts of the world. They encompass perspectives from the various art forms of dance, drama, music and visual arts and from countries including the UK, USA, Canada, Australia, New Zealand, Ghana, Uganda, Ukraine, Aruba, Egypt, Hong Kong and Thailand.

Christian Manhart
# UNESCO's Present Position towards Arts Education

Since its creation over 60 years ago, UNESCO has worked to mobilize the international community to support educational and artistic activities, with the aim to enhance dialogue and build peace among the people. Art is a tool for tolerance, social cohesion and peace building in our multicultural, connected societies. Young people must be taught to love and practice art: it will make them understand each other better. This love of art can be acquired from early childhood and maintained throughout all the life. It is our conviction that learning about creativity and the arts contributes to the building of prosperous and peaceful societies. Therefore, UNESCO encourages its Member States to support arts education, at school level and beyond.

The two **World Conferences on Arts Education**, held in Lisbon in 2006 and Seoul in 2010 helped to define clear objectives and strategies to achieve quality arts education for all. Lisbon gathered 1200 participants from 97 countries to share their experiences and practices. Seoul was attended by 650 participants from 95 countries, who adopted the **Seoul Agenda** as a concrete plan of action. It has been translated into the six official languages and is available on the UNESCO website under http://www.unesco.org/new/fileadmin/MULTIMEDIA/HQ/CLT/CLT/pdf/Seoul_Agenda_EN.pdf.

In order to give art and creation the place they deserve at the heart of society, in 2011 the General Conference of UNESCO proclaimed the fourth week of May as **International Arts Education Week**, to appeal to all UNESCO's partners, in particular governments, educational institutions and citizens around the world to celebrate the arts and their unique role in stimulating cultural diversity, dialogue and social cohesion. The week of **21-27 May 2012** marked the first edition of this Arts Education Week. Celebrations were held at UNESCO Headquarters with various activities including a workshop, a symposium, a ceremony and exhibitions. It gathered arts education specialists, artists, educators, researchers and NGO actors from all over the world. This first edition was co-organized with the Government of the Republic of Korea that also provided its generous financial support. UNESCO wishes to thank the Korean Government for their continued interest without which our Arts Education activities would not be possible.

However, in 2013 UNESCO was not in a position to organize such an event, due to its **current financial crisis**. In the field of culture, Member States decided to allocate the remaining regular budget for culture mainly to the 6 international cultural conventions and not to creativity and arts education. This unfortunately also means that only very reduced staff time is available for this programme, which previously had one person working full time.[1]

Thanks to extra-budgetary resources, UNESCO is still able to carry out some activities in arts education:

The UNESCO Bangkok office coordinates a **Network of Arts Education Observatories in Asia and the Pacific** in partnership with six specialized institutions in Hong Kong, Singapore, Kazakhstan, Korea, Australia and New Zealand.

The **UNESCO Moscow** Office implements a project "Arts Education in CIS countries: Building Creative Capacities for XXI Century" (with IFESCCO Intergovernmental Foundation for Educational, Scientific and Cultural Cooperation) to conduct analytical studies to identify main trends and prospects of arts education in CIS countries (Russia, Belarus, Armenia, Moldova, Kazakhstan, Uzbekistan).

Currently two **UNESCO Chairs** have been established in the field of arts education. The first established in 2007 at Queen's University, Ontario, Canada and the second in 2010 at the Friedrich-Alexander-University Erlangen-Nuremberg, Germany.

Also other programmes are implemented in favour of the arts and in particular to help young artists and craftspeople:

The **IFPC**, a quite old UNESCO Funds-in-Trust created by Member States was closed for many years. We revived it in 2012 with the establishment of a new Administrative Council and the set up of new statutes and operational guidelines. The first appeal for projects was launched from 1 March to 2 May 2013, which will be continued on a yearly basis. This Fund targets in particular young artists and designers 18–30 years old, to help them launching their career. But it can also support public and private institutions working with/for young artists. The Fund can contribute in a range between $10.000 and $100.000. We received some 1500 projects (half of them at the last two days before closing!) and 9 out of them were after a careful selection process finally chosen by the Administrative Council and received financial support.

The **UNESCO-Aschberg Bursaries for Artists** are designed to promote the mobility of young artists 25–35 years old, to improve their personal perspectives and develop a creative project by offering residencies worldwide. The focus is on creative writing, music and visual arts. Since 1994, over 700 fellowships in 149 institutions from 72 countries were awarded.

In partnership with the French Foundation "**Culture et Diversité**" for the project "Travel to learn the professions of the arts" we finance study tours for young designers and craftsmen and women from France to developing countries and vice-versa, in order to discover the artistic knowhow of other peoples. The main target groups are disadvantaged youth with the purpose of fostering equality of chances.

Finally, I wish also to mention UNESCO's **Creative Cities Network.** It consists presently of 41 Member Cities and 40 under evaluation. There are **seven** creative industry categories: **Literature, Film, Music, Crafts and Folk Art, Design, Media arts and Gastronomy.** This network has been launched in 2004 by UNESCO's Executive Board. Creativity and culture are playing an increasingly important role in urban renewal, and can be essential tools in solving today's urban challenges. We have recently received extra-budgetary funding for this programme from two Chinese cities, Beijing and Shenzhen.

Now we have to find ways to create synergies between these programs and those of the INRAE network, in order to find innovative and creative ways of responding to the challenges of contemporary societies by **building bridges** among people of different cultures, identities and beliefs.

## Editors's Note

INRAE understands that, during the General Conference held in November, 2013, the representatives of a number of National Commissions spoke highly about the importance of arts education. Unfortunately, however, the necessary budgetary changes were not enacted with the result that the Section of Museums and Creativity is now being dismantled, a process that will take several months. While this outcome may be disappointing for arts educators, it appears that arts education will continue to have a presence at UNESCO, notwithstanding the closing of this section. In a recent meeting with Mr. Christian Manhart, author of this chapter, INRAE learned that arts education is still mentioned in UNESCO's 4 year programme although without any Regular Funding. This means that activities will be undertaken only if extra-budgetary funds are provided by donors and that no regular staff will be working for this programme, only staff that would be financed under these extra-budgetary resources. Arts education will be situated under the umbrella of the 2005 Convention. This will take several months. Further information will be circulated when it is available.

Meanwhile, the UNESCO Chairs and Observatories in the field (which are funded by their host institutions, rather than by UNESCO) continue to work together to promote and monitor *the Seoul Agenda: Goals for the development of arts education*, and we continue to make plans to celebrate the International Week of Arts Education in the fourth week of May each year.

# Evaluation and Monitoring

Shifra Schonmann

# On Evaluation

## In Praise of Ambiguity and Clarity in Questioning what is Quality Arts Education?

## Opening

To introduce the viewpoint *On Evaluation* in only 2500 words (authors' request) reminds me of the old Jewish story about a Gentile who came before a Rabbi and said to him: *"Rabbi, convert me – but on condition that you teach me the whole Torah (Bible) while I stand on one foot"* (i.e very, very quickly). Shammai, for that was the name of the Rabbi, pushed him aside.

So that fellow went to another Rabbi; he was called Hillel and was known for his skill in facilitating things. The man came before Hillel and said: *"Rabbi convert me – but on the condition that you teach me the whole Torah (Bible) while I stand on one foot"*. Hillel was also about to push him away, but then he reconsidered, converted him, and uttered the famous sentence: *"That which is despicable (disgraceful) to you, <u>do not do</u> to your fellow man. This is the whole Torah, and the rest is commentary. Go and learn it."*

What I am trying to convey is that at the beginning, when I was trying to wrestle with the complexity of evaluation, I felt like Shammai, I was inclined to reject the attempt to articulate such an elusive concept, but then, like Hillel, I gave it another thought and the following is my try:

Evaluation in arts education is an impossible mission yet we should strive to make constant efforts to find solutions to carry out this mission.

This is a kind of paraphrase of the words of Scott Fitzgerald who said:

*"The test of a first-rate intelligence is the ability to hold two opposing ideas in the mind at the same time, and still retain the ability to function. One should, for example, be able to see that things are hopeless and yet be determined to make them otherwise."* (1936)

## Revisiting the Known by new Questions

We have all read or even written a chapter in the last handbook of *Research of Arts Education*, edited by Bresler (2007); we have all read or written reports on program evaluation, on classroom assessment; we all know current theories and their relevance to arts education and still can learn more, for example, from the *International Yearbook for Research in Arts Education,* edited by Liebau, Wagner and Wyman (2013). So much has been said already, written and spoken by our colleagues that I am afraid I cannot introduce news in the classical sense, **but I can revisit** (on one foot, so to speak) the ideas and topics which are **already known**, and **reframe** our knowledge within the struggle to hold ambiguity <u>and</u> clarity in the mind at the same time, and still retain the ability to function.

If this is the situation and we permit ourselves to revisit the known, I can try to raise doubts and ask questions, to set up anew the building blocks of knowledge (i.e. the questions) and to provide food for thought for further discussions. After almost fifty years of quite notable developments in the field of research in arts education we can ask:
- Do we really need to define what quality arts education is? Why is such a question not asked in the sciences? Why do the science disciplines not have to prove anything and the arts do?
- Can we say that there is a productive tension between the individual arts disciplines and the larger arena that is referred to as "arts" and "arts education"?
- Can we say that the individual disciplines have maintained their distinctive identities, organizations, traditions, specific skills and areas of practice and scholarship?

For many teachers and artist-educators *assessment* and *evaluation* are integral in the refinement and reflection of arts practices. What has been changed during the last decades is that the discussion now takes place under the gaze of other educators, and the scrutiny of the public at large. So, the question to be asked is this:
- How do we take the experience of practice and accepted <u>implicit</u> value of assessing the arts in educational contexts, and make assessment practices <u>explicit</u> and articulate to the public?

As we seek to evaluate both the art experience of individuals (be it dance or music or other forms of art) and the overall effects and effectiveness of art education programs, we can ask:
- How should we evaluate the hermeneutic circle of interrelationship of participants to programs?

In the field of evaluation, a great deal of talk has been about <u>change,</u> and substantial attempts have been made to introduce new practices.

My point is that evaluation in arts education is such a fundamental activity rooted in the practitioner's work that sometimes even leading figures in the field are not aware that the topic of evaluation stands at the core of understanding the nature of the field and the ways in which we want to develop its horizons. Exploring the interplay between the teachers, the students, the art (any form of it) as a subject in a defined context of school or any other educational context is a basis for constructing modes of knowing as inner structures of knowledge in use, leading to possible answers regarding what is quality arts education.

The following are observations on two main issues: ***language and curriculum,*** in an attempt to lead to clear premises and flexible approaches to quality arts education.

## Language

In the endless wrestling between ambiguity versus clarity in dealing with issues in arts education, the language we use should be defined anew, in each context. For example, let's examine the terms *assessment* and *evaluation*.

Although the terms *assessment* and *evaluation* are often used interchangeably, Elliot Eisner (2002) explains that: "*assessment* generally refers to the appraisal of individual student performance, often but not necessarily on tests. *Evaluation* generally refers to the appraisal of the program – its content, the activities it uses to engage students, and the ways it develops thinking skills." (p. 178). Unlike **program** evaluation, which according to Posavac and Carey (1997) "is a collection of methods, skills, and sensitivities necessary to determine whether a human service is needed and likely to be used, whether the service is sufficiently intensive to meet the unmet needs identified," (p. 2), **assessing individual achievements** is based on a collection of chosen criteria to be used in deciding whether the performance of a student are proper or not. By the term *performance* I do not mean only the acting skills, but the entire student's executions in the discipline. The terms have no fixed meaning and thus, as said, the language we use should be defined anew, in each context.

However, the problem is not with the ways in which one uses one term or another, but with the ideological commitments that they expose. Different practices usually reflect different ideological commitments. My main claim would be that developing evaluation and assessment strategies is a manifestation of a wider conceptualization about life in schools in general, and about how arts education should be developed in the schools. We should ask ourselves how clear do we want to be about that? Maybe ambiguity at some stages can help?

Narrative accounts of teacher's practice indicate that teachers have to rely on what they call their "gut feeling" or "intuition" in addition to their experience. Lyn McGregor, for example, who wrestled with the notion of *standards* in drama in the 1980s, reports that a few pupils told her that they did not like drama because they were "not good at it". She claims that "unlike a number of teachers, the pupils recognized that there are forms of achievements in drama and that for various reasons some pupils are better than others" (McGregor, 1983, p. 125). These opinions voiced by the pupils go hand by hand with Elliot Eisner's (1993) eight criteria for creating what he calls "authentic assessment" by which he tries to reshape the idea of assessment, however, the ambiguity-clarity dichotomy still remained.

Ambiguity-clarity dichotomy is rooted inherently in our very basic term: "*arts* education".

What is arts education? Is there one an Arts Education program? No.

Is there any subject, or discipline that is considered as "arts"? No.

So why are we speaking about Arts Education and not about a particular discipline as we do in science? Maybe we should not be too keen to find theories that embrace *all* the arts?

In the context of praising clarity, we may say that Arts Education constitutes a broad range of academic disciplines and as a relatively new field in education we want to create a close intellectual and creative community. Our common goal is to make connections across the fields of learning. To nurture the intellectual skills of inquiry, analysis, argument, and to cultivate creative expression, all are needed for a meaningful life. However, in the context of accepting ambiguity, we should tolerate chaotic constellations that admit intuitive authentic and original processes of evaluation and assessment in practices.

When speaking about *implementing standards, what do we mean by standards?* If we want to fix standards for quality in aesthetic education we need to understand that the concept of standards is multifaceted. The term is attractive – the word, standards, implies high expectations. But in thinking of a standard meal, there is nothing to rave about as Eisner used to say (Eisner 1995; 1998 and 2002). Do we need standards at all? What do they imply? According to my understanding we should not create standards in arts education, but we *do* need to look for criteria. A statement that one particular work of art is better or of greater aesthetic value than another assumes that there are criteria by which one can arrive at such a conclusion. I believe it would *not* be an exaggeration to claim that many attempts to define good art or quality aesthetic experiences have failed. Nevertheless, when we speak about art it seems everyone knows what we mean; this understanding is echoed in a number of studies (See: Schonmann, 2007a and 2007b), and leads me to comment on the second issue, which is the curriculum and its practical concerns.

## Curriculum

Along with the critical questions that I have posed, I clearly take the realistic stand that only those subjects that can be properly evaluated can be treated seriously in the framework of a formal curriculum and other educational settings. Moreover, ever since the ancient Greeks instituted dramatic contests on the analogy of the Olympic Games, people have looked for ways of assessing works of art. We want to know what to respect and why, thus the question that we have to make our main concern is not *how do the arts educate?* But *how do we educate to appreciate the arts?*

Intentions and decisions about the contents (i.e. *what* to teach) and the methodologies (i.e. *how* to teach) characterize disciplinary knowledge. If this is the case, then it can be argued that arts in education do not stand out as a discipline in the traditional sense because there is no consensus as to what we actually teach in this field. Neither are there any common claims to any definite methodology.

Arts in education, then, do not seem to fulfill the two conventional criteria (*what* and *how*) necessary to define a discipline in education.

Thus the difficulties of assessing students' achievements or evaluating educational programs rise to a level that explicit or implicit discussions that took place in the field remain incomplete and without a conclusion, leaving us with no clear-cut tools to appreciate the value of the arts in the curriculum. Moreover, we should constantly bear in mind that arts taught in school differ in significant ways from arts as they are found in non-school locations.

So, where does this leave us? If we take the realistic stand, as mentioned before, that only the subjects that can be properly evaluated can be treated seriously in the framework of a formal curriculum and other educational settings, then we can try to define <u>premises</u> (as basis to the criteria), whose language will fit the logic of curriculum.

## Premises and Approaches

Thus in the continuing search for constructing appropriate assessment and evaluation in arts in education which, in essence, I see it as a search for identity, I have tried (in other works of mine, Schonmann 1997; 2007a; 2007b) to define premises whenever an attempt is made to assess a student's achievements and whenever an attempt is made to construct curriculum and evaluate its quality:
1. "One size" does not fit everyone. The metaphor implies that different learning styles call for different types of assessment/evaluation. (*difference*)
2. Information should be gathered on the basis of using several elements from many diverse sources. (*plurality*)
3. The many variables should serve as a check on one another and provide support for a more reliable assessment/evaluation. (*reliability*)
4. There is a need to define ethical principles to guide the assessment/evaluation procedures. (*ethics-values*)

These four premises offer us, in principle, an opportunity to develop flexible approaches to assessment and evaluation.

These premises have served me as building blocks for admitting three different **approaches** to assessment ranging from clarity to ambiguity:
1. <u>The directive approach</u>: *pointing out which learning action leads to an artistic and aesthetic "right" or "wrong".*
   This approach accepts the basic idea of defining goals and finding suitable means for achieving them. However, instead of detailed criteria to monitor the progress of the student this approach proposes phases to control the process, not the student. This model is in the spirit of Tyler (1950); it is very clear and it is linear.
2. <u>The dialectical approach</u>: *organizing and prioritizing values that are particular in the nature of the art (any form or aspect of art that is studied) over others via a set of dialectical questions that create a profile of the student's achievement.*
   The dialectical approach is designed around cluster of questions: How can one know or discover whether the students have undergone a change? The deliberation goes through a series of dialectic questions at the end of which a student's profile is reached. It is based on a constructivist pedagogy which is inherently connected to arts.
   Questioning as a tool for teaching and assessment is a known strategy (Hubbard & Miller, 1993).
3. <u>The chaotic approach</u>: *Chaos theory offers us a new set of metaphors with which to make sense of the world* – such as the flow of a river, the collapse of the Berlin Wall (Hancock 1995). The idea of chaos in arts education is actually allowing the chaotic non-linear process of evaluation to develop our mental image about quality in arts.

## Concluding Comment

Evaluation in arts in education is a constant search for **identity**, that is to say: what is actually arts education? Evaluation in arts education is a constant search for the best options to construct its status. Thus, developing the language of evaluation while trying to play judiciously with the curriculum, both with ambiguity and with clarity, is in fact refining the ability to hold two opposing ideas in the mind at the same time, and still retain the ability to function, to make constant efforts to find solutions to carry out the mission of evaluating what is quality arts education?

## References

Bresler, L. (Ed.) (2007). *International Handbook on Research in Arts Education*. New York: Springer.
Eisner, E. (1993). Reshaping assessment in education: some criteria in search of practice. *Journal of Curriculum Studies* Volume 25, Issue 3, pages 219-233.
Eisner, E. (1995). Standards for American Schools: Help or Hindrance? *PHI DELTA KAPPAN*, 76 (10), 758-760.
Eisner, E. (1998). *The Kind of Schools We Need*. Heinemann: Portsmouth, NH.
Eisner, E. (2002). *The Arts and the Creation of Mind*. New Haven: Yale University Press.
Fitzgerald, S. (1936). "The Crack-Up". http://www.esquire.com/features/the-crack-up
Hancock, A. (1995). Chaos in Drama: The Metaphors of Chaos Theory as a Way of Understanding Drama Process. *n.a.d.i.e Journal, 19*, 1, 15-26.
Hubbard, R. S. & Miller Power, B. (1993). *The Art of Classroom Inquiry*. New Hampshire: Heinemann.
Liebau, E., Wagner, E. and Wyman, M. (Eds.) (2013). *International Yearbook for Research in Arts Education*. Volume 1. Waxmann: Münster.
McGregor, L. (1983). Standards in Drama: Some Issues. In: C. Day & J. L. Norman (Eds.), *Issues in Educational Drama*. London: Falmer Press (pp. 123-133).
Posavac, E. J. & Carey, R. G. (1997). *Program Evaluation Methods and Case Studies*. NJ: Prentice-Hall.
Schonmann, S. (1997). How to recognize Dramatic Talent When You See It: And Then What? *The Journal of Aesthetic Education, 31*, 4, 7-21.
Schonmann, S. (2007a). Wrestling With Assessment in Drama Education. In L. Bresler (Ed.), *International Handbook on Research in Arts Education*. New York: Springer (pp. 409-422).
Schonmann, S. (2007b). Appreciation: The weakest link in Drama/Theatre Education. In L. Bresler (Ed.), *International Handbook on Research in Arts Education*. New York: Springer (pp. 587-600).
Tyler, R. W. (1950). *Basic Principles of Curriculum and Instruction*. Chicago: University of Chicago Press.

Lode Vermeersch

# The Evaluation of Public Policies on Arts Education: Not just 'this-leads-to-that'

*In this article we will briefly examine the practice of evaluation in arts education. First we will explain that evaluation in arts education is a complex and multifaceted practice and different types of evaluation can and do play a role. After having explored the issue of the evaluation of public policies on arts education in general, we will examine some of its most important components more closely.*

## Evaluation in Arts Education: A Complex and Multifaceted Concept

Educational practitioners, policy-makers as well as scholars in the field of arts education often rely on evaluation. The meaning of that concept is however not always made clear. As evaluation is a complex and multifaceted concept; there are several underlying dimensions, including the scale or level of the evaluation, the way the evaluation is being elaborated (e.g. qualitative vs. quantitative measurement), the techniques used (e.g. written test, survey, assignment, observation, participatory evaluation), the aim of the evaluation (summative vs. formative evaluation), the position of the evaluator (internal evaluator vs. independent external evaluator), and the moment of evaluation (prospective or exante evaluation, ongoing or process evaluation, retrospective or expost evaluation).

Here we want to discuss one of those key dimensions: the scale or level of evaluation (Lauret, 2009; Eisner, 2002). Put simply, an evaluation can be either small-scale or large-scale in terms of the people it affects. In the first case it assesses the act or performance of an individual or the outcome of this act or performance. This type of small-scale evaluation is usually called an 'assessment' and with regards to arts education it focuses on what the individual does (e.g. the learning, making, performing of a pupil) and what that effort leads to (e.g. a work of art). This type of evaluation can and should also take into account the context in which this happens, because for instance the context of a student-at-work is different from the context of a student's exhibition. Evaluation can also be broad-based when it describes and evaluates not the achievement of a single person but the performances of populations, for example an age group, or an organization such as a school or an arts organization. A large scale evaluation can even be nationwide, as is the case for some standardized tests for school-based arts education (Myford & Sims-Gunzenhauser, 2004).

The evaluation of a public policy or a policy measure can be considered broad-based because it evaluates the quality of an effort to make a successful decision for (many) others. Because policy decisions affect more than one single individual, policy evaluations are always large-scale evaluations even though they may depend on the study of one or a few cases. The policy effort under scrutiny in the evaluation procedure might be a single or even isolated policy measure, like a funding scheme for enhancing creative partnerships between schools and artists (Smith, 1977), but it just as well might refer to larger frameworks that govern specific decisions of policy-makers, such as a general policy discourse on the aims of artistic and cultural education (Hope, 2004).

## A Typology of Evaluation in Arts Education

In the table below we summarize some of the most important types of evaluation in the field of arts education according to the subject of evaluation (first row). Some types of small-scale evaluation are in the columns on the left while typical large-scale evaluation types are in the columns on the right (second row).

| What can be evaluated? | An artistic or cultural product | The artistic experience (cognitive and affective) or behaviour of an individual | The artistic experience (cognitive and affective) or behaviour of a group or population | Policy/policy measures concerning arts education | Educational system/process/material |
|---|---|---|---|---|---|
| Scale | Small-scale | Small-scale | Large-scale | Large-scale | Large-scale |
| Concept | Criticism Assessment | Individual assessment | Large-scale assessment or broad-based evaluation | Policy evaluation Policy Analysis | Curriculum evaluation Program or Project evaluation |
| At the center of evaluation | The artwork itself: *book, dance, song, play, ...* | The act or performance of the individual: learning or being able to… *Create Present Understand Reflect Teach* | The act or performance a group or population: learning or being able to… *Create Present Understand Reflect Teach* | A specific policy measure A specific funding scheme A strategy framework | Programs Curriculum Books Educational tools |
| Level of implementation | Students Artists | Students Participants/visitors of cultural institutions Artists Teachers Principals | Classes Schools Age groups | Policy makers Policy measures Policy programmes | Teachers Cultural institutions Publishers Etc. |
| Some typical ways of evaluating (evaluation design) | Criticism Public discourse on arts | Tests (assignments) Feedback | Tests Survey | Evaluation research Policy studies Policy analysis | Curriculum evaluation Self-evaluation |

| Some typical evaluation tools/techniques | Reviews Journals | Tests Interviews Portfolios Peer assessment tools Co-assessment tools | Tests Survey | SWOT-analysis Feasibility study Policy review Cost-benefit analysis | Reviews |
|---|---|---|---|---|---|
| Some quality aspects included in the evaluation | Originality? Technical quality? | Features of activity? What is learned? Is a certain level of attainment achieved? | General competence level? Comparison in-group and between-groups | Relevance? Efficiency? Effectiveness? Effect and impact? | Has the quality of education improved? |
| Aim of the evaluation | Judgment/ appraisal in order to make improvement | | | | |

Although all types of evaluation mentioned in the typology above are different, it is important to stress that they do have some things in common:
- the aim of appraisal and critique by providing well-established arguments (Majone, 1989);
- the idea that evaluation can stimulate improvement;
- the basis of information and evidence;
- the possibility to use several evaluation techniques and tools;
- the importance of a theoretical framework to frame and interpret the evaluation results.

In the next paragraph I will elaborate these elements specifically for the evaluation of policy and policy measures on arts education.

## Evaluating Public Policies on Arts Education: From Taking Temperature to Suggesting Treatment

### Appraisal and Critique

Evaluating a single piece of art could be described as an attempt to organize and analyze the complex elements of an aesthetic response. It is an attempt to make that response, which is initially preconceptual and more intuitive than logical, more conceptual and logical (Abbs, 1994). In its core, evaluating an arts education policy functions in a similar way. It is also a method for "drawing out the value" of a, in this case, policy strategy or measure in order to make some kind of judgment about it. The idea that a policy strategy or measure needs to be evaluated lies in the fact that we – sometimes *intuitively* – know there might be gaps between the different components of policy making and policy implementation. These components are: the policy objective and its relation to a real-life problem, the values embodied in the policy, the actual policy-based action that is implemented, the values that are expressed in the policy language that precedes or accompanies that action, the outcomes and actual impact of that policy-based action. Just like an artwork a policy on arts education can come up short on several aspects.

## Information and Evidence

Evaluation requires information that is collected and carefully examined. Collecting the right information or evidence is of utmost importance as a starting point for any evaluation, but it should not to be mistaken for the evaluation process itself. As Jörissen (2013) noted regarding policy evaluation in arts education, monitoring could be considered a first step; it is not the evaluation process itself. Monitoring is taking the temperature, not making a diagnosis or suggesting a treatment. For that both careful consideration and critical review of the collected data and information are needed.

## Techniques and Tools

In the making of art as well as in the making of policies there are several routes to "success". As a consequence, like the evaluation of a work of art or the assessment of the output of an artist or student, a policy evaluation can be conducted in several different ways. On a higher level, the domain of arts education itself is quite complex: there is a distinctive body of knowledge that is hard to be compared with any other subject or type of education, there are different dimensions in arts education (productive, reflective, critical, historical etc.), there is the arts education scene that is quite complex, the diverse ways of implementing a public policy, etc. (Bamford, 2013; Gardner, 1988; Smith, 2001). As a result, it is no surprise that evaluation matters can be approached in different ways and different formats and paradigms for inquiry are possible. Some of the most typical instruments for policy evaluation research are: cost-benefit analyses, risk-benefit analyses, project evaluations, impact estimation, feasibility studies, needs assessments, policy reviews, etc. (Castiglione, 1991). No matter which formats or tools are used, the final argumentation should always be embedded in thorough methodological investigations (Van der Knaap, 1995).

## Theoretical Framework

Because an evaluation leads to some kind of judgment or appraisal, all evaluation is value-bound or at least has some normative components (Nevanen et al., 2012). To gain insight into the values, the normative assumptions and the preferences embedded in the policy is essential in a policy evaluation (Bresler, 1998). If for instance a policy measure tries to foster the arts and cultural involvement of young people, it is key to know why policy-makers think that involvement is worth supporting. What is the reason (one or maybe several), and can we agree with it? Notwithstanding the fact that a policy analysis and policy evaluation cannot determine whose values are best, values are central to understanding the choices and decisions policy-makers make (Castiglioni, 1991). And because values or systems of values, norms, assumptions and preferences are not developed in a vacuum, it is important to know how different values and systems interact with each other (Hope, 2004; Van der Knaap, 1995). Disclosing the theoretical values embedded in a policy is one the evaluators first and hardest tasks.

> *"All policy, including arts policy, is created and executed in a political context and social environment. Consequently, it reflects all multiple conflicting factors that are inherent in, and characteristic of, human affairs. Representing this complexity coherently while avoiding either confusion or oversimplification is a difficult task."* (Castiglioni, 1991, p. 5)

## Policy Evaluation: A Critical Look at some Typical Ingredients

A public policy evaluation typically evaluates the nature, causes, processes, outcomes and effects and impact of a certain public policy that addresses a certain societal problem (Nagel, 1961). These are also the necessary ingredients for a solid evaluation of a public policy on arts education. For arts education, societal problems can relate to several things, but they are usually linked to: the way arts education is designed and planned (e.g. is there a coherent and sequential arts curriculum? How can we make sure that students learn basic arts knowledge and competences?), the way it is implemented in real life (e.g. are the arts educational practices in the classroom or in out-of-school classes effective practices?), or the outcomes or impact of arts education (e.g. do teachers know the purposes and possible effects of arts education? How can we make the arts more attractive in schools?).

An evaluation of a public policy on arts education can answer several questions. One question is that of relevance: is the proclaimed policy indeed really a policy, and is it one that is really needed? (Smith, 2001; Gonzalez Garibay & De Cuyper, 2013). This evaluation criterion implies that the arts education policy is specific enough, that the plan of action addresses a problem that really relates to arts education and not simply to arts or education or some other societal or political issues (Smith, 2001). This question is easily forgotten since the most common and perhaps most essential evaluation questions deal with effectiveness and efficiency. In essence, the question of effectiveness asks whether the effects of the policy are consistent with its aims and objective. The efficiency of an arts education policy raises the question whether or not the aims and objectives embedded in the policy are achieved, and if they are achieved in an efficient way.

Both effectiveness and efficiency are slippery notions in this field, both for policy makers and for evaluators of public policies (Smith, 2001; Eisner, 2002). Both terms imply the possibility to link inputs or resources (e.g. the amount of public funding spent on arts education, the staff that is responsible, the way a policy measure is shaped or even more general the system of schooling) directly to effects in terms of outcomes (e.g. amount of partnerships, amount of projects in schools) or in terms of impact (e.g. level of artistic skills in a school population). Although this model is important, it goes without saying that this type of thinking is not without any challenges or constraints. Establishing causality is just one of the elements that cause headaches among policy evaluators in the field (Schad & Wimmer, 2008). In arts education it is hard to identify all variables at stake (Smith, 2001) and there are a lot of inputs and outcomes that cannot be measured easily (e.g. people's motives to be interested in arts, their thinking about art, etc.) and a lot that *can* be measured but are hard to measure in a standardized way. It is therefore tempting for any evaluator to just look at things that can be measured and measure what is easy to measure. We also note that the discourse on arts education is often plagued by beautiful but quite vague words and complex concepts: arts, culture, passion, creativity, innovation, amazement, imagination, artistic research, play, … Broad, generic and often beautiful terms like that are needed to capture the full flavor of arts and arts education, but when imprecise and vague they are hard to use in an empirical evaluation. So the question of research design, terminology and operationalization are challenges.

In summary, it is certainly hard to tell the whole story of the quality of an arts education policy simply based on evidence about inputs and outcomes and "this-has-led-to-that" information. When done thoroughly, i.e. on the basis of a traditional rational-objectivist perspective and the right methodological skills, such investigation should provide forceful and hopefully relevant arguments to contribute to the quality of a policy. The result might, however, also be misleading because it is often not possible to have a fully neutral evidence-based policy evaluation based on an objective or "hard" way of framing facts about causes and effects, nor is it desirable (Majone, 1989; Van der Knaap, 1995). Every evaluation is to some extent subjective and context and interpretation must not be excluded, especially not in arts education. Therefore, we agree with Van der Knaap (1995) that a rational-objectivist perspective on evaluation should be complemented with an argumentative-oriented one.

We could conclude now that policy evaluation in arts education is a very complex and tricky matter, but our main message – if there should be one – is rather that in spite of those conclusions it still is very important. All the questions mentioned above, whether they are about relevance or effectiveness or efficiency, ultimately raise the question whether or not a public policy is qualitative and more desirable than any other alternative policy or even lack of policy. In the field of arts education that important question is still rarely asked and almost never answered (Bamford, 2013; Castiglioni, 1991; Hope, 2004; Schad & Wimmer, 2008).

## References

Abbs, P. (1994). *The educational imperative: A defense of Socratic and aesthetic learning.* New York: The Falmer Press.

Bamford, A. (2013). The Wow and what now? The Challenges of Implementation of Arts Education. In: Liebau, E., Wagner, E., & Wyman, M. (Eds.). *International Yearbook for Research in Arts Education, Volume 1.* Münster: Waxmann, 175-187.

Bresler, L. (1998). Research, Policy, and Practice in Arts Education: Meeting Points for Conversation, *Arts Education Policy Review*, 99 (5), 9-15.

Castiglione, L.V. (1991). Evaluating Policy Analyses in Arts Education and Art, *Design for Arts in Education*, 92 (6), 2-12.

Eisner, E. (2002). *The Arts and the Creation of Mind*. New Haven: Yale University Press.

Gardner, H. (1988). *Art, Mind and Brain: A Cognitive Approach To Creativity*. New York/Oxford: Basic Books.

González Garibay, M. & De Cuyper, P. (2013). *An evaluation framework for the Flemish integration policies*. HIVA-KULeuven: Leuven.

Hope, S. (2004). Art education in a world of cross-purposes. In: Eisner, E. W. & Day, M. D. (Eds.). *Handbook of research and policy in art education*. Mahwah, NJ: Lawrence Erlbaum and Assoc., 87-91.

Jörissen, B. (2013). Definition and Concepts of Monitoring and Evaluation. In: Liebau, E., Wagner, E., & Wyman, M. (Eds.). *International Yearbook for Research in Arts Education, Volume 1*. Münster: Waxmann, 99-101.

Lauret, J.-M. (2009). *European Agenda for Culture. Open Method of Coordination. Working Group on developing synergies with education, especially arts education. Intermediate report*. European Commission.

Majone, G. (1989). *Evidence, Argument, and the Persuasion in the Policy Process*. New Haven, CT: Yale University Press.

Myford, C. M., & Sims-Gunzenhauser, A. (2004). The evolution of large scale assessment programs in the visual arts. In: Eisner, E. W. & Day, M. D. (Eds.). *Handbook of research and policy in art education*. Mahwah, NJ: Lawrence Erlbaum and Assoc., 637-666.

Nagel, E. (1961). *The Structure of Science*. Harcourt, Brace & World: New York.

Nevanen, S., Juvonen, A., Ruismäki, H. (2012). Qualitative evaluation processes in arts educational projects, *Procedia – Social and Behavioral Sciences*, 45, 548-554.

Schad, A. & Wimmer, M. (2008). The cultural policies of arts education – a policy analysis approach, paper prepared for the 5th International Conference on Cultural Policy (ICCPR), Istanbul.

Smith, R. A. (2001). Formulating a Defensible Policy for Art Education, *Theory into Practice*, 23 (4), 273-279.

Smith, R. A. (1977). A policy Analysis and Criticism of the Artist-in-Schools Program of the National Endowment for the Arts, *Art Education*, Vol. 30 (5), 12-19.

Van der Knaap, P. (1995). Policy Evaluation and Learning: Feedback, Enlightenment or Argumentation?, *Evaluation: International journal of theory, research and practices*, 1 (2), 189-216.

Michael Wimmer

# Let us be brave! – Towards a Political Contextualisation of Arts Education

During these days we are confronted with disturbing reports mainly from Southern European countries making clear the extent of the decline of the living and working conditions of broad sections of the population. Is it the increase of unemployment rates among young people up to an incredible 60%? Is it the lowering of the purchasing power of ordinary people, the increase in suicide rates or in drug consumption or is it the rise of radical political movements? The message is clear: This part of Europe is facing a relapse of social achievements and with it the continent as a whole is entering a period of growing social fractures. After the unification of the East and the West it may even fall apart again and this time the fracture lines run from North to South as well as from the rich to the poor or those who are (still) visible in the public arena and those who aren't any more.

The hazard of the European welfare states has also consequences for the cultural and educational sector when it is confronted with massive cuts of public and private support. A recent report on the decline in bookshops in the heart of Athens brought it – at least for me – to the conclusion that, because of the disastrous economic situation, Greeks can less and less afford to buy books. The result is a mass extinction of bookstores that can no longer survive without customers. Here we find just one piece of evidence that the conditions of the cultural infrastructure correlate with the cultural behaviour of people affected by economic and political circumstances.

At the last World Summit on Arts Education in Wildbad Kreuth "Polylogue II"[1], Susanne Keuchel presented a first draft on possible correlations between the provision of arts education and the quality of social life demonstrated in indices like peace and anti-corruption.

Following Keuchel's considerations, against the background of the worsening of living and working conditions of a broad range of Europeans, two consequences could be taken into account. One is a possible negative correlation when an increasing number of people are going to lose their future perspectives at the same time that arts education is celebrated as a cultural and education policy priority. The other is a reflection on how these economically and socially excluded cohorts of people can be reached by the provision of new methods of arts education which are appropriate in their current situation. In any case, we can assume that they have meanwhile withdrawn into their own "cultural spaces" far from what traditional arts education provision is about.

---

1   http://worldsummit2013.bkj.de/speakers/keuchel-susanne.html

The issue that I want to raise in these remarks is about the changing political, social and economic context in which arts education provision takes place and how the political implications of arts education must be taken into account in the further development of the sector.

## Fragile Relationships between Arts and Civic (Political) Education

There is quite a longstanding controversy on the relationship between civic education and arts education. At first sight, these sectors seem to be quite separated, each with its own tradition, expert language, objectives and institutions. Following the interpretation of Max Fuchs[2], politics has to do with power whereas culture is concerned with the communication of questions of meaning. Policy is expected to reach decisions quickly whereas the field of arts and culture is expected to take its time to check arguments over and over again. The concept of autonomy is often invoked to prevent the arts from any social (and thus political) use.

When taking into account diverse practices it becomes evident that the outlined demarcation for categorical separation does not really work. In fact, there are manifold arts projects which deal with existential problems that have something to do with the state of our society: unemployment, environmental degradation, violence, loneliness, poverty. Reflecting problems of this kind, Fuchs argues for a broader understanding of "politics" which finds its correlation in the history of the Avant-garde of the 20th century and their attempt to reconcile the arts with the living conditions of the people.

Another commonality lies in the ability to judge, either politically or aesthetically. In both cases we are deciding on the basis of critical reflection rather than making spontaneous decisions taking into account not only the issue that has to be decided but also the context in which the issue arises.

## State of European Developments

It seems remarkable that the sector of arts education so far – if at all – has made only modest efforts to find new relationships with civic education. On the contrary, it has developed only a low interest in the (socio-)political context in which arts education activities are taking place[3]. This can be observed particularly in Europe, where even a mention of the fundamental crisis which nations have been facing for five years is commonly regarded as irrelevant.

Perhaps this denial of reality is due to a disinterest in the priority setting of the sector so that, instead of critically reflecting on the changing working and living realities of their students, arts educators rely mainly on the perpetuation of traditional rhetoric.

---

2  http://www.bpb.de/gesellschaft/kultur/kulturelle-bildung/59942/kulturelle-und-politische-bildung (07.01.2014).
3  As a result not only in the research which became the major source of Anne Bamford's „Wow-Factor" arts education practices in totalitarian regimes are compared with those in democratic ones as if the fact of different political constitutions can be neglected.

As a consequence, these proponents have to limit themselves to stereotypical questions, such as whether dancing in school produces better results in mathematics, while in Europe the cultural fabric is in a process of dramatic alteration (and with it individual and collective perspectives particularly in the most dynamic age groups).

Now I'm not saying arts education could – at least in its current constitution – make a significant contribution to solving the crisis. I confine myself at this point to arguing that the changes in the social conditions in the professional discourse should be taken into account. This would be the prerequisite to ensure that arts educators are not merely dependent on what is going on around them but can participate as co-actors, who co-decide which function the sector can or in a more normative way should play in further societal development. I am referring to a statement of the legendary German cultural politician Hilmar Hoffmann, who in the 1970's described the content of what is at stake in arts and cultural education in terms of "culture as the system that justifies a distinctive shape and material value of society. The arts are then the aesthetic forms of expression precisely of this culture"[4].

If we are able to agree with this statement even today, we cannot avoid accepting that what we call society has changed considerably and with it its cultural values. However, this has not yet led to a reorientation of arts education. England seems to be one of the exceptions, when it tried with projects such as Creative Partnerships to make use of arts education for further market liberalization hoping that the opportunities for young people in the emerging markets of cultural and creative industries would improve – an experiment that has since been terminated by the liberal-conservative government.

## On the Way to Post-Democracy

A number of social scientists are analysing developments in the current crisis. Most of them come to rather sobering findings, stating that a devaluation of democratic values leads to post-democratic constitutions of national societies and thus questioning current forms of (political) participation[5].

Besides Wolfgang Streeck who, describes in his book "Die gekaufte Zeit"[6], the decline of democratic capitalism as a constituent of the post war order, I found the contribution of Claus Offe "Two and a half theories of democratic capitalism"[7] helpful to analyse the current status quo and link it to our topic of interest, arts education.

Offe begins his historical outline with the idea of a social-democratic theory of democratic capitalism from the 1970's. Its quality lay in a strict decoupling of (unevenly distributed) socioeconomic resources and (equal) political rights. The constitutional intention was to avoid the conversion of ownership of assets into political power. This was intended to counteract the increasing inequality caused by market forces and was oriented towards the prevailing conceptions of social justice, when it came to politically influencing the design of the market dynamics and the distribution of economic goods.

---

4   Hofmann, Hilmar (1979): *Kultur für alle*. Frankfurt, S. 126.
5   Fe Crouch, Colin (2004): *Post-democracy*. Oxford.
6   Streeck, Wolfgang (2013): *Die gekaufte Zeit*. Frankfurt.
7   Published in German in: *Transit – Europäische Revue: Zukunft der Demokratie*. Nr. 44 Frankfurt.

## About the Loss of Political Hegemony

When (since 1989) a market-liberal theory became dominant, Offe analysed a new phase characterized by the attempt to carry out a strictly symmetrical separation of the rules of the market and public policy. At this stage the market forces were to be allowed to develop free of government influence, while the political system was to be restricted to the provision of a public infrastructure and services (including educational and cultural provisions). The basis for this concept of social transformation was a "post-ideological" political culture that led the citizens to be distanced from and indifferent to most political issues in order to guarantee a necessary stability. The rest was to be managed by the dynamics of the markets.

The increasing dominance of the financial industry ushered a third phase. Offe describes the current crises and their logic of social organization as a betting game characterized first and foremost by an end to previous social theories. Its dynamics – at least so far – no longer requires any normative theory or justification based on traditional European (cultural) values. Instead, the owners of financial resources have – almost like a coup without democratic legitimacy – taken over the agenda of policy-making. In a reversal of the asymmetry of the 1970's now the "imperatives of markets" dominate public action (and not vice versa). As a result, politics is less and less able to counteract the predominance of accumulation, profit, efficiency, competitiveness, austerity and commodification as the only remaining guiding principles, debasing traditional values such as social rights, political redistribution or sustainability.

The exceptionality of the current situation lies in the dominant goals of economic decision-makers who have struggled to achieve a largely unchallenged position to enforce their new brutal realities without any legitimizing promise such as "progress", "justice", "freedom" or "stability". Consequently, they make democratically elected politicians look increasingly weak. The only remaining "chance of survival" for the state seems to be its transformation from "tax state" to "debt state". This means to negate the interests and demands of stakeholders on the "demand side" and to reduce the provision of services and infrastructure. The results can be observed not only in Greece.

## About the Changing Social Context of Arts Education

This three-phase model is mirrored – in my hypothesis – in the value of the arts education sector. After all, arts education provision was originally understood as an eminent contribution to the realization of more social justice ("cultural policy as a continuation of social policy"). Regarding theoretical approaches that, to this day, continue to justify arts education programs in public policy, one of the main arguments remains the expected inclusion of socially disadvantaged young people. Of course the original impetus to make use of a changing cultural behaviour to improve political participation is gone.

The subsequent market-liberal phase has changed both the form and content of arts education programs largely without reflection. Dating from this period we are confronted with a language regime of "management", "target-group orientation", "efficiency", "third party funding" or simply "impact" as action-guiding parameters. At the same time, the ability of the sector to claim a "value-oriented market correction" reduced the chance to synergize the artistic and political dimension of arts education.

Instead, representatives mutated to confirmers of a "post-ideological" socio-political constitution, which offered to compensate for the declining importance of the political with new forms of co-operation with market forces. Since then, a preoccupation with the diversity of artistic expression has fostered a better form of togetherness, superior to the degradation produced by an ignorant policy.

Nevertheless – and here a possible asynchrony is emerging – arts education obviously still serves as one of the few remaining insurers of the unbroken strength of nation-states, given the increasing helplessness of politicians and administrators in relation to the global financial sector. This would explain the rise of arts education in recent years in some European countries. From this exceptional position an outstanding (socio-)political mission for arts education can be derived.

If this analysis is plausible, the question can be raised: what constitutes the social relevance of arts education in a phase of post-democratic development, in which financial investors have taken over the economic and political regime and the chances for political intervention have fallen dramatically?

## Arts Education in the Current Period of Transition

In the absence of a theoretical foundation the sector (still) has a choice. The previous lack of a socially critical discourse nourishes the temptation to be content with an ornamental if not veiling function in times of refeudalization of social power relations. In a nutshell this means singing and dancing, to escape the frustrations of everyday life for at least a few hours. In the meantime, politics continues to take place increasingly dominated by market interests, while those taking part in arts education programs turn their backs to politics. This is even more true when the cultural elites have taught arts educators in strange alliance with boulevard media (which pursue its own economic interests) to distinguish themselves and their commitment from the political elites, even to despise them.

And yet there is also the option to politically recharge arts education activities and to put them in relation to what Hofmann defined as the main objective of arts education. The present social analyses make it clear that Europe is not going through a temporary cyclical crisis of its capitalist economics, but through a fundamental cultural transformation that fundamentally affects an appreciation of the values of the people. This is the existential experience of millions of young people, whose living conditions are currently dependent on some financial jugglers. They have to find their way in a completely uncertain future "without any spiritual resonance that is able to foster their moral and their civil fantasy"[8].

---

8 Sandel, Michael (2013): Solidarität. In: *Transit – Europäische Revue*: *Zukunft der Demokratie*. Nr. 44, S. 114.

## From "Talking about People" and "Talking to People" to "Talking with People"

So how about making young people "experts" of their own situation and trying to talk with them instead of talking about them? As an adult, I do not even like to say it, but we have to be aware in propagating arts education activities, that it is not the young people but the adults who have produced the current state of those modern societies in which they find no perspectives. A new dialogue, based on the democratic participation rights of all concerned – could be the basis of an attempt to reconstruct social life and to produce new trust between generations. Especially when the fundamental achievements which have distinguished the character of Europe are at stake: not profit and efficiency, but freedom, democracy, solidarity and justice.

On the basis of these discussions, it might be worth trying to implement new models of participation, especially in the field of arts education and its research. Offe's model of a more substantive change that moves to the centre the interests and preferences of those who are the participants of arts education activities could be a guiding principle.

Susanne Keuchel

# Arts Education Development Index (AEDI) – A Comparative International Empirical Research Approach in Arts Education

Past experience has shown that international indices, even if they focus on a few key indicators, can be useful to show development needs, success and, more than anything, to stimulate constructive competition between countries.

The success of international empirical studies like PISA[1] or indices like "Education For All (EFA) Development Index (EDI)"[2] poses a justified question, if such an empirical instrument in the field of arts education could also activate more international competition in arts education.

The following summarizes the background for the development of such an international comparative empirical research approach, named Arts Education Development Index (AEDI), first results of an international pre-test, the need of rework and possible future benefits of AEDI. The research approach was developed by Prof. Dr. Susanne Keuchel, Prof. Dr. Eckart Liebau and Dr. Ernst Wagner in cooperation with experts from the International Network for Research on Arts Education (INRAE) in 2012 with the goal to support the implementation of the Seoul Agenda.

## 1. Aims and Background for the Conception

It is extremely difficult to compare national arts education activities on international level. This difficulty arises in part as a result of *different institutionalised structures of arts education*. This can illustrate for example by the international music school statistics provided by the European Music School Union. As the Union point out, their data mainly relates to the public, extracurricular music schools, whereas generally neither private institutions nor freelance music educators are included in the statistics.[3] So it is not possible to present a complete picture of music activities generally in countries such as Germany with a higher amount of private music schools and freelance music educators or

---

1 Organisation for Economic, Co-operation and Development (OECD): Program for International Student Assessment (PISA). PISA 2012 Assessment and Analytical Framework, Paris 2012.
2 UNESCO (Ed.): Education For All (EFA) Development Index (EDI): The 2012 Education for All Global Monitoring Report, Paris 2012.
3 European Music School Union (EMU) (Ed.): EMU 2010. Statistical information about the European Music School Union, Utrecht 2011, p. 13f.

England, where music services usually don't take place outside schools but are included in school offers.

Adding to the difficulty are *different national school and education systems*, such as half-time or all-day schools, single or multiple school systems – which affect the organisation of arts education in curricular and extracurricular contexts. If you look at the Eurydice Report[4] for example, which focuses on schools and excludes non-formal arts education outside schools, problems of comparing different school systems in arts education become obvious: How is it possible to compare countries with an all-day-school system with countries with a half-day school and probably a few school arts educational offers, but a broad non-formal arts educational sector outside school?

*Different national political systems of cultural funding* further complicate international comparisons. The difficulties in comparing arts education "investment" within different political systems of cultural funding were recently shown in a national research project on arts education in Germany called mapping//arts education,[5] in which several structural indicators were compared for 16 federal states in Germany.

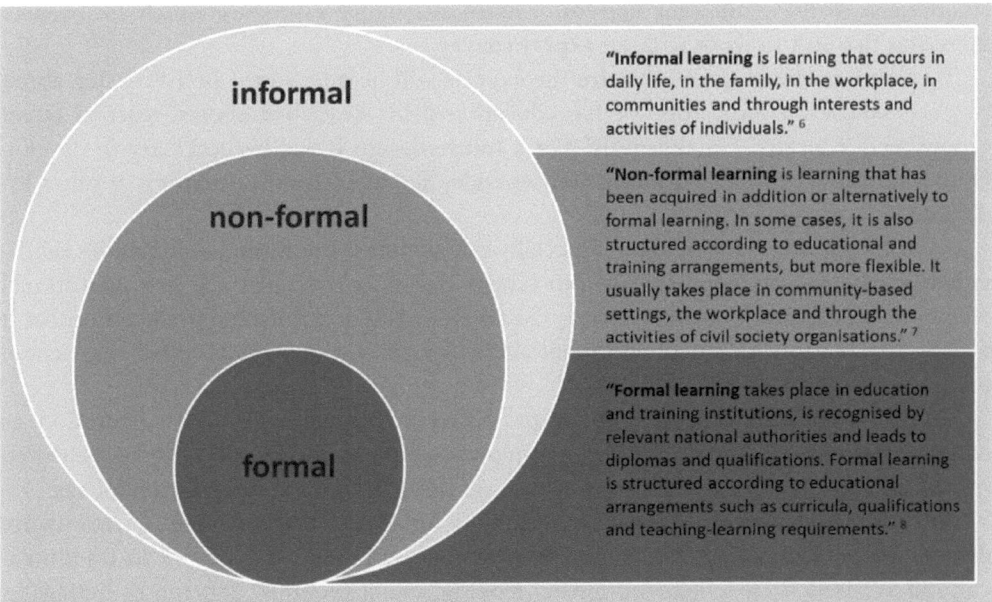

Figure 1: Fields of Education (definitions by UNESCO)

This research approach was adapted to free researchers from the various institutions and allow them to work with the different ‚fields of education‘, as defined by UNESCO: the

---

4  European Comission/EACEA/Eurydice (Ed.): Eurydice Report. Arts and Cultural Education at School in Europe, Brussels 2009.
5  Keuchel, Susanne: Arts Education by Numbers. Cartography and quantitative measurement of Arts Education in Germany. In: *International Yearbook for Research in Arts Education*. Eds.: E. Liebau, E. Wagner and M. Wyman. 1/2013, p. 129-137.
6  ibid.
7  ibid.
8  ibid.

formal, non-formal and informal education fields, which are the main focal points of AEDI. The simultaneous integration of all three fields enables international compatibility of various education systems.

Moreover, the informal education field is also important for an international comparison in arts education – especially under the presumption that in some countries cultural and artistic traditions are maintained intensely but possibly are not represented in formal or non-formal arts education services. It is also interesting to analyse whether there is a relation between the existence of formal and non-formal arts education services and arts education activities within the informal fields.

## 2. Methods and Research Design

Specific national statistics about arts education in the fields of education hardly exist. So it will be necessary to use several different sources such as analysis of the existing curriculum, existing statistics from national unions, population surveys or time-budget studies. Because of these different sources or as an alternative estimates, which are needed, there was the idea to work with an **expert survey**.

By a **standardized questionnaire** the experts will be questioned in a first step about two arts education indicators for the education fields described above: 'reached target groups' and 'educators' qualification'. For a future design it will be necessary to develop further indicators connected to the Soul Agenda, like intensive of mediation or other indicators.

Concerning the available data, especially curriculums, the formal field will be subdivided twice: into arts education within school classes (curricular) and arts educational offers outside classes (extracurricular). Elsewhere existing national analyses prove that it usually is easier to give statements about curricular and extracurricular offers, e.g. school orchestra or drama club.[9]

To gain an overview of the scope of the different national fields of arts education, as other surveys e.g. PISA[10] do, the target group of each field of education will be measured by different age groups: one primary school age and the other secondary school age.

In order to identify art education structures for conducting an initial questionnaire design, arts education will be refined in a first step to creative activities in traditional cultural sections such as playing music, making/taking pictures, dancing or acting. In later surveys there is an option to a) either limit the creative activities to further due to practicability or b) extend them to other artistic activities, such as media art or receptive activities, e.g. visits of theatres etc.

---

9 Keuchel, Susanne (2013): mapping//kulturelle-bildung. Editor Mercator-Stiftung, Essen.
10 PISA aims to evaluate education systems worldwide every three years by assessing 15-year-olds' competencies in three key subjects (reading, mathematics and science).

|  | | Artistic-creative activities ... [making music, making pictures, dancing, acting] | | | |
|---|---|---|---|---|---|
|  | | formal | | non-formal | informal |
|  | Age group ... | curricular | extra-curricular | | |
| Access ⇨Seoul Agenda: Goal 1 "Test-"Indicator: **Reached target groups** | 8-year-olds (primary school) | | | | |
| | 15-year-olds (secondary school) | | | | |
| Quality ⇨Seoul Agenda: Goal 2 Test-Indicator: **Qualification of educators** | 8-year-olds primary school) | | | | n/a |
| | 15-year-olds (secondary school) | | | | n/a |

Figure 2: The Questionnaire's Structure

To determine the reach of target groups, the percentage of the various age groups in the respective fields of activity and learning was gathered in the questionnaire. For the indicator 'educators' qualification' the percentage of the active educators was captured in each field with pedagogical and/or artistic qualification.

Because at the present time structural data and empirical studies in the field of arts education hardly exist on an international level, the instrument presented here is also intended to be used to improve the empirical data on arts education internationally. So for all the indicators respondents are asked whether the answers are based on existing data sources or whether they are based on estimates.

## 3. Background and Function of the Pre-Test

To ensure the practical application of AEDI on an international level INRAE conducted an international pre-test with INRAE-Experts[11] in eight different countries in five continents with the indicators described above in 2012 and 2013.

The primary function of the pre-test was to test the instruments for practicability in an international context and to collect initial data about some countries, even if they are not significant. Completion of the standardized questionnaire was not the only intention of the pre-test. The experts were also asked to give a precise feedback on the model's suitability for international comparisons, on the mentioned validity and on specific suggestions for improvements.

In the process of the pre-test it turned out, that research to identify the requested data needs far more time than estimated because it requires extensive secondary analyses, especially in federal state systems.

---

11 Many thanks for hard work by supporting the pre-test to Robin Pascoe, John O' Toole (Australia), Liane Hentschke (Brazil), Larry O'Farell (Canada), Eckart Liebau, Susanne Keuchel (Germany), Richard G. Whitbread, Samuel Leong (Hong Kong), Shifra Schonmann (Israel), Ralph Buck (New Zealand), Aud Berggraf SæBø (Norway) and Chee Hoo Lum, Shuxia Tai (Singapore).

These are the reasons, why the significance of the collected present data is very limited. In the following they will just be used to demonstrate opportunities for analyses.

## 4. Analysis Opportunities

The research approach is characterized in its name as an index with the goal of enabling international comparison. But AEDI provides more analysis opportunities which can be located in four focal relevant themes as demonstrate in the following:

### 4.1 Monitoring of International Data

AEDI in its approach and basic idea is designed not just with the intention of collecting structural data, but also of producing an overview of existing data and empirical studies. So one analysis option is the possibility of monitoring the empirical data situation of arts education worldwide.

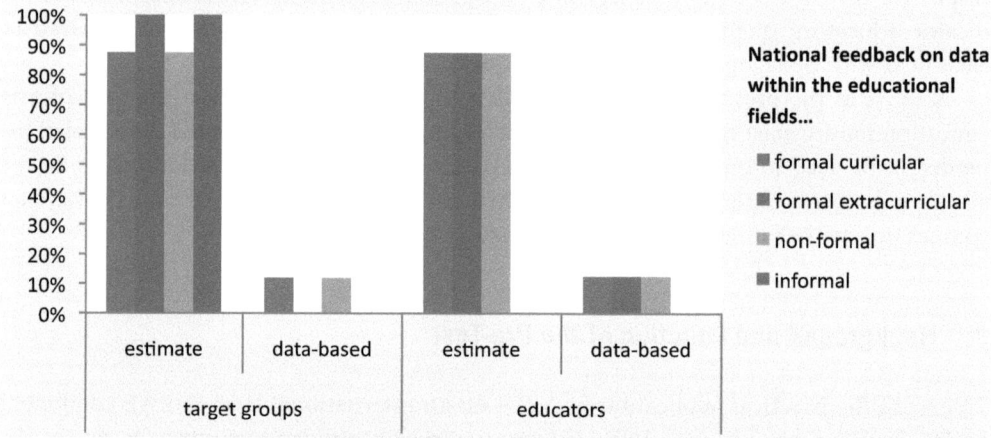

Figure 3: Existing nationwide data of reached target groups and qualification of educators regarding artistic activities in different fields of education

Generally, the feedback of experts, who participated in the pre-test, from countries with comparatively high educational levels point out the insufficient state of statistical data in arts education. Partial exceptions are the formal and the non-formal fields, for which in some cases data exist, presumably from school statistics or institutional statistics. If this feedback would be verified by valid data it becomes obvious that there is a real lack of empirical research in arts education.

## 4.2 General Findings about Organisation Structures

AEDI also could help to identify general findings on arts education organisational structures. For instance, on the basis of the experts' feedback there is a correlation between the reach of target group within the formal curricular education on the one hand and the reach of target groups as well as the educators' qualification within the non-formal education on the other hand, as it is presented in the following figure:

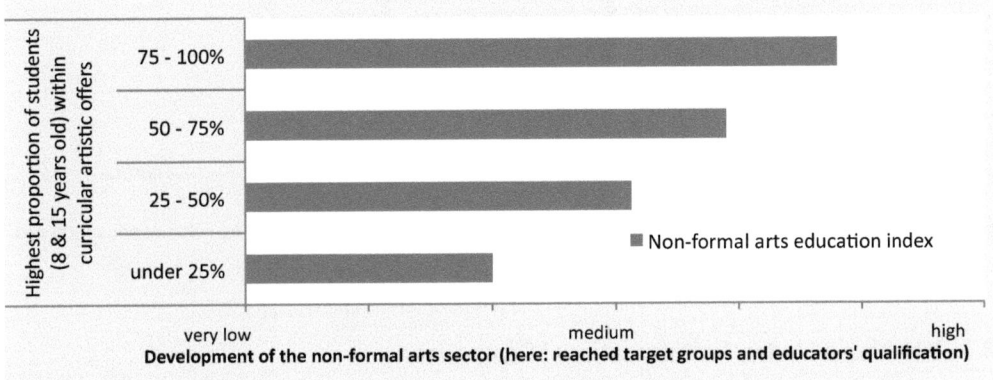

Figure 4: Extension of non-formal education differentiated by reached students within curricular artistic offers in eight countries

If this finding can be verified based on valid data, that countries with a highly developed curricular arts education sector also provide this level within their non-formal offers, this would be revealing. It would not just dispel the prior outlined presumption, according to which a wide range of non-formal arts education would relieve a less developed curricular one, but also support the perspective, that a comprehensive curricular arts education sector is rather the premise for a manifold non-formal arts education sector.

It would also be enlightening if the following diagnosis could be proved with valid data: The reach of the curricular artistic sector in the pre-test is internationally much higher for the 8-year-olds than it is e.g. for the 15-year-olds. The offers for the 15-year-olds in this context are also not compensated by intensified non-formal structures. This leads to the question, why the 15-year-olds should be served less in arts education than the 8-year-olds.

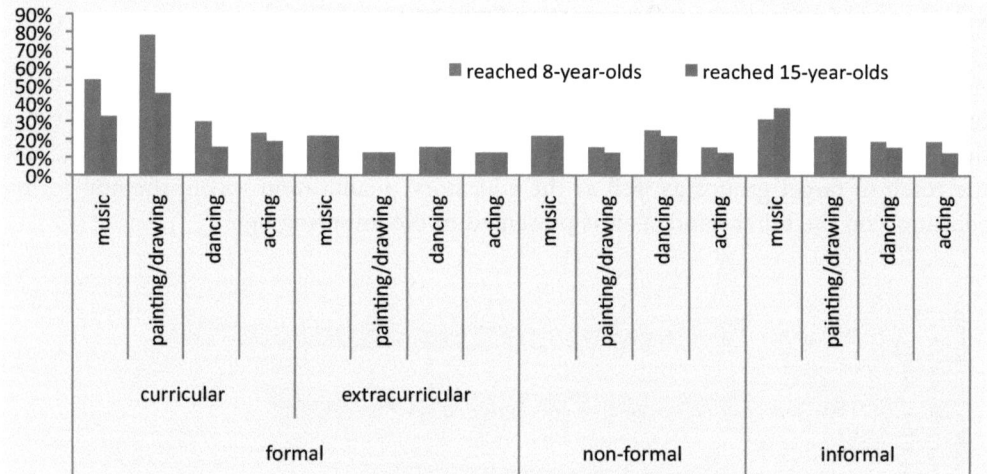

Figure 5: Average reach of target groups regarding artistic activities, differentiated by fields of education and age group

## 4.3 Working as Index for International Comparison

Designed as an index AEDI can be used for international comparisons. Generally it can be argued, that a few quantitative data as indicators are not sufficient to draw a conclusion on the efficiency of arts educational systems and especially the quality of offers. However, in practice there can be found examples where this happens in other contexts for the purpose of contributing international comparisons and by this international competition.

When dealing with indices, it is essential to be able to estimate the significance of the implemented indicators in a realistic manner and to avoid generalizations or over-interpretations of any kind. The way in which the use of various indicators leads to different results, can be demonstrated strikingly with the few data of AEDI.

For example, by comparing the national arts educational structures with AEDI it is necessary to take the predefined research design into account and think about how to handle the formal field that was – in favour of a better characterization – separated into the curricular and the extracurricular fields.

Including the data of both mentioned sub fields equally in the index without weighting, the formal educational field is predominant compared to the non-formal and informal contexts. Taking the corresponding effects into account, New Zealand ranks first with its far reach of target groups within the formal fields of education. If one stays with the original idea that the three fields are weighted equally – which involves the necessity to divide the formal educational field by two, since it is composed of the curricular and the extracurricular field –, Canada ranks first due to the fact that in this country a high reach of target groups within the non-formal and the informal fields of education can be observed.

|  | Reach of target groups | | | Reach of target groups and educators' qualification | | |
|---|---|---|---|---|---|---|
|  | all fields, formal weighted higher ranking | formal field only ranking | all fields weighted equally ranking | all fields, formal weighted higher ranking | formal field only ranking | all fields weighted equally ranking |
| Australia | 6 | 6 | 6 | 5 | 6 | 5 |
| Brazil | 5 | 6 | 4 | 8 | 8 | 8 |
| Canada | 2 | 4 | 1 | 1 | 1 | 1 |
| Germany | 7 | 4 | 7 | 4 | 4 | 4 |
| Israel | 8 | 8 | 8 | 7 | 4 | 7 |
| New Zealand | 1 | 1 | 2 | 2 | 2 | 2 |
| Norway | 3 | 1 | 3 | 3 | 3 | 3 |
| Singapore | 4 | 2 | 4 | 6 | 6 | 6 |

Figure 6: Weighted and non-weighted comparisons amongst the countries regarding the reach of target groups as well as reach of target groups and educators' qualification

Another modified ranking amongst the countries that included the educators' qualifications in addition to the target groups[12], illustrates how crucial it is to use as many indicators as possible in order to describe the outcome of a system. So in a ranking list Germany is in seventh place concerning the reach of target groups, but shifts to fourth place when both aspects are taken into consideration.

Due to the increase of indicators, the ranking amongst the countries could change continuously. Hence, researchers are encouraged to establish more indicators for this context in a long-term. In doing so, one must keep in mind that the model has to stay manageable for the experts.

## 4.4 Using Index for Linking to Other Studies

AEDI can also be linked to other arts education studies. Conceivable is a connection to qualitative international research projects, for which AEDI as an index can offer a basis to group the participating countries into different arts education structural types and then put this grouping directly into the context of the qualitative results of the particular studies.

---

12 Unfortunately, while translating the AEDI questionnaire from German into English the translator made a serious translation error. Originally, it was asked how many qualified school teachers and how many other educators are participating in arts educational programmes within the respected educational fields, and what kinds of artistic trainings and pedagogical qualifications they have. Due to the translation error this crucial information wasn't available. For that reason, the qualification of school teachers and educators was combined to one group in which the data of the teachers' qualification was weighted higher within the formal educational field (2/3). Outside school, it wasn't possible to analyse data concerning the pedagogical qualification; the data simply consists of the information whether the educators have or have not an artistic training.

Another possible link is the connection with existing international indices on different topics such as PISA, Human-Development-Index, Global Peace Index, Corruption Perception Index, Democracy Index etc. This can be used to outline the value of arts education for national systems according to the Seoul Agenda, and at the same time show potential links between the national significance of arts education and other social developments. An interesting research question in this context could be for example, if countries which succeeded in PISA also invest in a broad infrastructure of arts educational offers. Is the key to success here perhaps not the focus on core subjects, but rather the support of a wide range of educational offers?

## 5. Feedback of the Expert for Modification

All participating experts, involved in the first pre-test, stressed the necessity of reworking AEDI and this also pointed out the difficulty of developing international research designs. In three areas it was possible to frame some important ideas for improvement as well as to point out problems which still need to be solved regarding AEDI, as listed up in the following table:

|  | **Current Problems and Necessary Modification of the Model** |
| --- | --- |
| *Insufficient data* | • Enlarge the questionnaire's category *"based on data/estimate"* by classifying the last option into *"estimate based on subject-specific experiences"* and *"uncertain estimate"* |
|  | • Involve more experts, most notably section-specific ones |
|  | • Involve also experts from different federal states in federal states |
|  | • Include particular national institutional structures (e.g. inclusion of WorldCP) |
| *(Intercultural) Problems of Definitions* | • Give definition-help for the differentiation between formal and non-formal fields of education |
|  | • Invest more work into defining terms (e.g. „theatre" or „drama") |
|  | • Invest more work into definition of art education processes (When is dancing "dancing" as an arts education process? How do we classify dancing in the disco or karaoke singing?) |
| *Proposal for Expanding and Differentiating/ Restructuring* | • Expand the arts educational activities (e.g. media art activities) |
|  | • Integrate additional focal points (e.g. social-cultural or gender-distinctions) |
|  | • Give open space for further basic information about the country-specific situation of arts education |

## Conclusion – Use and Future

Initial, useful advice to further development of AEDI was provided by the experts in the pre-test. But it became rather obvious as well, that a continued exchange of ideas and further pre-tests are still necessary for the development of a final index.

Even if there is a need to invest more time and work into AEDI the investment could be useful because there are many advantages to a continuous monitoring of art education, including the following aspects:

a) Collecting more expertise about structural relations (organization of arts education depending on different educational systems, correlations between arts education in formal, non-formal and informal contexts, etc.)
b) Analyzing interdependencies between the national development of arts educational structures and other national topics (e.g. PISA, different political systems, national aspects like corruption, economy, etc.)
c) Establishing a basis with AEDI to systematise different national arts educational systems and link them to other studies concerning arts education, especially qualitative ones
d) Providing a political rationale for implementing the goals of the Seoul Agenda on a national level.

Tatiana Fedorova and Liubava Morevo

# Arts Education in the CIS Countries: National Reports and Regional Observatory on Promoting Creative Capacities in the XXI Century
# (The UNESCO/IFESCCO Pilot Project)

Establishing a common ground of understanding on the important role of arts education within the international community as well as encouraging exchanges of ideas, knowledge and practises in the field are among the goals of the UNESCO Arts Education programme. The existing attitudes, practices and experiences in arts education that characterise national traditions may be approached as treasured manifestations of both cultural diversity and heritage in the fleeting world of today.

In this world, where globalization blurs boundaries, cultural diversity is best represented and valued in the constant dialogue of cultures and traditions. The role of the UNESCO in this respect is to support this dialogue and to enable people to be tolerant and cooperative without losing their identity. Promoting understanding of the role of arts education in the development of intercultural dialogue, encouraging and assisting implementation of the Universal Declaration on Cultural Diversity (2001) and the Convention on the Protection and the Promotion of the Diversity of Cultural Expressions (2005) are the best lines to achieve these goals.

The UNESCO's efforts and vision of arts education have been concretized through research and enquiry, and organization of regional and global expert meetings. Holding the World Conferences, making advocacy of strategic documents such as "Road Map for Arts Education" (Lisbon 2006) and "The Seoul Agenda: Goals for the Development of Arts Education" (Seoul 2010), and supporting arts education resource bodies like Observatories and UNESCO Chairs are of particular importance. To achieve the goals defined and principles elaborated, the Organization acts at multiple levels of which the regional one has proved to be quite efficient.

The UNESCO fundamentals are shared by the Intergovernmental Foundation for Educational, Scientific and Cultural Cooperation (IFESCCO) of the Commonwealth of Independent States (CIS), the mission of which is "to contribute to the further development of humanitarian cooperation and intercultural communication" in various fields including education, culture, and youth matters. Therefore, co-operation between the two Organizations at the regional level has become quite a natural result. A number of joint UNESCO/IFESCCO projects were launched by UNESCO's Moscow Office, which is the Organization's only cluster office located in Europe. It is mandated to operate for Armenia, Azerbaijan, Belarus, Republic of Moldova and the Russian Federation.

Picture 1: Covers of the two Main Reports.

The long-term UNESCO/IFESCCO pilot project **"Arts Education in the CIS Countries: Development of Creative Capacities in the XXI Century"** was initiated by the UNESCO Moscow Office in 2009 and was successfully implemented in partnership with the UNESCO Offices in Almaty and Tashkent. The experts involved were from all CIS countries including Armenia, Azerbaijan, Belarus, Kazakhstan, Kyrgyzstan, the Republic of Moldova, the Russian Federation, Tajikistan, Ukraine and Uzbekistan.

The project aimed at supporting the arts education systems in the CIS countries and facilitating UNESCO priorities and principles within the national strategies for development of the arts education field. In particular, the project envisaged the conducting of case studies in the field of professional arts education, arts-in-education approaches and education through arts, including the analysis of existing educational system, training programs and trends in their development.

The studies were carried out in close cooperation with the related research and educational institutions, professional communities and governmental agencies including culture and education Ministries, universities, culture and arts organisations and other as well as in close consultancy with the National Commissions for UNESCO of the involved countries. The research was based on information collected about approaches used in arts education and challenges that are to be met in the near future.

In every CIS country, arts education is a unique phenomenon organically combining tradition and innovation, human and national values, artistic forms and genres, various types of activities and manifestations; most importantly, it is concerned with the issues of both personal and social development. Historically preserved traditions of arts edu-

Picture 2: Covers of the Analytical Papers.

cation have some general traits and are national cultural properties; they are primarily looked at as a means to influence spiritually the development of a person.

Furthermore, world-wide, native cultural-historical values appear to be an indispensable educational factor fostering the generation of national and cultural self-consciousness, underpinning multi-cultural interaction and deepening a sense of personal responsibility for the future prosperity of the native country. Clarifying and amplifying the role of arts education in conveying principles of social responsibility, social unity, cultural diversity, and intercultural dialogue proved to be an important task for all the CIS countries.

Project activities were also aimed at the improvement of cultural and educational policies in the field of arts education, as well as enhancing the interaction between the Ministries of culture and education of the CIS Member States. The emerging consolidation of professional and expert communities became an important result of the project. During the project implementation, the specificities of the Arts Education systems in the CIS countries were brought to light and the related recommendations were elaborated by leading experts in the field. Analysis of precise materials and elaboration of the recommendations were conducted with regard for international experience and basic documentation in this field, as well as the UNESCO strategic documents, including the Road Map for Arts Education and "The Seoul Agenda: Goals for the Development of Arts Education".

Within the First Stage of the UNESCO/IFESCCO Project, the national analytical reports were prepared. They based on the collection and thorough analysis of information on current programmes, approaches used and challenges that may emerge in the short run concerning arts education in the CIS countries. The authors of the national analytical reports also focused on elaboration of the relevant recommendations for the further

Picture 3: Website of the UNESCO-Observatory on Arts Education (Screenshot).

development of the arts education systems and enhancement of cooperation subject to international practices. The national Analytical Reports covered all forms of arts education and every level of national arts education systems; they addressed various art forms including music, dance, theatre, visual arts, design, artistic crafts, film and media.

Along with the prepared analytical reports of the CIS countries, three important documents, analyzing and at the same time summarizing the results of the project were prepared by the expert community and published. In particular, an analytical review "Arts Education in CIS countries: Building creative capacities for 21$^{st}$ Century", a policy brief "Arts Education in CIS countries" and a presentational booklet "Strategic Guidelines for the Development of Arts Education in the CIS Countries" explain to the external reader the system of arts education in CIS countries, the problems and the prospects of its improvement.

The analytical papers gave an opportunity to record the uniqueness of arts education in the CIS countries, the developmental potential of which is rooted in the continuity of educational models of Soviet times and the originality of national cultural traditions. The papers reflect the current state of arts education systems in the CIS countries, the potential of arts education for the solution of urgent challenges of modern times.

The creation of the data base Internet portal "Observatory on Arts Education in the CIS countries" (http://ae.cis.iite.unesco.org/observatory/index.php/en/) is one of the most important and substantial results of the project. The input of the Arts Education Institute of the Russian Academy of Education in opening the Internet portal was essential. The Observatory comprises all basic international documents about arts education, documents regulating the activities in the field of arts education in CIS countries, analytical reports issued during the implementation of the above-mentioned UNESCO/

IFESCCO project by 10 involved countries, as well as the latest news about projects, events, research, publications, communities and information about the participating countries.

The benefits of introducing the arts and cultural practices into learning environments reflect a balanced intellectual, emotional and psychological approach to the development of individuals and societies. Such an education not only strengthens cognitive development and the acquisition of life skills – innovative and creative thinking, critical reflection, communication and inter-personal skills, – but also enhances social adaptability and cultural awareness for individuals, enabling them to build personal and collective identities as well as tolerance, acceptance and appreciation of others. The positive impact it has on the development of society ranges from cultivating social cohesion and cultural diversity to preventing standardization and promoting sustainable development.

Jan Jaap Knol

# On the Mapping of Cultural Education in Europe and More
# A Plea for Political Urgency

"Utility is the great idol of the age, to which all powers must do service and all talents swear allegiance. In this great balance of utility, the spiritual service of art has no weight and, deprived of all encouragement, it vanishes from the noisy Vanity Fair of our time.[1]"

Those who are concerned with the future of art – and with the future of arts education in particular – can agree with these dystopic words that are loaded with disenchantment.

There is every reason for concern if you consider the consequences of the neo-liberal economization of all aspects of society, including education. Or the excessive consumerism and the rapid evolution of a malleable media culture with an ever-shrinking attention span where fact and fiction are continually interwoven. Replace 'utility' with 'market' or 'economic growth' and the words are more salient than ever.

These words were written at the end of the 18th century by Friedrich Schiller, in letters to the Danish Prince van Augustenburg, setting out his ideas about aesthetic education formulated in the days of the French revolution. Against the backdrop of the mounting political turbulence in Europe, Schiller argued for the pre-eminence of beauty. He argued that the way to freedom is through beauty and beauty alone. Only beauty can strike a balance between the natural, competing urges and appetites of man on the one hand and the compulsive striving for unity on the other.

I use this brief cultural-philosophical preamble to introduce an argument developed as follows. First, I will delve more fully into the disenchantment with the position of arts education I touched on above. Second, I will explore the relevance of international monitoring and mapping as an instrument for moving from disenchantment to action. Thirdly, I will argue that any cultivation of this disenchantment is fruitless. The task at hand is to transform these concerns into an education and cultural politics that is both rooted in ideals, and is practical – a framework within which arts education engages with today's education issues.

First, I would like to address the current disenchantment. Education policy in many European countries – and, in fact, many parts of the world – has increasingly fallen prey to economization. The development of the Lisbon agenda of 2000, for example, saw Europe poised on the brink of becoming the world's most dynamic knowledge economy

---

1   "Der Nutzen ist das Grosse Idol der Zeit, dem alle Kräfte frohnen und alle talente huldigen sollen. Auf dieser groben Waage hat das geistige Verdienst der Kunst kein Gewicht, und, aller Aufmunterung beraubt, verschwindet sie von dem lermenden Markt des Jahrhunderts." Friedrich Schiller, *Über die ästhetische Erziehung des Menschen*, Zweiter Letter, 1801.

with ambitious plans for growth. However, a few years later, we are unfortunately left with no choice but to admit that these ambitions have crumbled in the face of the debt crisis. There was absolutely nothing wrong with a number of goals originally identified by the agenda – such as reducing high school drop-out rates and promoting life-long learning. Disenchantment arose, however, from the feeling that education is being forced to play second fiddle to the economic system.

In the last ten years, international comparisons, such as PISA (Programme for International Student Assessment), have increasingly demonstrated improving education results. In the Netherlands in recent years, as in other countries, international competition has led to a one-sided focus on the basics: cognitive language and mathematics skills. This has done nothing to boost the status of the already neglected arts subjects. As a consequence, arts education policy has become conflicted. Where cultural politics encouraged museums and theatres to develop and deepen education programmes for children, the education policy received no such stimulus. Art was deemed a marvellous subject, but not one that most schools should put much effort into. Fortunately, a counter movement is beginning to surface under the motto 'quality education for arts and culture'. Members of the present Dutch cabinet responsible for education and cultural policy are preparing a joint covenant to safeguard the quality of arts and education culture in the future; a re-appreciation of creativity and expression in education seems to be emerging.

This deep-felt disenchantment is not confined to arts subjects and is not unique to the Netherlands. There is a more widespread unease regarding the position of the humanities within education, resulting in constant readjustments to structure. Unfortunately management and bureaucracy have gained the upper hand in education policy and the urge for control has spilled over into standardization and measurable targets. As a result, teachers feel their individual freedom and professionalism is curtailed.

In 2010, Martha Nussbaum published 'Not for Profit'[2] here she makes a powerful case against the obsessive focus on economic growth and the technocratization of education. Nussbaum demonstrates how this emphasis erodes our ability to become critical, independent-minded citizens who respect diversity – qualities more essential than ever in a world in which immigration levels have risen so significantly. This excessive utility and malleability mind-set is a threat to democracy. Nussbaum champions the core values that we also increasingly connect with arts education: individual development, the power of the imagination and creativity, open-mindedness and cultural-historical awareness.

The question is, can we ascribe the disenchantment we are experiencing only to the relentless drive for economic profit and standardization. Flemish writer David van Reybrouck draws attention to the new cultural-ethical divide line between so-called liberal-minded, highly educated citizens of the world and those less highly educated who are rarely found in parliament and who have adopted new forms of nationalism[3]. He points out that, in recent decades the intellectual elite began to side-line a notion such as edifi-

---

2  Martha C. Nussbaum, *Not for profit. Why Democracy needs the Humanities*, 2010.
3  David van Reybrouck, Er is niets mis met een goede populist, article in Dutch Newspaper NRC Handelsblad, 26 August 2008 (http://vorige.nrc.nl/opinie/article1962942.ece/Er_is_niets_mis_met_een_goede_populist).

cation – a classic carrier of the ideals underlying arts education – which precisely coincided with the burgeoning of the commercial mass media. I quote from van Reybrouck: "Cultural relativism delivered the low-educated to the market long before the process of cultural emancipation had reached completion." He argues for a cultural education offensive, a permanent mandate that – in his words:

> in no way needs to be paternalistic, as was so often the case in the past, nor wholly popularist which is currently the norm. There is no disgrace in edifying the population – it is a necessity. It is a form of lasting civic development, from infants school via adult education to cultural coverage. Every democratic state under rule of law has need of it.

Thus Reybrouck draws the same conclusion as Nussbaum.

The combination of the commercialization and technocratization of education and the ruined ideal of edification unite to create an enormous sense of disenchantment.

This now brings me to the second section. Can international monitoring and mapping be effective in reducing this disenchantment? Let me begin by saying that greater monitoring of arts education from a transnational perspective is more than welcome. We know relatively little about each other. Effective monitoring and mapping systems can lead to more factual information about objectives, instruments, actors, results, current themes and developments. Systematic, international comparisons of arts education are extraordinarily important, all the more so because the object of this type of education, the arts, is such a prominent part of the international context.

Member states in Europe began working towards a form of collaboration in this regard in 2001. It began informally in Rotterdam, on the fringes of the conference 'A-must or -amuse?', a title that echoes the age-old dilemma of arts education. An informal network, ACE-NET, was set up. This group was comprised of civil servants involved with arts education policy working at ministries and other government bodies. The network, initially headed by the Netherlands, was continued by France, Austria and Flanders. Meetings are incredibly inspiring and participants tend to come away wiser than before. My colleague Teunis IJdens from the Netherlands, a monitoring and evaluation specialist, emphasizes the importance of this type of dialogue as a means of monitoring – for both policy and practical implementation. Fact-gathering alone simply is not enough.

Nonetheless, a great deal is happening in the area of research. Launched recently a new Arts Education Monitoring System is a collaborative project between Austria, Germany, England, Hungary and Spain. The Community of Knowledge on Arts and Cultural Education which was founded earlier has, unfortunately, been unable to move forward due to lack of funding. I am very interested in hearing about examples of excellence in arts education. In which context, under which conditions, for example, do children best develop their artistic abilities and what can we, as nations, learn from one another in this regard?

I also feel that is essential to see whether we can take all these initiatives and draw on them to create a lasting portal with policy-related, scholarly and practical information about arts education. This is one instance in which solid direction and financial support from Brussels would be extremely welcome now. Moreover, it is vital to draw a comparison with developments in other continents – Asia, North and South America, Africa and Australia.

At this point, I will return to the question of whether monitoring and mapping can play a role in banishing disenchantment with the marginalization of arts education.

In 2009 Eurydice, the European research network into education systems in Europe, explored the position of arts education in European countries. In March, Eurydice published a similar study on the position of sport and physical education. It is fascinating to compare the two, although the two studies were conducted along different lines. What both areas – sport and art – have in common is the fact that they account for a relatively small part of the curriculum. What struck me most, however, was the difference in urgency, illustrated by comparing the two opening sentences of the reports. The introduction to the physical education survey is upbeat and dynamic: "During childhood and youth, physical education at school provides an excellent opportunity to learn and practise skills likely to enhance lifelong fitness and good health."[4] The report on arts education begins as follows: "Education in European countries is subject to many competing demands which have an influence on arts and arts education".[5] This statement comes across as a little flat. However heartfelt and sincere the remainder of the report is, there is no avoiding the conclusion that – at least five years ago – there was no clear political focus when it came to the necessity of the research. One would hope that the mental health of children would receive as much attention as their physical condition. The difference in emphasis is more a reflection of the political context and in no way a criticism of the researchers.

My expectation is that the various forms of monitoring and mapping and a long-term portal of this kind will clearly lead to more information and, as a reference point, be helpful in forming policy at national and European level. But as long as these actions are not accompanied by a greater political urgency, I am afraid that their impact will remain limited.

This brings me to the third part of my argument. However clearly formulated, cultivating disenchantment is pointless. Cultural pessimism often goes hand in hand with a rosy picture of the past and can act as an anaesthetic that numbs rather than prompts action. Hence, to use the words of David van Reybrouck – forget complaining and forge ahead. It is more productive to explore the possibilities and harness disenchantment as a force for action.

Let us start with the possibilities. Is there really a reason for so much doom and gloom? We live in a fascinating time. The impact of our ubiquitous information and communication technology can be compared to the invention of printing. The internet presents an unlimited platform for cultural production and consumption. Because production and consumption intermingle, young people are adept at making the most of the opportunities available. A search of the internet will soon turn up the most amazing examples of young creativity. Last week, I saw a fantastic video clip online – an ani-

---

4  Physical and Sport at School in Europe. Eurydice report, March 2013, p. 7 (http://eacea.ec.europa.eu/education/eurydice.../documents/thematic_reports/150EN.pdf).
5  Arts and Cultural Education at School in Europe. Eurydice report, September 2009, p. 7 (http://eacea.ec.europa.eu/education/eurydice%20/documents/thematic_reports/113EN.pdf).

mation with Lego people made by Morgan Spence, just 13 years old, winner of a Young Scot Award. Spence made it for the famous trance DJ Paul Oakenfold[6]. In the Netherlands the Kunstbende holds an annual competition for young people and produces talented winners time after time. Wouter Hermans, a young student, was last year's winner in the Film and Animation category. He made a clip about a boy who dreams of a life as an artist. One of the protagonist's first lines says it all: "First I've got to escape this soul-destroying school." Thankfully, as long as there are young people there's a future – certainly for art!

Another promising aspect is that politicians and policy-makers are increasingly voicing the importance of creativity. However, this too is driven by economic motives, such as the ability to gain a competitive edge. There is more to it than that. Creativity is also seen as essential for solving social issues relating to sustainability and quality of life. The scale of these issues, combined with the influence of new media on our knowledge society, demands skills such as collaboration, the ability to problem-solve and, above all, creativity. Skills that are typically cultivated by a good arts education, as well as other subjects taught at school. Languages and technical subjects can equally train creative abilities. But the arts subjects – the realm of the imagination – present unique possibilities in this regard, particularly if they challenge pupils to adopt an open, inquisitive and free way of thinking.

It seems to me that the greatest pitfall to avoid here is that ensuing discussion about 21st century skills does not descend into bureaucratic clichés. Creativity cannot be summoned and resists standardization and predictable results. It is wise to remember that creativity and imagination alone do not represent the entire spectrum of arts education. Arts education is also about historical awareness and knowledge-sharing.

The best medicine for disenchantment is, ultimately, a fundamental re-evaluation of education: a vision of education that reaffirms multiple focuses on development in the broad sense, reinstates edification as an ideal, and relieves education of technocratic new-speak that leads to standardization and conformism, not inspiration. Education is not an 'industrial process' but a 'personal process', proposes Ken Robinson[7]. His principal message is that we need differentiation, not more standardization: education that takes account of the great differences between children and does not work on the basis of averages. Moreover, he argues for investing in the quality of teachers to support their children's learning process.

The increased importance of creativity in combination with a re-evaluation of the formative role of education creates enormous opportunities for arts education. It also, of course, encourages expectations and calls for ambition: an unassailable place on the curriculum, the best teachers, the most challenging educational programmes, and the integration of new media. It calls for the courage to experiment and transcend disciplines. Politicians need to have faith in teachers and create opportunities for *quality arts education*. This entails attention for training teachers, for the status of the profession, for the facilities they need and which are needed by their peer educators at cultural institutions.

---

6   https://www.youtube.com/watch?v=KcCND-43ucE
7   http://sirkenrobinson.com/

The focus on confidence in teachers and the quality of art lessons in practice is what I mean by a *practical* education and cultural politics.

We also need an ideals-driven politics. Education and arts education, in particular, must uphold the ideal of edification – they owe it to the past and to the future. Friedrich Schiller, author of the European hymn, expresses this far more eloquently than I: "In a narrow circle the mind grows narrow. The more one expands, the larger his aims."[8]

---

8   "Im engen Kreis verengen sich sein Sinn, es wächst der Mensch mit seinen grössern Zwecken". Friedrich Schiller, Prologue Wallenstein's Camp (line 59-60), 1798.

Benedicte Helvad

# Monitoring

ACEnet, the European Network of civil servants, working in the field of arts and cultural education, has been very useful in my country, Denmark, and has completed many concrete activities. In this network we have been inspired to make an overview on art, culture and education in the EU countries. This overview along with discussions within the group on specific themes provide us with a strategic tool that helps members in policy-making. ACEnet is an important platform for sharing knowledge and fostering collaboration between policy makers and scientists. The ongoing dialogue in ACEnet helps members to identify the needs of research and enables us to benefit from results from all over Europe.

Denmark has conducted a mapping project on art and culture in the Nordic countries schools over the past past ten years. The report was completed in June 2013 and translated into English. An expected but unsettling conclusion is that very little research has been done on art and culture in schools of the Nordic countries. The challenge, now, is to fill in the gaps.

## Importance of ACEnet

I can begin by confirming that, in Denmark, ACEnet has been very useful. The informal exchange of information and cooperation between EU countries on Arts Education has been vital. It has provides us with an overview on Arts Education in Europe. Also, we have been inspired by news from other countries, including other ways of working and other approaches to organisation. Our discussion about Anne Bamford's research and reactions in different countries is a good example.

Cooperation between the European Commission and ACEnet has been very important. So, it was considered a splendid idea when ACEnet members were invited to join the OMC group "Synergies between education and culture". In this group we had an opportunity to work in greater detail on cultural experiences in schools. In the process, we became aware of the differences and similarities that we have in Europe with regard to this issue. The working methods of this group were very helpful. We appreciated the subgroup meetings between plenary meetings of the whole OMC, the use of researchers and specialists during the meetings, and the homework which included the making of lists and the sharing of reports on national activities. The only thing missing from that collaborative period is an official list of the activities collected and a catalogue of examples. That would have been helpful.

The ACEnet enables members to learn from one others' success and – at least as important – from one others' failures. Policy-making is an essential issue for a network like ACEnet. The members are all civil servants working with policy-making in their countries. So knowing what is going on and how politicians are reacting in various countries is important. Also, cooperation and communication in the context of ACEnet and EU-initiatives promote a feeling of being EU-citizens.

With respect to global issues, ACEnet discussed UNESCO's Roadmap and its role in preparation for the second UNESCO World Conference on Arts Education held in Seoul. This has given us a feeling of responsibility. We have taken part in international discussions and have also been responsible for implementing the recommendations in our own countries.

## Monitoring and how to use it

I mentioned Anne Bamford's research and our discussions within ACEnet as good examples of sharing knowledge between countries. We need to know what kind of documentation we have on arts education. And we need to share the research that is available. This means that it is important to have an overview on research – to be able to find and use what we need. Even more important is a need to know the gaps and to help one other to fill in those gaps. Consequently, it is important to build relevant networks to collect, to spread, to share and to map knowledge and to develop further research.

## Network – An Example

I have referred to ACEnet as an excellent kind of network. In Denmark we have another network of great importance that focuses on art and culture for children and young people. It is the Network for Children and Culture . The tasks of this network are, for example, to inspire, initiate, coordinate, support and give advice on matters of art and culture for children and young people. The members of this network belonging to the Ministry of Culture in Denmark are the Danish Agency for Culture, The Danish Film Institute, the municipalities, the Ministry of Education and the Ministry of Social Welfare. With these members we have assembled the most important policy-makers in art and culture for children and young people and therefore we have a great potential to develop good initiatives for this purpose.

Another important network is the network on researchers on art and culture for children and young people in Denmark. These two networks (or representatives from them) meet now and then to share knowledge, to debate on actual research, to discuss new tasks and needs and to try to map what we have so far on certain subjects. The cooperation between administration and scientists gives us a strong platform for developing relevant activities in monitoring and evaluation and for showing the relevance of this for Denmark.

## Nordic Mapping Project (Mapping of Research)

In Denmark we have been in charge of a project on mapping research on art and culture in the schools in the Nordic countries over the past ten years. The Nordic Council of Ministers has funded the project and we have a group of contributors from all the Nordic countries. We believe we have a common Nordic view on childhood and we want to benefit from this.

## The Nordic View on Children

One explanation of the Nordic view would be that all the Nordic countries believe in democracy as a right. We believe in children as "beings" and not only "becomings". This means that it is important to give children a right to a childhood with qualities for their specific age and not only to prepare them to be schoolchildren or adults. Children have a right to art and culture and a right to enjoy art for art's own sake – just like you and me – and not always for a purpose, decided by adults.

There are not many results to report, as yet, because the mapping is still in process, but one of the preliminary results is that we unfortunately have very little research on art for children in the Nordic countries. This result demands new strategies! Anne Bamford has conducted research in most of the Nordic countries, so we will add a special chapter in our report with her comments. We will also add a chapter about national strategies in all of the Nordic countries.

## Concluding Remarks

We all share the belief that creativity changes the world and we think that there is some evidence supporting this belief. But we know very little about what we have and how to find it. This is why we need international cooperation. I know that the Netherlands and Germany are already mapping this kind of research. I am sure other countries have some mapping research also.

Does the effort pay off? It does. If you agree with this, the next step will be to use our different networks to share these mappings in order to develop the best opportunities to give children and young people access to art and culture.

Fianne Konings and Barend van Heusden

# Evaluating Partnership, or how to Evaluate the Contribution of Cultural Institutions to an Integrated Curriculum for Culture Education in Primary Schools

## Abstract

Each year, many thousands of children and youngsters take part, with their school, in educational projects that have been designed and developed by cultural institutions, such as museums and theatres. Although the importance of these cultural educational programs is being stressed by governments and cultural institutions, the (added) value of these activities for the school and for the pupils is unclear.

Our research focuses on the ways in which cultural institutions and their educational programs contribute, or could contribute, to an integrated curriculum for culture education and to the cultural development of children. In this article an instrument is presented that allows us to *analyze* and *evaluate* the contribution of cultural institutions to an integrated curriculum for culture education.

The question to which we wanted to find an answer is: Can we systematically describe and evaluate the ways in which an institution contributes to an (integrated) culture education curriculum of one or more schools, and can we draw any conclusions about the added value of the cultural education program offered?

This article consists of three parts: First, we explain from a theoretical perspective how the contribution of a cultural institution can be analyzed. In order to do so we focus upon the contents of the cultural education programs and upon the tuning process taking place between schools and cultural institutions about these contents.

Secondly, the theoretical framework is used to analyze the two aspects, the contents and the tuning respectively, in educational programs of cultural institutions. This will be illustrated with an analysis of a film project about fairytales developed by a youth-theatre for, and in consultation with a school for primary education in the Netherlands.

Thirdly and finally, we conclude by answering the research question. In this section we will also discuss the potential of the instrument and its practical value for the evaluation of cultural educational programs and activities.

*Keywords:* Cultural education, cultural institutions, cultural education programs, integrated cultural education.

## 1. Introduction

In this article we will provide an – affirmative – answer to the question: Can the ways in which an institution contributes to an (integrated) culture education curriculum of one or more schools be systematically described and evaluated, and can any conclusions be drawn about the added value of the cultural education program offered?

In order to analyze what the contribution of a cultural education program to an integrated curriculum for cultural education could be, we will have to explain what we mean by the concepts *cultural institution, cultural education program* and *integrated curriculum for culture education.*

We take the concept of *cultural institution* in a broad sense as encompassing all sorts of institutions, from a youth theatre or art museum to a heritage institution, a music school, or a center for the arts that has the task to develop cultural education programs for schools.

A *cultural education program* is a program developed for schools. Such a program can last a couple of weeks or be confined to a single activity. It can take place in school or in the institution. It can be (mainly) productive, receptive or a combination of the two.

Our view of an *integrated curriculum for cultural education* is based on the theoretical framework developed by Barend van Heusden in the research project *Culture in the Mirror (CIM)* (cf. Van Heusden 2010). This framework will be explained in the next section (*Contents*).

It will be argued that a cultural education program can be analyzed with respect to two main aspects, namely the *contents* of the program, and the *tuning* that takes place between school(s) and a cultural institution. The theory of contents is based on the 'Culture in the Mirror' *(CIM)* theoretical framework for an integrated curriculum for culture education (van Heusden 2010). The theory of tuning is based on an extensive review of the literature related to this topic.

## 2. Contents

A cultural education program is analysed on the basis of the *CIM* theoretical framework. *CIM* is a theory of culture and culture education (van Heusden 2009; van Heusden 2010). According to the theory, the main goal of culture education is to help children in developing their cultural (self-)consciousness, i.e. their ability to reflect on culture in the broadest sense.

The following section is based on several publications by van Heusden (1997, 1999, 2003, 2007, 2008, 2009a, 2009b, 2010a, 2010b, 2011). We will explain what is meant by culture, cultural (self-)consciousness and an integrated curriculum for culture education.

### Culture

Van Heusden uses a broad and a narrow definition of culture. Culture is our intentional behaviour (the broad definition), which is what distinguishes us from other animals.

This means that we are aware of our memories and use them to interpret an ever-changing actuality. This intentional behaviour has three characteristics: (1) Humans experience a difference between the situation they are in (the 'here and now') and their memories. (2) They can cope with this difference and adjust to the new situation and (3) lastly they can reflect upon their memories and upon the process of adjustment. This capacity for self-reflexivity underlies the narrow definition of culture. Culture in the narrow sense, or cultural (self-)consciousness, is our ability to reflect on memories and behaviour (i.e. on culture in the broad sense).

Culture – in the broad sense – is conceived as the continuous process of adaptation of our memories to the situation we are in. We use our memory to recognize a continuously changing reality – to give meaning to it, and we adapt our memories to 'fit' the new situation.

We adapt to our environment using four basic thinking skills, namely: *perception, imagination, conceptualization* and *analysis*. For example, when we arrive at a holiday destination, let's say a tropical island, we perceive and take in the environment. For instance, we notice the weather, the location of our room, and a variety of other sights, sounds and smells. When it is very hot, we can imagine how it would be if we had chosen an Alpine holiday destination. We can imagine how cold it would be and enjoy the warmth of the current location. We can also go over other possible holiday destinations in our mind and by comparing and contrasting, emphasize the conditions at our current location.

Culture as adaptation is a continuous process. We continually perceive, imagine, conceptualize and analyse, and organize our behaviour on the basis to the outcome of this process.

These basis skills are expressed through four types of media. These are:
- The body (e.g., the mind, in gestures, or in a dance)
- Objects (e.g., a chair or an art object)
- Language (e.g., spoken words, a poem)
- Graphics (e.g., a painting, or a population growth graphic visualisation)

## Cultural (Self-)Consciousness

One aspect of culture is cultural (self-)consciousness (or culture in the narrow sense). Humans have the ability to reflect on themselves, on others and on culture in general. When we reflect upon our own adaptations, we use the same four basic cognitive skills, namely (self-)perception, (self-)imagination, (self-)conceptualization, and (self-)analysis, and the same media types (body, object, language and graphics). Meditation, for instance, would be an example of reflective perception. Another example of self-perception would be watching the news, where we look at the actions of our culture daily. An important form of expressing self-imagination is art. In theatre, we give meaning to ourselves, others and culture in general through language, body and objects. In film, we make use of the graphic medium and in dance, we use the body. We conceptualize ourselves in the field of history. We interpret our past and label what we find worthwhile to remember. When we reflect upon and analyse our world, as we do in science, we search for underlying structures.

## An Integrated Curriculum for Culture Education

We can now, in the light of this theory of culture, define the focus of cultural education in school as cultural (self-)consciousness. Cultural education should be about culture. This sounds rather obvious, but what about school projects, for instance, which ask children to reflect on 'trees', or 'water'? Such projects only become cultural education when children are asked to reflect upon what the trees, or the water, mean to us (for instance, where do we plant trees, and why? What does it mean to live in a city nearby the sea?). Or, to refer to Mondriaan (Dutch spelling), why did he paint the trees the way he did?

The main goal of cultural education thus becomes the development of the cultural consciousness of pupils.

To achieve this goal, we have to be knowledgeable about how children of a certain age perceive, imagine, conceptualize and analyse the world. We have to know what children of a certain age are able to do with their body, with objects, language and graphical notation. In the *Culture in the Mirror* research project the research literature on the development of the basic cognitive and medial skills of children ranging from 4 to over 18 years old is reviewed.[1]

So when we strive to implement an integrated curriculum for culture education, we try to reach and develop the cultural self-consciousness of pupils of a certain age. But what makes the curriculum 'integrated' is the taking into consideration of different aspects of a pupil's background, education and development, and structuring the curriculum accordingly. In order to do this, we take into account the culture of the pupil (his or her memories and lived actuality). We also need to know about the educational program of the school, about what has gone before and what will come after. Moreover, we want to know what educational material is covered in other (non-cultural) courses. This body of knowledge grounds the coherence of a continuous cultural education curriculum within the educational program of a school.

Generally speaking, the contribution of a cultural institution to an integrated curriculum for cultural education is mainly supportive. The school is the architect of the cultural education of its pupils. So when a cultural institution wants to contribute to the cultural education of pupils, it has to work closely with schools, taking into consideration the developmental stage of the pupil and the school program of the pupils.

## Conclusions

When analysing the content of a cultural education program developed by a cultural institution, we examine the contents, its relatedness to the school program and the way in which it connects to the developmental stage the pupils are in. More specifically, we look at:

---

1  Theisje van Dorsten (4-10 years), Welmoed Ekster (10-14 years) and Emiel Copini (14-18+).

Contents:
- Which cultural issue is central in the program: what aspect of culture is reflected upon?
- Basic skills: which basic skills are developed by reflecting on these issues (perceiving, imagining, conceptualizing and analysing)?
- Media: which media (body, objects, language, graphical notation or a combination of these) are used in the reflection process? Which medial skills are trained?

Coherence (in school):
- What happens before and after the cultural project? How does it fit within the curriculum? Which education themes are being covered in non-cultural courses (which skills, or mediums)?

Connectedness (to pupils' development):
- What is the relation to the culture of the pupil? (How) are the issues connected to the cultural (self-)consciousness of a pupil of a certain age?

## 3. Tuning: Collaboration

### Collaboration

One of the starting points of this research was the question: why is the collaboration between schools and cultural institutions mostly occasional and seldom lasting? On the basis of a review of the research on coordination and collaboration in cultural education in the Netherlands and on collaboration in cooperation in general, the insight emerged that for collaboration one needs tuning, but for tuning one does not need to collaborate (Konings 2011). The main goal in cultural education is to connect to the culture and cultural consciousness of pupils. As the school is primarily responsible for the pupils education, the cultural institution not 'only' has to connect with (and know a lot about) the ability of pupils to reflect on a certain issue through basic skills and media. If cultural institutions really want to substantially contribute to the development of pupils and to an integrated curriculum for culture education, they must work together closely with schools and get to know both about the culture of the pupils and about the educational program.

### Trust: Reference, Goal Setting, Collective Action and Formalization

We will therefore now analyse the dimensions of the collaborative process that takes place between schools and cultural institutions for implementing in the context of the designing of culture education projects.

In the literature on collaboration, 'trust' is an important concept (Klein Woolthuis 1999; Nooteboom 2002, 2009; Vlaar 2006; Vlaar et al. 2006), which also plays a significant role in the tuning relation of schools and cultural institutions. Klein Woolthuis

(1999) distinguishes three aspects of trust, namely trust propensity (willingness to trust), cognition based trust (trust in knowledge and abilities) and affect based trust (feelings of trust) (p. 45-46). For cultural education, trust in the capacities of the employees of the school and the cultural institutions is crucial (Klein Woolthuis 1999). But in culture education, trust in the respective capacities of schools and cultural institutions is not always present. This quote in a publication on collaboration in cultural education gives an illustration of this 'distrust':

"Centres for the arts find that schools pay to little attention to the quality of cultural activities. Employees of centres are often critical. They find that the quality of cultural activities in schools can always be better. The question is whether you can exchange thoughts about this issue with educators? Teachers of primary schools often assume that they know enough to give instructions and teach about the cultural activities. They trust their knowledge and skills and sometimes do not recognize that their expertise is generally at a low level" (Hagenaars et al. 2006).

In this example the cultural institutions and specific art centres appear not to trust the capacities of schools for supporting culture in school.

Although there are still differences of opinion about the concept (and impact) of trust on collaboration[2], it is widely held that trust has effect on organisations and collaboration (Voortman, 2012). Although we are not researching trust in culture education, we look for aspects of trust that will help us analyse the tuning between cultural institutions and schools on the cultural educational program of a cultural institution.

We focus on the dynamics that have a positive effect on trust. A direct effect on and increase of trust is realized through *collective action* (Nooteboom 2002; van Delden 2009) and *formalization* (Vlaar 2006; Vlaar et al. 2006). Collective actions are about working together on a task. When the working together is a success, then the trust grows. Formalization refers to the process (conversations, including those in the corridors) and the products (project-plans, contracts and evaluations) in an interaction between two parties. Both, the process and the products are important in knowing and understanding (and trusting) each other.

Two other aspects have an indirect effect on trust, namely *goal setting* and the frame of *reference of the participants*. There is a relation between goal setting (van Delden 2009) and collective action. Van Delden (2009) argues that when a clear mission is absent the working together won't work, referring to this situation as a "seeming cooperation". Finally, the collective action and the formalization continually influence the reference of participants (Vlaar, 2006; Vlaar et al., 2006). When there is successful joint experience, the reference grows as well as the trust.

---

2  See also Nooteboom (2009, p. 150-151): "From a social science perspective, some take the view that trust is viable, without necessarily becoming blind or unconditional. […] A committed partner does not immediately exit from the relationship in case of unforeseen opportunities or problems, but engages in 'voice'."

## Conclusion

In the analysis of the tuning of a cultural institution with a school about a program of a cultural institution, the following issues and aspects will be looked at:
- Frame of reference of the school and the cultural institution and shared frame of reference (contents: theme, skill and medium)
- Goal setting: what are the goals of the activity (with respect to the content)? What are the goals of school? What are the goals of the cultural institution? What are the shared goals?
- Joint/collective action: who determines the focus of the project? Who does what (management, teacher, art teacher, employee cultural institution)? Who is responsible?
- Formalize: between whom is the conversation held (management level, teacher level)? What are the conversations about? What is written down (project plan, evaluation and contract) by whom?

## Instrument of Analysis and Illustration

### Analysis: Methodology and Instrument

The theoretical input leads to a framework that allows us to analyse the contribution of cultural programs, developed by cultural institutions, to culture education in primary schools. This instrument is presented in figure 1 and will be illustrated with a case study (Thomas 2011) of a cultural educational program designed by a cultural institution for a primary school.

| Who, what (where), how, and why (when)? | |
|---|---|
| Tuning | Content |
| Shared reference | Issue/topic of cultural education (which aspects of culture) |
| Collective goal setting | Basic skills (perception, imagination, conceptualization, analysis) |
| Collective (joint) action of school and cultural institution (determining of roles) | Media and media skills (body, objects, language, graphic notation) |
| Formalizing<br><br>Verbal/process: conversations before, in between and after<br>Written/product: project-plan, contract, evaluation (in between, afterwards) | Connection:<br>- cultural (self-)consciousness of pupils at a certain age<br>- cultural background of pupils<br><br>Coherence:<br>- what happens before and after<br>- what is the relation to non-cultural courses |

Figure 1: A framework for the analysis of cultural education programs

The case-study is based on an analysis with the instrument of documents and interviews. In the next section the instrument is illustrated with a film-project of a youth theatre which was developed for a particular school. The analysed documents were the project-plan, educational material, evaluation, a document for the ability to repeat the project and a DVD of the end-presentation. The documents were analysed with the instrument.

On the basis of this analysis the art director of the youth theatre and the manager of the school were interviewed and the final analysis was made. The analysis is audited by an external partner. In this case the PhD-student Drs. (MA) F. Konings analysed the project and her supervisor, Prof. Dr. B. van Heusden audited the analysis. He mainly focused on the grounding of the argument.

## Case: Film-Project of a Youth Theatre

The film-project the youth theatre developed was about fairytales. The youth theatre designed the project for, and in conversation with a school for primary education. For a period of two years, the artistic leader of the theatre was in contact with the manager of the school about the project.

In the four weeks the project lasted, each class filmed a fairy tale which was selected by the artistic director, with input of the pupils. The pupils were from different cultural backgrounds, and were invited to present fairytales from their own culture in class. They came up with 35 fairytales. The artistic director selected four tales and added six other fairytales to the project (one for the frame-story which connected the films of the pupils, one for a performance of the youth theater itself, and four for four different age groups). In the project the pupils developed (imagined) scenes, played the scenes, made the decors and the props and taped the film. They were supervised by media teachers. In the end, the films were brought together in a frame-story and edited by professionals. The film was presented to children and parents along with a performance of a Turkish fairy tale by the youth-theatre.

Below we give the analysis of the project:

| Tuning | Content |
|---|---|
| Shared reference:<br><br>The basis for the starting of a conversation between school and youth theatre is the desire of both partners to realize a project for the children.<br>Both sides agree on the subject: fairy tales. For the youth theatre, fairy tales are part of their repertoire. The school had an experience with a fairy tale project ten years earlier.<br>They did not talk about a shared experience concerning the meaning of fairy tales for the school and children of different ages. | Issue/topic of cultural education:<br><br>Ten fairytales from Europe (the Netherlands and Germany), Africa, and the Middle East (including Turkey) |
| Collective goal setting:<br><br>The school set the conditions for the project. The cultural institution chose the contents.<br><br>The school wanted a project which would make the children more creative. The project could take up to three weeks and all classes had to participate in it.<br><br>The youth theatre aims at working with schools, because this is what it is funded for.<br>The goal for the children according to the artistic director, was to experience how stories can be manipulative. She did not explicitly state this in the conversations with school and the project plan.<br>The explicit goal was to experience a story by "living" it (like an artistic director).<br><br>The choice of the film was the artistic director's, who finds putting on plays with children is not very useful, because there are usually difficulties with language and presentation for an audience. For the manager of the school it didn't matter whether the project involved making a film or a live performance. | Basic skills:<br><br>Productive imagination: making scenes, playing scenes, making decors, props, costumes, and filming.<br><br>Receptive imagination: reading and 'living' fairy tales. Watching a theatre performance.<br><br>Pupils of fourth grade: conceptualization and analysis. Conversation after the performance of the youth theatre with the actors about performing the Turkish fairy tale. The children of the fourth grade also played and filmed a Turkish fairy tail. |
| Joint/collective action:<br><br>On the management level, there was some exchange during the preparation. Six conversations took place in the course of two years.<br><br>During the project, a problem emerged related to the teacher's skills. The external teachers, i.e., the media teachers, had very little background in teaching in class. Therefore, from the second week of the project onwards, the school teachers worked together with the external staff.<br><br>The media teachers were visual artists who had little experience with making a film. The youth theatre provided much support during the project. | Media:<br><br>Filming: graphic, productive (adults do the editing/assembling)<br><br>Writing scenes: language, productive<br><br>Playing: body, language, productive<br><br>Making decors and costumes: objects, productive |

| Formalization: | Connectedness (children) and coherence (school): |
|---|---|
| Process:<br>Six conversations on management level in the preparation of the project.<br>A conversation between the artistic director and two Turkish mothers.<br>Consultation on management level during the project.<br><br>Two meetings for school teachers (only) prior to the project.<br>Daily consultation between school teachers and external teachers.<br><br>Products:<br>- Teachers got three newsletters from the youth theatre prior to the project, and three during the project.<br>- A project plan from the youth theatre.<br>- An evaluation from the youth theatre.<br>- Information about, and lessons for toddlers from the youth theatre.<br>- A manual about the project from the youth theatre for future projects. | Connectedness on to pupils:<br>The Cultural consciousness: not taken into account<br>The Cultures of the pupils: minimal, pupils contribute 35 fairy-tales in the beginning of the project. The artistic leader selects four.<br><br>Coherence with schoolprogram:<br>- the project is a stand alone.<br>- There are no preconceived relations with other courses. The manager notes that the pupils made some scenes in the language lessons. This was due to lack of time. The artistic director saw goats made by children on the windows of the toddler class who filmed "the wolve and the seven goats". |

Figure 2: Analysis of the cultural education program: A film-project of a youth theatre for all age groups in a primary school

Our conclusion was that this project was definitely a typical example of culture education. A very specific and characteristic aspect of culture, fairy tales, had been chosen as central topic, around which the activities were organized. Despite some tuning, the project did not contribute in any significant way to an integrated curriculum for cultural education.

The school did not formulate any specific goal for the children, other than that they should be creative. The youth theatre, on the other hand, had a clear goal and invested a lot in the tuning process. But this was mainly focused on the organizational aspects of the project (its practical side), rather than on the contents.

## Conclusions and Discussion

We have been searching for a means that would give us insight in the added value of cultural programs offered by cultural institutions to primary schools. Each year children visit cultural institutions and/or participate in cultural education programs, but the added value for the school curriculum and the development of children is not so clear.

We have sketched an instrument that allows us to systematically describe and analyze a cultural program or project. Such an analysis would provide us with a basis on which to draw conclusions about the value of program.

The two main aspects of the instrument/framework are 'contents' and 'tuning'. With regards to the contents of a program, we ask what cultural issue is central in the program: What do the children reflect upon? We then focus upon the basic skills that are developed (i.e. perception, imagination, conceptualization and analysis), the medium skills that are trained (the body, objects, language, graphics or a combination of these). We also look at how the project connects to the age and cultural background of the children (connectedness), and at the relation to the school-curriculum (coherence). What do fairy tales mean to a five-year old child? Or to an eight-year old? Is a seven-year old child able to shoot a film scene? If so, how should he or she be instructed? What media skills do we want to develop or train? Why these skills at this age? Why in relation to this theme? What happens before and after this project? How does it connect to the curriculum?

In our case study, the issue, fairy tales in general, is not so relevant for the project. Each class is working on one specific fairy tail and looks at other fairy tales during the end presentation. The focus is, according to the goals, on the imagination of the children in there ability to show this imagination in film. The children ought to 'live' the story and show this in film. In the lessons the focus is on writing and playing a scene. To film it, the children push the on-button on the camera. The final editing of the film is done without the children.

The skills and abilities of the children are not taken in account. The toddlers and children from first till sixth grade did all the same. There was no difference between a four year old and a twelve year old. They all had to 'live' a fairy tale and film it. Even though the culture of the children was a starting point for the collection of the fairy tales, the artistic director alone choice four fairy tales out of 35 added tales by children. She herself added six other fairy tales to the project.

The project had no connection whatsoever to other activities in school. The school had no intention to integrate it in the school program or relate it to other, eventually non-cultural subjects.

Looking at the tuning, we analyze what the differences in the frames of reference of the school and the cultural institution are, and where they match, if at all. In our case study example, the school and the theatre shared an interest in fairy tales, but this frame of reference was not discussed. We also analyzed the setting of the goals. In the casestudy, the school had formulated quite general goals ('to improve creativity') and the theatre tried to realize these goals. As a consequence, the cultural institution took the lead in deciding what would happen and now and then 'overlooked' the possible involvement of the schoolteachers in the developing of the project. No collective action on the teachers' level was organized. On the management level, there was some collective action, although, as we mentioned earlier, the director of the school set the boundaries and the cultural institution had to work within these. We saw the same thing on the level of the formalization. All the documents were produced by the cultural institution and conversations during the development phase took place only on management level.

The program analyzed did not contribute to an integrated curriculum in culture education. This shouldn't come as a surprise, as the school did not intend to develop such a culture education curriculum. However the value of the project for the children's education is also far from clear, as neither the school nor the cultural institution reflected upon what the children would or could learn from it.

We now come to our final question: What is the potential of this instrument and what could be its practical value for the evaluation of cultural education programs and activities?

The instrument may be used to answer the question whether and how a cultural institution program may contribute to a school's culture education curriculum. This is done through the analysis of contents and tuning. In many cases, as in the one discussed here, the answer will be negative. One of the reason is that there are still very few schools that have developed an integrated curriculum for cultural education.

For research the potential of the instrument is set in testing it in a variety of cases and developing the instrument to make statements that do more justice to the current cultural educational programs. This must be done in order to develop it into an instrument that strengthens the conversations between schools and cultural institutions.

The instrument certainly also has practical value for cultural institutions at this moment because it gives insight into the contents and tunings of their cultural program. This insight can be used as a basis for the conversation between schools and cultural institutions about the cultural consciousness of children they want to develop, their goals and the ways in which they want to reach these goals. In the case-study we see that the two different languages of the school and the institution did not always match and, consequently, that opportunities were missed.

The instrument thus serves as an opportunity to start, or deepen, the conversation between institutions and educators. But before we can start that conversation we have to evaluate what's happening. The instrument can also be of help in this important process.

## References

Hagenaars, P., Lieftink, J., Vingerhoets, C. (2006). *Samenwerken is een kunst. Een inventarisatie van en een handreiking voor samenwerking en netwerkvorming tussen Centra voor de Kunsten en het primair onderwijs.* Utrecht: Cultuurnetwerk Nederland.

Klein Woolthuis, R. (1999). *Sleeping with the enemy. Trust, dependence and contract in interorganisational relationships.* Enschede: Universiteit Twente (dissertation).

Konings, F.E.M (2011). *Culturele instellingen en de doorlopende leerlijn cultuuronderwijs. Een analyse-instrument.* Utrecht: FCP.

Nooteboom, B. (2002). *A Cognitive Theory of the Firm. Paper for a workshop on theories of the firm, Paris, November 2002.* Rotterdam: Rotterdam School of Management, Erasmus University Rotterdam.

Nooteboom, B. (2009). *A Cognitive Theory of the Firm. Learning. Governance and Dynamic Capabilities.* Cheltenham: Edward Elgar.

Thomas, G. (2011). *How to do your Case Study.* London: SAGE Publications Ltd.

van Delden, P. (2009). *Samenwerking in de publieke dienstverlening. Ontwikkelingsverloop en resultaten.* Delft: Eburon (dissertation).

van Heusden, B. (1997). *Why literature? An inquiry into the nature of literary semiosis.* Tübingen: Stauffenburg Verlag.

van Heusden, B. (1999). The emergence of difference: Some notes on the evolution of human semiosis. In: *Semiotica Special Issue on Biosemiotics,* 127 (1/4), pp. 631-646.

van Heusden, B. (2003). De maker. Notities naar aanleiding van *Wij zagen ons in een kleine groep mensen veranderen* van Tonnus Oosterhof. In: *Spiegel der Letteren*, themanummer 'Literatuur en nieuwe media' (editors Jan van Looy and Barend van Heusden), 45, 4, pp. 361-377.

van Heusden, B. (2007). Het leven nagebootst in taal: een cognitieve benadering van de Literaire mimesis. In: *Neerlandistiek.nl 07.08c*.

van Heusden, B. (2008). *Cultuur in de Spiegel: naar een doorlopende leerlijn geïntegreerde cultuureducatie, Projectplan voor subsidiepartners*.

van Heusden, B. (2009a). Dealing with Difference: From cognition to semiotic cognition. In: *Cognitive Semiotics,* Issue 4, 2009.

van Heusden, B. (2009b). Semiotic cognition and the logic of culture. In: *Pragmatics & Cognition* 17,3, pp. 611-627.

van Heusden, B. (2010a). *Cultuur in de Spiegel naar een doorlopende leerlijn cultuuronderwijs*. Groningen: RuG en SLO.

van Heusden, B. (2010b). *De structuur van cultuur, of: wat weet de schildpad?* (Oratie).

van Heusden, B. (2011). *Presentatie Cultuur in de Spiegel, naar een doorlopende leerlijn Cultuuronderwijs*. Dag van Taal, Kunst & Cultuur, February 2011.

Vlaar, P. (2006). *Making Sense of Formalization in Interorganizational Relationships. Beyond Coordination and Control*. Rotterdam: EUR (dissertation).

Vlaar, P., van den Bosch, F., Volberda, H. (2006). *Coping with problems of understanding in interorganizational relationships: using formalization as means to make sense*. Rotterdam: ERIM Report Series Research in Management.

Jessy Siongers, Dries Vanherwegen and John Lievens

# The Multiple Layers of Arts Education in School

As a policy topic, arts education is certainly not confined to 'culture'. Policy makers in education, media, well-being and youth also give significant attention to programs of arts education. Across these domains, mediating, integrative and participation enhancing functions are ascribed to arts education in schools. Besides the obvious mission of creating cultural knowledge, interest and competences, it is believed that arts education paves the way for lifelong cultural learning experiences and that it fosters the necessary social and behavior skills for school and adult life (Winner, Goldstein & Vincent-Lancrin, 2013). The majority of both policy makers and arts educators are convinced of these outcomes of arts education. Nevertheless, while a number of studies find indications for a positive relation between enrolment in arts educational programs and broader cultural participation (e.g. Nagel & Ganzeboom, 2002; Nagel, Ganzeboom et al., 1997; Kracman, 1996; Kraaykamp, 2003), more in depth research is needed to gain insight in the educational processes that underpin the reported wider benefits.

However, the cultural and artistic sector seems rather suspicious when it concerns large-scale surveys on arts education, assuming that large-scale measurements would fail to capture the diversity of approaches that exist within arts education and to grasp the total value of arts education and the impact it has. We strongly believe that surveys can improve our understanding of the diverse ways schools pay attention to the arts and the – arts as well as non-arts related – outcomes of it. That being said, research on arts education is still in its infancy and indeed a lot of the ongoing surveys fail to capture the complexity and diversity in arts education (see also Winner, Goldstein & Vincent-Lancrin, 2013). Most of surveys that have been carried out so far focused on only a small part of what takes place in schools with concern to the arts. They mostly concentrate on the arts subjects, e.g. Nagel, Damen & Haanstra, 2010; Kinder, Lord et al., 2000; see also Klopper & Power, 2010; Winner, Goldstein & Vincent-Lancrin, 2013) while research hardly focuses on more project-based initiatives (e.g. attending contemporary dance, or organizing school plays). We believe that research on arts education may benefit from a multi-level and multi-actor approach that grasps the different contexts in which arts education takes place within a school (e.g. at the playground or in the classroom) and that measures input, process and output by taking into account the perspectives and experiences of all school actors (pupils, teachers and principals).

In this contribution we will elucidate these different perspectives and show how empirical research can take them into account by drawing on a recently finished study in Flemish (Flanders is the Dutch speaking part of Belgium) secondary schools that used a multi-actor design. In order to grasp the complexity and diversity of arts education in Flemish schools we went to 84 secondary schools during spring 2013, where a total of 5086 pupils completed a questionnaire in their class. In addition approximately 2000 parents, 1100 teachers and 65 principals completed a coupled questionnaire.

## Different Methods

Schools but also teachers within schools differ in their emphasis on arts education and their methods. Therefore, the mapping of art education in schools may certainly not be restricted to what happens in art classes. Art classes are often – and this certainly is the case in Flanders – restricted to the junior school year, while in the senior years secondary school arts education is generally only available to the more affluent youth (Bamford, 2007). Thus, the competencies and interests that young people develop in the field of art and culture are influenced by various actors within the school and art education happens on several occasions and locations of which the arts class is just one. Therefore, measuring arts education and its impact has to take into account aspects such as the school culture, the view teachers have on arts education and the way art is embedded in school life.

The bulk of the existing studies however only focus on the formal aspects of arts education (e.g. Nagel, Damen & Haanstra, 2010; Kinder, Lord et al., 2000) as well as some of the most visible and easy countable indicators such as the existence of a specific course on arts or the time devoted to that course or other forms of arts education. Most of the formal aspects are however highly influenced by national legislation and neglect the huge variation that exists within countries and within schools.

According to Bamford (2007) one could create a continuum, ranging from the more formal to the more informal aspects in cultural learning. The rather formal forms, according to Bamford (2007), refer to forms of arts and cultural education in a structured educational setting with a certain regularity, and a trajectory to be followed (mainly art subjects, musical or creative courses), while rather informal forms refer to workshops, projects, (city) trips, extra-curricular activities, museum or theatre visits, etc. In our study we tried to cover as much as possible of this continuum of cultural learning in schools. The indicators we used to measure formal and informal curricula on art are shown in Table 1.

Nevertheless, many of these activities, even the ones that Bamford calls informal, encompass quite formal aspects of cultural learning. Both the formal and informal curricula are predominantly part of an official school policy towards arts and arts education. Both have proven their relevance with regard to the development of cultural competences. However, the more normative outcomes such as cultural interests and cultural tastes are most likely more influenced by the so-called "hidden curriculum". While the formal and informal curricula are habitually part of an official school policy towards arts and arts education, the hidden curriculum is not. It is a side effect of education and refers to the implicit messages a school sends about culture and arts through the institutional environment and values. It captures "the unconscious and unintentional learning arrangements and processes that potentially or actually influence students" (Klaassen, 1996: 83). Concerning the creation of interest and value formation, the hidden curriculum is often considered more important than the manifest curriculum (Klaassen, 1996: 84; Sachs & Smith, 1988; Ehman, 1980; Elchardus, Kavadias & Siongers, 1998).

This hidden curriculum may amount to a latent content of the official curriculum, but also embraces the additional learning effects associated with the process of teaching and the organization of the school. These are things that the students hardly notice, but nevertheless could have a huge impact. An example of such a latent transfer is the filter function, which is fulfilled by the teacher. A teacher is indeed bound to the official curriculum, but in the daily practice, the subject material is filtered with certain interpretations and beliefs inherent to the personality of the teacher (Klaassen, 1996; Pajares, 1992; Wren, 1999). Therefore we also measured the cultural interests, tastes and practices of the teachers.

In addition, the hidden curriculum also pertains to the dominant patterns of interaction found in schools or what is also called the school climate. Studies on non-cognitive outcomes of education provide strong evidence that that desired attitudes and competencies are not so much achieved as a result of what pupils are taught, but by the way in which the school is organized (Klaassen, 1996; Campbell, 2008). For example, the general finding in studies on citizenship education is that teaching democratic citizenship is most successful in a democratic setting where participation is encouraged, where opinions can be openly expressed and discussed and where there is freedom of expression for both pupils and teachers (see for instance: Campbell, 2008; Elchardus, Kavadias & Siongers, 1998; Hahn, 1998). In the same vein, it is important to look at the school culture and the way arts and culture are integrated in school life. Therefore we asked not only principals but also teachers about their vision on culture and arts education.

Finally, the spatial and structural setting of the school encompasses an important aspect of the hidden curriculum of a school. The way schools are spatially organized, furnished and decorated, the look of the classrooms, all these aspects formulate latent messages. Therefore, we incorporated these spatial elements in our study. The researchers completed an observation report for each school visited in which they reported on the visibility of culture and arts in the school.

## Different Actors

As noted, our study adopted a multi-actor approach. To achieve a better understanding of cultural education we asked principals, teachers as well as pupils about the cultural activities that were organized in their school, if they participated in these and how they perceived these different activities. This resulted in school-level data which were essential for a complete understanding of arts education practiced. Beside these school actors, parents were also questioned.

Multi-actor data have the advantage that they capture multiple perspectives on the same phenomena and allow a measurement of contextual effects, therefore capture a richness and depth that may otherwise be missed. One-actor data (e.g. a survey among pupils only) can only estimate effects of contexts through the characteristics that are measured, with the disadvantage that such measured characteristics do not cover the complete context effect.

## Different Levels

We also adopted a multi-level analytical approach. Individuals interact with the social context they belong to (Hox, 2002). Pupils are influenced by the social groups and contexts – schools and classrooms – to which they belong; the properties of those groups and settings are in turn influenced by the pupils. When studying art education and its outcomes we therefore have to take into account these contextual and compositional effects.

Three levels were taken into account in our study: the student level, the classroom level and the school level. Student indicators were measured by questioning the pupils themselves. Some of the effects of the higher levels (classroom and school level) were measured directly. For instance principals were asked about the school policy on cultural education, the school infrastructure and about the art subjects and cultural projects that were organized in their school.

However, the variation that exists in the impact that schools and art education have on art- and non-art outcomes cannot be attributed solely to these directly measured school or classroom indicators. Research has shown that schools differ considerably in their student outcomes, even after taking account of – at an individual level – students' ability and family background and – at the school level – school policy indicators (Hamnett, Ramsden & Butler, 2007; Opdenakker & Van Damme, 2007; Perry, 2012). In these studies differences in outcomes are related to differences in the social composition of the students in the school (the "compositional" effect), meaning that school level aggregated variables make a significant contribution in the explanation of different outcomes (after taking into account the same variable at the individual level). The likely rationale for such an effect exists, in part, because students are not randomly assigned to schools. For indicators concerning school composition we relied on information gathered from the pupils themselves (see Table 1) and the information gathered from their parents. Yet, where in studies on school outcomes one has traditionally focused on the SES and ethnic composition of the school, we have broadened these composition indicators to cultural background indicators, such as the cultural participation of the parents, the cultural objects at home and the extent to which they are encouraged by their parents to participate in arts and culture. These indicators informed us on the cultural capital (cfr. Bourdieu) of pupils within a given school. Our first analyses show that the school composition based on cultural background differs tremendously across the Flemish schools. We believe that this cultural school composition also has an impact on the way in which arts education is organized in schools and the extent to which it is successful in those schools. Both elements are the subject of our current research and analyses.

## Concluding Thoughts

The research design outlined above permits a comprehensive view on arts education, its underlying processes and also its outcomes. Yet, even this design is far from perfect.

One evident restriction is the lack of a longitudinal approach, which does not allow for causal interpretations. However, longitudinal large scale surveys have the disadvantage that they have to cope with a strong and non-random loss of respondents which makes longitudinal research also very expensive. The bulk of reviews on cultural education research therefore indicates experimental research as one of the more promising routes.

Another important restriction is the lack of an international scope. Our research focused on the micro- and meso-level, or the classroom and school level. Schools are however regionally embedded and have to cope with national legislations. An even more neglected level is the country level. Cross-national comparison of arts education is a largely unexplored are of research (one of the exceptions is Bevers, 2005). More information and research on national policies, structures, educational approaches and curricula is needed. This macro level determines the canvas for the other layers. Most of the European countries pay attention to arts education in their curriculum. However, there is considerable variation in the way arts education is approached and implemented in national legislations. Some countries organize arts education as a cross-curricular learning area, others integrate it into existing subjects, and in still other countries it is taught as a separate subject. And also broader educational policy measures and the national culture influence arts education. For instance, policy evolutions relating to the 'maximum bill' (an upper limit on school expenses) in primary education in Flanders limit – especially in the more rural schools – the possibilities for arts education outside the school and force schools to look for alternatives (which may sometimes lead to very creative solutions). Also the legislative, social and cultural contexts of regions or countries make specific forms of arts education more or less plausible and effective. So let this be a plea for more and more profound international collaboration in arts education research.

Table 1: Overview of indicators measured

|  | Pupils | Teachers | Principals |
|---|---|---|---|
| **Formal Curriculum** | | | |
| Policy | | • Cross-curricular team/core group of teachers who are responsible for cultural activities in school: existence, participation in it and realizations | • Vision of the school on cultural education<br>• School policy with concern to cultural education (does the school has a policy plan on culture? integrated approach or isolated activities?) |
| Courses | • Artistic or creative classes they follow | • Artistic or creative courses they give | • Artistic classes that are organized |
| **Informal** | | | |
| Extra-curricular activities outside the school | • Cultural excursions (museum visits, theatre visits, cultural projects at school, library visits, …)<br>  – Organized?<br>  – Did one participate?<br>  – Evaluation<br>  – Pedagogical approach | • Cultural excursions (museum visits, theatre visits, cultural projects at school, library visits, …)<br>  – Organizer?<br>  – Did one participate? | • Participation in school competitions by making use of cultural products or contents |
| Extra-curricular activities inside the school | • Creative activities, workshops in school (playing music, dancing, photography, singing, theatre, drawing, …)<br>  – Organized?<br>  – How often did one participate? | | • Extra-curricular initiatives (choir, reading club, theatre group …)<br>• Media channels made by pupils (school journal, school radio, school blog, …)<br>• Creative activities, workshops in school (playing music, dancing, photography, singing, theatre, drawing, …)<br>  – Organized?<br>  – For which pupils?<br>• Cross-curricular and extra-curricular cultural projects |

| | | | |
|---|---|---|---|
| **Hidden** | | | |
| *Position of arts education in the school* | | • importance attached to arts education in comparison to other subjects<br>• importance attached to the development of cultural competences and interest in relation to other competences and values<br>• Teachers view on arts education and on culture | • importance attached to arts education in comparison to other subjects<br>• importance attached to the development of cultural competences and interest in relation to other competences and values |
| *Cultural participation and interest of actors* | • creative hobby's (outside school)<br>• cultural participation (outside school)<br>• perception of art museums<br>• cultural interests<br>• cultural education outside school | • Teachers cultural activities, tastes and interest | |
| | • do teachers use cultural products in courses (music, film, visual arts, literature, architecture) | • use of cultural products in courses (music, film, visual arts, literature, architecture)<br>• use of cultural hobby's in the lessons | |
| **Context** | | | |
| *School infrastructure* | | | • Infrastructure for cultural activities (auditorium, availability of musical instruments, camera's, …) |
| *Background of the pupils* | • cultural background<br>• socioeconomical background | | |

## References

Bamford, A. (2007). *Kwaliteit en Consistentie: Kunst- en cultuureducatie in Vlaanderen*: CANON, Cultural Unit, Ministry of Education Flanders.

Bevers, T. (2005). Cultural education and the canon: A comparative analysis of the content of secondary school exams for music and art in England, France, Germany, and the Netherlands, 1990–2004. *Poetics, 33*(5), 388-416.

Campbell, D. E. (2008). Voice in the classroom: How an open classroom climate fosters political engagement among adolescents. *Political Behavior, 30*(4), 437-454.

Ehman, L. H. (1980). The American school in the political socialization process. *Review of Educational Research, 50*(1), 99-119.

Elchardus, M., Kavadias, D., & Siongers, J. (1998). *Hebben scholen een invloed op de waarden van jongeren? Een empirisch onderzoek naar de doeltreffendheid van waardevorming in het secundair onderwijs*. Brussel: Vakgroep Sociologie-Onderzoeksgroep TOR, Vrije Universiteit Brussel.

Hahn, C.L. (1998). *Becoming Political. Comparative Perspectives on Citizenship Education*. New York: State University of New York Press.

Hamnett, C., Ramsden, M., & Butler, T. (2007). Social Background, Ethnicity, School Composition and Educational Attainment in East London. *Urban Studies, 44*(7), 1255-1280.

Kinder, K., Lord, P., Stott, A., Schagen, I., Haynes, J., Cusworth, L. et al. (2000). *Arts education in secondary schools: Effects and effectiveness*. Slough: National Foundation for Educational Research.

Klaassen, C. (1996). *Socialisatie en moraal. Onderwijs en waarden in een laat-moderne tijd*. Leuven/Apeldoorn: Garant.

Klopper, C., & Power, B. (2010). Illuminating the gap: An overview of classroom-based arts education research in Australia. *International Journal of Education through Art, 6*(3), 293-308.

Kraaykamp, G. (2003). Literary socialization and reading preferences. Effects of parents, the library, and the school. *Poetics, 31*, 235-257.

Kracman, K. (1996). The effect of school-based arts instruction on attendance at museums and the performing arts. *Poetics, 24*(2-4), 203-218.

Nagel, I., Damen, M. L. & Haanstra, F. (2010). The arts course CKV1 and cultural participation in the Netherlands. *Poetics, 38*(4), 365-385.

Nagel, I., & Ganzeboom, H. B. G. (2002). Participation in Legitimate culture: Family and school effects from adolescence to adulthood. *The Netherlands' Journal of Social Sciences, 38*(2), 102-120.

Nagel, I., Ganzeboom, H. B. G. et al. (1997). Effects of art education in secondary schools on cultural participation in later life. *Journal of Art & Design Education, 16*(3), 325-331.

Opdenakker, M. C., & Van Damme, J. (2007). Do school context, student composition and school leadership affect school practice and outcomes in secondary education? *British Educational Research Journal, 33*(2), 179-206.

Pajares, M. F. (1992). Teachers' beliefs and educational research: Cleaning up a messy construct. *Review of educational research, 62*(3), 307-332.

Perry, L. B. (2012). Causes and Effects of School Socio-Economic Composition? A Review of the Literature. *Education and Society, 30*(1), 19-35.

Sachs, J., & Smith, R. (1988). Constructing teacher culture. *British Journal of Sociology of Education, 9*(4), 423-436.

Winner, E., Goldstein, T. R., & Vincent-Lancrin, S. (2013). *Art for Art's sake? The impact of art education*. OECD – Centre for Educational Research and Innovation.

Wren, D. J. (1999). School Culture: Exploring the Hidden Curriculum. *Adolescence, 34*(135).

# Competencies and Assessment

Ernst Wagner

# The Concept of Competencies in Formal and Non-Formal Arts Education – The Perspective of Research

Since 2000 we have been able to observe a change of paradigms in educational systems, especially in OECD countries: the general trend leads from input to outcome orientation. According to the OECD, "That means that not only "input" [… like curricula, teacher qualification, time resources …] but equally the 'output' is important; e.g. the students should know which learning outcomes and what knowledge they should have achieved after participating in a course, module or study program. Learning outcomes are statements of what a learner knows, understands and is able to do after she or he has completed a learning process."[1]

Avoiding a further increase in the already existing gap between arts education and education in the fields of science, technology, engineering and mathematics (STEM-education, which is generally considered essential in order to meet global competition in the future), is only one motivation for discussing a possible shift in arts education. But how would a competence-based "outcome model" work? What are the consequences for arts education and for research in arts education if we apply these concepts?

## Concept of Competencies

In the current discussions "competence" is defined as the ability of an individual to do a job/task/assignment, to solve a problem properly. Competence can be evaluated and measured by using predefined and differentiated levels. This definition of competence, developed in the 60s and 70s of the last century mainly by psychologists,[2] can easily be applied to arts education, especially at school: students are given assignments where they are able to demonstrate their knowledge, skills and motivation by solving a specific task and the results are then graded by the teacher. To find out what is new – also for arts education – one has to take a closer look at the specific combination of three different dimensions in the definition: the combination of knowledge, skills and behavior. To be competent, a person:
- should be able to interpret a situation in which they have to act, e. g. understand the given problem and have an idea of the strategies required to solve the problem.

---

[1] Dorfler, Ressler, *Competence-oriented Course Evaluation and Follow-up Measures*, Grauz 2009 http://www.oecd.org/edu/imhe/43977332.pdf.
[2] Dreyfus, Hubert L./Dreyfus, Stuart E., *A Qualitative Stance: Essays in honor of Steiner Kvale*. Edited by Klaus Nielsen et al., Aarhus University Press 2008, pp 113-124.

- needs to have a repertoire of possible options to complete the given task and must be able to select the best possible option.
- must have the knowledge, range of skills and motivation that are needed to carry out and fulfill the requirements of the task.
- has to evaluate this process and the results in a self-critical way (the metacognitive aspect) in order to gather information about how to solve similar problems in the future.

The following example may show more clearly how this rather abstract concept could be applied to the field of arts education also in regard to competence-levels. In a visual art lesson with 10-year-old students the following assignment is given to the students: "*Think of a storyline for a fantasy film where a young person has a nightmare. Create a picture showing the most dramatic part of the dream from this young person's point of view.*" It seems obvious how the four points of the competence-process mentioned above can be adapted to this assignment. At this point, it would be of more interest to see how a concept of different competency-levels can be used in the context of art education. A model with five levels of skill acquisition, as the one suggested by Dreyfus and Dreyfus, appears to appropriately reflect the possible range of developments.

1. Dreyfus/Dreyfus identify the first level as the level of the "Novice" and characterize it as "rule-based behavior, strongly limited and inflexible".
   *Solving the assignment mentioned above, a novice would only be able to use learned schemes and patterns of representation to illustrate the thoughts, ideas and images she already has in mind before starting to work on the picture. When something happens in the picture, she hasn't expected (e.g. because she has not the skill to realize it), he will try to correct the "mistake".*
2. The second level is the level of the "Advanced Beginner", who "incorporates aspects of the situation".
   *This person would take what he or she already knows from experience and adapt it to the task, e.g. by using appropriate colors and forms of composition, and by exploring news ways of representation.*
3. The "Competent", who has reached the third level, acts consciously regarding long-term goals and plans.
   *The Practitioner can develop a rather complex output-driven strategy to solve the task e.g. in regards to the size of the picture, the materials and techniques to be used, time management, process planning (e.g. making various drafts, selecting, executing, doing corrections), etc.*
4. The "Proficient" sees the situation as a whole and acts from personal conviction.
   *Using the skills of levels 1 to 3 proficiently, this person is able to create an individual expression, showing his personal involvement in relation to the requirements of the task.*
5. The fifth and final level is the level of the "Expert", who has an intuitive understanding of the situation and zooms in on the central aspects.
   *The expert finds the right balance between personal expression and the expectations of the audience (teacher/classmates). He/she acts creatively in a spontaneous way and is able to focus on specific details without losing the overall perspective.*

Reviewing this attempt of adaption to an ordinary situation in art education, it seems that these criteria for evaluating the outcome fit properly, even though they are mostly used intuitively and never made transparent. If one formulates these criteria explicitly, the consequences for the way of teaching are obvious. The definition of levels shows that a new perspective of competencies differentiates between the **output** – in this case the picture (which is evaluated as a excellent, good, adequate, insufficient, poorly executed, bad solution) – and the **outcome** – the complex competencies performed in solving the assignment.

## Potentials and Challenges for Research

Some of the potentials and challenges of this concept of competencies in regard to research are:
1. A positive result of the change from input to outcome-orientation is that research in arts education can develop a new and innovative focus. We know very little about the learning processes in arts education, especially how a gain in competencies can be observed. And we know next to nothing about the outcome. We know a lot about the output (we can see e.g. the performance of a student on stage, the picture created, or the piece of music played), but nothing about the complex outcome: the acquired competencies.[3] If one follows the outcome-orientation concept, one has to describe precisely the different, exactly defined dimensions of competencies, and the level the student is reaching in these dimensions.
   To give an example: a student should draw a blossom. When the student is able to understand that the illusion of depth in the perception of nature is based on the phenomenon of overlapping/intersection, etc., he will be able to see the surface structure of the blossom autonomously (without help of the teacher). That means transferring a 3-dimensional space into a 2-dimensional plane and is a cognitive activity which can be trained. Finally, the student can use this principle for a naturalistic drawing of, e.g. a blossom on a specific level (this means to solve the assignment as a nature study). If we want to implement the concept of competencies into arts education seriously, we have to analyze the learning processes such tasks involve through empirical research.[4]
2. The given example of drawing a blossom shows that there are many more questions research should face. I have described the activities of the student, when he or she solves this task, by differentiating three dimensions of competencies which are related to visual art and required in this assignment: to perceive/observe (here: nature), to perform the cognitive process of transferring pure, wordless perception into representation and to design/create/show. This analysis is done intuitively and reflects on my own experience in drawing. And it is aligned with international approaches in curriculum developments. But this cannot be the only base. There are scientif-

---
3   Only if one has own experiences in these art-forms, one can imagine what the processes are leading to a specific output and what broader kind of outcome happens.
4   The concept of competencies delivers a critical model of description for these aspects.

ic methods to construct these models in regard to competence dimensions as well as skill acquisition levels, and to substantiate them through empirical research.

3. The third challenge is a conceptual one. Competencies are defined as skills that are necessary in order to master daily life situations. Two aspects must be clarified here: What is daily life – now, and if we take children into account, in the future? We must define the most relevant, exemplary situations in which the students will need specific visual, linguistic, musical or theatrical competencies, in order to cope with and master in these situations.

4. Some theorists agree that an orientation along the tasks of daily life cannot be the only focus for teaching, especially in the arts. For them the second focus is defined by domain specific situations, like composing a piece of music, painting a self portrait, writing a poem, choreographing a dance. To legitimize these fields within the lessons at public schools and their funding through public resources, one has to explain how the competencies developed in these domains can contribute to self formation (Bildung). This question touches on all kinds of research that focuses on the transfer of outcome.[5] And it must be based on a domain specific concept of cognition that underlies creativity.

5. Looking at the specifics of the arts one can find – beyond these areas – competencies that cannot be described by means of a competence-model as defined by Dreyfus and Dreyfus (see above), but that are perhaps essential for arts education in their own way. The "wow-effect", which Anne Bamford claimed to be specific for arts education, is one example.[6] We all know this effect from our own experience. At first glance the wow-effect can hardly be described. The quality of a good, excellent piece of art, which strikes the producer as well as the audience as impressive and surprising is one example. The wow-effect happens abruptly (especially in reception) or as a kind of a continuous flow-effect (mainly in production). It means a form of total consent between the subject and the object, where the distinction between both is transgressed/exceeded. It is of interest how this "wow-effect" could be brought into dialogue with the terms and concept of competencies. First help could come from esthetic theory (as a discipline of philosophy) where different convincing descriptions of esthetic experience already exist.

---

5   See study „Arts for Arts Sake" (Winner, E./Goldstein, T./Vincent-Lancrin S., Arts for Arts Sake, OECD, 2013).
6   Bamford, A., *The WOW Factor*, Münster, 2006.

Eckart Liebau

# Limitations of the Competence-Approach

The common sociological view of the school system stresses five functions: Qualification, selection, integration, legitimation and something like custodianship where schools are seen as a kind of "storage", a protected parking place for young people. The focus on competencies is a modern version of focussing on qualification. But in a pedagogical view there are other dimensions relevant, too. Qualification meets only a specific dimension in a holistic approach of *Bildung*.

*Bildung (both education and formation)* can be translated as the ability to actively participate and be willing and prepared to participate in different fields of life, culture, arts, public discourses, politics, science, work, religion – the different spheres of society and justice, to quote Michael Walzer (1983). The more uncertain future perspectives become, the more important such a wide concept of *Bildung* is. Furthermore, considering how little we know in which way our labour-based society will change, redefining *Bildung* in a more general approach is a challenge we have to face. This is of major importance not only for the educational system but for the purpose of our future society. So this is the first critical point: the concept of competences is characterized by defined goals in defined fields of qualification, the so called domains. It is helpful for describing specific aims in curricula, but it is not helpful to find out, what the curriculum should be good for.

The second point is: The concept is not really open to contingency and complexity. It is based on tests defining grades of competence by testing abilities activated in situations of testing. So we do not know anything about the real abilities in real situations, about the performance in real life or even in real teaching and learning situations.

More important is the third critical point: the concept of competence cannot describe how Bildung happens, because it is only centered on the person, the personal abilities. It lacks the view of the world. But Bildung happens only in the interaction of the person and the world, by developing both of them at the same time in a process of interdependence, facing the strange things happening in the process, and the open and contingent results. You must hear the music you produce in order to react to it. You can't be sure that the click will happen. And you can't be sure which kind of a click will happen … arts education has always to cope with open and contingent results.

The impact of arts education has increased due to globalization. Regarding communication and intercultural dialogues, education through the arts and through cultural experiences are a decisive *conditio sine qua non for modern education*. Some school subjects have traditionally focussed on developing aesthetical qualities and qualifications (arts, music, literature, physical education, drama, dance at some schools), but also extracurricular activities such as choirs, orchestras, bands, drama groups have developed promising approaches. Of course you need competencies for competent performances. So you have to learn and to train, to train and to train again. But you have to know why. And you must know that the process may not strictly follow the plan ...

The students must be given the chance to find out for themselves, must gain practical experience. You don't know what theatre really is if you never enter a stage or turn on the lights.

When one examines the needs of the young generation including children and adolescents, one can discover the pedagogical needs and the pedagogical relevant dimensions for schooling and teaching. Schools should be places for young people to grow up in, not places for disciplined qualification for the needs of the market, Paul Goodman once postulated (1960). Schools are, of course, part of society and must match the needs of culture and society. But predominantly they must match the needs of the young generation. Schools are public places with rooms open for encounters. Why should students not use the corridors for exhibitions? The hall for recitals? Why should they not adopt parts of the school building for a day, week, a month? For many kids these days it's the only chance to take responsibility, to be needed, to be important. This means defining the time spent on education not only as preparing a near or far away future, but as a moment in time that counts. A moment that is precious in itself.

Every period of life is precious in itself, as we are taught by Rousseau and Schleiermacher. Any school of this kind cannot depend on teachers and students only. We expect schools in the future to be less bound by the physical walls of the school building, but to connect the students with a range of learning resources: on the one hand with the world of labour and politics; on the other hand with publicly sponsored places of education like universities, museums, theaters, sports clubs, zoos, botanical gardens, parks, castles. Such a school can truly be considered as a cultural centre, not only for the girls and boys who come there daily, but for a wider public, too. Without such a vision you can train competences as much as you want – but it won't help.

## References

Goodman, P. (1960). *Growing up absurd: Problems of Youth in the Organized System.* Random House, New York.

Walzer, M. (1983). *Spheres of Justice: a defense of pluralism and equality.* Basin Books, New York.

Ellen Winner, Thalia R. Goldstein and Stéphan Vincent-Lancrin[1]
# Does Arts Education Foster Creativity? The Evidence so far

**Introduction**

The arts are commonly associated with creativity. Artists are our prime social role models for creativity and innovation. Even practiced in an amateur capacity, the arts are typically seen as activities like play, where one can express one's imagination, express one's self, and be "creative". These assumptions generally inspire educational programmes based on the arts, with the hope that students' creativity will be enhanced and possibly transfer to other academic subjects.

Why should arts education engender creativity? One hypothesis grows out of Hetland, Winner, Veenema and Sheridan's (2013) analysis of visual arts teaching. The authors found that visual arts teachers continually asked student to take risks, experiment, try new things, and thus to extend themselves beyond what they had done before. This was coded by Hetland et al. as asking students to "stretch and explore". If this kind of discourse is common in all kinds of arts classes, we might expect arts classes to train students to be more creative, at least in the domain of the art form in question. Whether this habit then transfers to other areas is an open question.

We distinguish sharply here between "little-c" and "Big-C" creativity. Big-C creativity refers to the kinds of major innovations that revolutionise a domain: e.g. Einstein's theory of relativity, Darwin's theory of natural selection, Picasso and Braques' invention of cubism, Martha Graham's invention of modern dance (Csikszentmihalyi, 1996). These are innovations that leave a domain forever changed. Little-c creativity refers to the activity of discovering how to solve a problem on one's own (even if the solution is already known by others) or solving problems in unusual ways. This kind of behaviour requires thinking in new ways, but does not lead to big changes in a domain. No child can be Big-C creative: one must first master a domain before one can change it (Gardner, 1993; Winner, 1996).

When psychologists and educators attempt to quantify creativity, they most typically use the Torrance Tests of Creativity developed by Paul Torrance in 1966. These tests, consisting of both a verbal and a figural (visual) measure of creative thinking, assess four aspects of "divergent" thinking: fluency, flexibility, originality, and elaboration. Sample tasks on the verbal form include imagining how to improve a stuffed toy animal so that it would be more fun to play with; imagining what would happen if something improb-

---
[1] This chapter is an edited passage from the OECD report *Art for Art's Sake: The Impact of Arts Education*, published in June 2013. The analyses given and the opinions expressed herein are those of the authors and do not necessarily reflect the views of the OECD and of its members.

able occurred, such as people gaining the ability to move themselves from location to location by winking; or coming up with unusual ways to use a common object such as a brick. The figural form includes drawing and giving a title to the drawing, and naming an unusual looking design by answering the question "What might this be?".

These tests are "domain-general" in that they are meant to assess a general factor of creativity, rather than level of creativity in a specific area such as music or mathematics or visual arts, etc. Thus some have questioned the predictive validity of these tests (e.g. Baer, 1994). However, Millar (2002) demonstrated that children who scored high on these tests were more likely than those who scored low to enter creative professions as adults – they become entrepreneurs, inventors, authors, software developers, and were more likely to get awards for creativity, or to become involved in the arts. It is most likely that these creative adults were little-c rather than Big-C creative.

Plucker (1999) reanalysed Torrance's data using structural equation modeling and demonstrated that about half of the variance in adult creative achievement could be explained by Torrance's divergent thinking test scores – which was more than three times the variance explained by IQ. Creative achievement was again most likely not Big-C creativity (as this kind of creativity is so rare). Creative achievement was measured by number of publicly recognised creative achievements such as inventions, published articles, creativity awards, as well as by judges' ratings of the level of creativity of participants self-listed three most creative achievements. Plucker's (1999) finding suggests that despite all of the criticism of domain-general paper and pencil tests of creativity, such tests actually do predict later creative achievement.

A very different measure of creativity was developed by Getzels and Csikszentmihalyi (1976) in a study of adult visual arts students. The authors argued that true creativity does not consist in solving a known problem, but often calls for finding a new problem to solve. This was a domain-specific measure of visual arts creativity and it was termed a measure of "problem finding" rather than problem solving. Visual arts students were given a wide variety of objects and were told to make a drawing that incorporated any of the objects they wished. Problem finding was measured in a number of ways, including time spent exploring the objects, and time spent experimenting with a drawing on paper before reaching "closure" on the drawing. We know of no attempts to develop problem finding measures of creativity in other arts domains.

The renewed focus of schools on preparation for standardised tests is criticised for not being the way to enhance creativity. Many arts educators have bemoaned the fact that by cutting out the arts from school curricula we deprive children of one excellent route to becoming more creative. And of course creativity is considered an important outcome – both for educational reasons as well as for economic development. But is there an established link between any form of arts education and performance on standardised tests of creative thinking? Does studying the arts lead to enhanced critical and creative thinking either within arts class or outside of the arts?

## Empirical Evidence Linking Arts Education and Creativity

The OECD report *Art for Art's Sake?* reviews the extant research on the impact of arts education on a variety of outcomes, including creativity (Winner, Goldstein and Vincent-Lancrin, 2013). We covered most of the literature since 1950 in a large number of languages.

## Multi-Arts Education

A number of studies have investigated the claim that "multi-arts" instruction (i.e. a variety of non-specified forms of arts education) boosts creativity. Moga, Burger, Hetland and Winner (2000) meta-analysed ten correlational studies assessing the claim that arts instruction boosts creativity. All of these studies used as their outcome measures standard paper-and-pencil creativity tests, and compared the creativity test scores of students who took arts courses versus those who did not. The weighted mean effect size was positive and statistically significant. However, correlational studies are vulnerable to the possibility that the people who take up arts education are more inherently creative, i.e. correlations may not indicate a causal impact of arts education. Therefore, the same meta-analysis also examined three quasi-experimental or experimental studies with verbal and figural creativity outcomes. By contrast to correlational studies, the results from these studies found no significant relationship between participation in arts education and Torrance-style measure of creativity.

A small number of subsequent (quasi-)experimental studies do, by contrast, point towards a link between mulit-arts education and creativity. Byun (2004) studied the impact of the Arts Educational Program with Picture Books (AEPPB) on creativity among 111 children aged 5-6 from similar socio-economic backgrounds living in Korea. While the control group received the usual programme, the 61 young children in the experimental groups had three types of instructional activities with picture books. While the two groups showed no difference on both tests at the beginning of the intervention, the experimental group exhibited statistically significant higher scores in various tests of creativity after participating in the programme. Garaigordobil and Pérez (2002) assessed the effects of the Ikertze arts programme on verbal and figural creativity with 6-7 year old (first grade) children. The intervention involved 89 experimental and 46 control students who were randomly assigned to either a treatment or a control group. The experimental groups followed the Ikertze arts programme that implements a coordinated pedagogy based on the parallel exploration of related concepts in visual art, music, and drama, whilst the control group followed the traditional curriculum in arts education. The authors found a positive effect of the multi-arts programme on verbal and figural creativity, as measured by the Torrance Tests of Creative Thinking and one other test.

These results do not allow us to conclude that any multi-arts education will have similar effects, though it does make it clear that arts education taught in certain ways can boost some aspects of creativity. Although there is a robust correlation between multi-arts education and general creativity, and a number of positive findings, there is not enough evidence thus far to support the hypothesis that multi-arts education raises children's performance on paper-and-pencil creativity tests. Experimental studies have so far failed to produce findings that can be generalised. And even when studies did report a positive effect, no evidence was reported that the students used their increased creativity skills anywhere but on these measures of creativity.

## Specific Art Forms

*Art for Art's Sake* also reviewed the literature assessing creativity outcomes for specific art forms. There is little empirical evidence that music education fosters creativity and only weak evidence for visual arts education. We were not able to find any studies examining specifically whether music education improves children's domain-generic creativity. For visual arts, Korn and Associates (2007) assessed a programme at New York's Guggenheim Museum called Learning Through Art (LTA) in which students created visual arts projects. On three qualitative measures, LTA students performed better at problem solving than control students but LTA students also scored lower than control students on a measure of experimentation. In other areas no differences between groups were found. Catterall and Peppler (2007) compared two groups of third grade students in inner-city schools – those receiving high-quality visual arts instruction over the course of 20 and 30 weeks and those at the same school not receiving any special visual arts instruction. Children in the arts groups rated themselves significantly higher than control-group students on one of these measures – originality. However, since the measures were self-ratings, we cannot be very confident that students actually became more original – only that they believed they had.

We identified two experimental studies assessing the relationship between theatre/drama education and creativity or problem solving, both of which point towards a positive effect. Warger and Kleman (1986) examined the effects of theatre on the creativity scores of four kinds of 6-10 years olds. These children were either institutionalised behaviour disordered, non-institutionalised non-behaviour disordered children, institutionalised non-handicapped children, or non-institutionalised non-handicapped children. In each group, children were randomly assigned to 30-45 minutes per day of creative dramatics for two weeks, or to a control group that received no creative dramatics training. The drama group for all four subgroups outscored the control group on Torrance's tests of fluidity, originality, and imagination. Hui and Lau (2006) reported that drama training improved creativity, expressive communication, and creative drawing. In total, 126 children in grades one and four were randomly selected to receive drama lessons. Sixty-nine children were randomly selected to form the control group which received other instruction, such as sports. All participants completed the Wallach-Kogan creativity tests, tests for creative thinking-drawing production, and a story-telling test created and scored by the experimenters. Children in the drama project generated more creative responses, tended to provide more creative drawings, were more expressive, and provided more interesting stories than those who were not in the project.

We do not know why theatre training appears to have, bearing in mind the limited evidence, stronger effects on creativity than visual arts training. However, one possibility is that theatre training boosts performance on verbal creativity tests due to the strong effect that theatre training has on verbal skills, reviewed earlier.

For dance education we identified two quasi-experimental studies and two experimental studies assessing the relationship between dance classes and creativity or problem solving. These studies assessed dance taught as a separate discipline rather than integrated into the academic curriculum. Kim (1998) compared the effects of 15 sessions of creative versus traditional dance instruction over eight weeks on creative thinking in 7th grade girls. Students in the creative but not traditional dance programme gained significantly in creative thinking. Minton (2003) compared the effects of one semester of dance training versus no training on 15 year olds' creative thinking, measured by the figural forms of the Torrance Test of Creative Thinking. Creativity scores for those receiving dance instruction grew significantly stronger over one semester than did scores of those receiving no training. In an experimental study, Caf et al. (1997) found that dance classes help hypoactive children develop creative thinking. Reber and Sherrill (1981) showed that dance can be used to teach creative skills to deaf students. Hearing-impaired children were tested on the Torrance figural creativity measures. Half were then assigned to 10 weeks of dance training, and half to no training. The students receiving dance instruction improved on all three tests of creative thinking over and above those not in dance classes.

## Conclusions

The claim that arts education nurtures children's creativity seems self-evident. After all, the arts are inherently creative activities. Surprisingly, however, we found little evidence for this hypothesis in the area of multi-arts and visual arts education, though we found studies supporting this hypothesis in the area of theatre and dance. One reason lies in the design of the studies. Even though most results are positive, most studies are correlational and do not allow us to determine the direction of causality. Often, they are also based on small sample sizes and would not have enough statistical power to be generalised.

One explanation for the lack of overwhelmingly clear findings that arts education boosts creativity is that the measures used are typically paper-and-pencil tests of creativity. Perhaps these are poor measures. In addition, there is no reason to think that arts education will make children more creative unless the arts are taught in a way that really pushes children to explore and invent. It is likely that many arts classes ask children to do rather routine things – sing in a group, make Christmas decorations for the school hallway, etc. It is also possible that, like in other disciplines, one needs to reach a certain level of proficiency or mastery before being able to have a more inventive approach to the practiced art, and even more so before such creativity can transfer to other disciplines or practices. However, creativity may be highly domain specific, in which case we would not see transfer of creativity from an art form even to another art form, much less to an academic subject.

Even though it is possible (and perhaps even plausible) that arts education can foster creativity, there is still little evidence that this is the case. Perhaps because many people take an impact of arts education on creativity for granted, creativity outcomes have also rarely been included in research on the impact of arts education.

## References

Baer, J. (1994). "Why you shouldn't trust creativity tests", *Educational Leadership*, Vol. 51/4, pp. 80-83.

Byun, Y.H. (2004). *The Effects of Arts Educational Programs with Picture-Books on Creativity and Designing Rubrics for Assessing Young Children's Creativity*, Doctoral Dissertation, Sungyunkwan University, [in Korean].

Caf, B., Kroflic, B. & Tancig, S. (1997). "Activation of hypoactive children with creative movement and dance in primary school", *The Arts in Psychotherapy*, Vol. 24/4, pp. 355-365.

Catterall, J.S. & Peppler, K.A. (2007). "Learning in the visual arts and the worldviews of young children", *Cambridge Journal of Education*, Vol. 37/4, pp. 543-560.

Csikszentmihalyi, M. (1996). *Creativity: Flow and the Psychology of Discovery and Invention*, Harper Collins, New York, NY.

Garaigordobil, M. & y Pérez, J.I. (2002). "Efectos de la participación en el programa de arte Ikertze sobrela creatividad verbal y gráfica", *Anales de Psicología*, Vol. 18/1, pp. 95-110.

Gardner, H. (1993). *Creating Minds: An Anatomy of Creativity Seen Through the Lives of Freud, Einstein, Picasso, Stravinsky, Eliot, Graham and Gandhi*, BasicBooks, New York, NY.

Getzels, J. & Csikszentmihalyi, M. (1976). *The Creative Vision: A Longitudinal Study*, Wiley, New York, NY.

Hetland, L., Winner, E., Veenema, S. & Sheridan, K. (2013). *Studio Thinking2: The Real Benefits of Visual Arts Education*, 2nd edition, Teachers College Press, New York, NY. First edition: 2007.

Hui, A. & Lau, S. (2006). "Drama education: A touch of the creative mind and communicative-expressive ability of elementary school children in Hong Kong", *Thinking Skills and Creativity*, Vol. 1/1, pp. 34-40

Kim, J. (1998). *The Effects of Creative Dance Instruction on Creative and Critical Thinking of Seventh Grade Female Students in Seoul*, unpublished Doctoral Dissertation, New York University, New York, NY.

Korn, R. & Associates, Inc. (2007). *Educational Research: The Art of Problem Solving*, Solomon R. Guggenheim Museum, New York, NY.

Millar, G.W. (2002). *The Torrance Kids at Mid-Life*, Ablex, Westport, CT.

Minton, S. (2003). "Assessment of high school students' creative thinking skills: A comparison of dance and nondance classes", *Research in Dance Education*, Vol. 4/1, pp. 31-49.

Moga, E., Burger, K., Hetland, L. & Winner, E. (2000). "Does studying the arts engender creative thinking? Evidence for near but not far transfer", *Journal of Aesthetic Education*, Vol. 34/3-4, pp. 91-104.

Plucker, J.A. (1999). "Is the proof in the pudding? Reanalyses of Torrance's (1958 to present) longitudinal data", *Creativity Research Journal*, Vol. 12/2, pp. 103-114.

Reber, R. & Sherrill, C. (1981). "Creative thinking and dance/movement skills of hearing-impaired youth: An experimental study", *American Annals of the Deaf*, Vol. 126/9, pp. 1004-1009.

Warger, C.L. & Kleman, D. (1986). "Developing positive self-concepts in institutionalized children with severe behavior disorders", *Child Welfare*, Vol. 65/2, pp. 165-176.

Winner, E. (1996). *Gifted Children: Myths and Realities*, BasicBooks, New York, NY.

Winner, E., Goldstein, T.R. & Vincent-Lancrin, S. (2013). *Art for Art's Sake? The Impact of Arts Education*, OECD Publishing, Paris.

Robin Pascoe

# Arts Assessment: A Need for Critical Engagement

Assessment in the arts is a vexed, contentious issue; caught in the crossfires of competing values and external pressures for demonstrated accountability in education. As arts educators we **must** engage with assessment – on its own terms. In this chapter I explore field experience in drama assessment for Year 12 students in Western Australia to show some possible pathways forward for arts assessment.

## Putting Assessment in the Arts into Context

In the context of increased scrutiny and accountability in education (e.g. van Damme, 2013, and other presentations at The World Summit on Arts Education – Polylogue II) the role of assessment in the arts requires our attention. The traditionally held view that the arts are un-assessable, even ineffable, springs from the argument that responses to the arts are "purely subjective" and resistant to quantitative measurement.

Amongst my teacher education students I hear this argument rehearsed and reinforced by teachers and principals they work with when on School Professional Experience. What this perception has led to is a deep-seated popular opinion that the arts cannot be assessed (for example, see Hatton, 2007, for discussion of this issue). And this is a perception I even hear anecdotally among arts educators themselves. What seem to be playing out are firmly established values-based differences that have led to a consequential disengagement from arts assessment.

I would argue that, as arts educators, there is a need to engage with the assessment issue. Rather than opting out from the debate, we must participate. Elsewhere (Pascoe, 2006), I have argued the case for both *assessment competence* and *assessment literacy*. Assessment literacy is the capacity to make the arts assessment case, talk the assessment specific language, communicate a coherent point of view amongst ourselves, with our students and the community. We need to make the case for ourselves and to take the argument about arts assessment to assessment specialists and talk to them in their jargon. We cannot opt out. If we allow ourselves as arts educators to be disengaged and disempowered in this context, we further marginalise arts education.

To support this case I share with you experiences with assessment of Drama for Year 12 in Western Australia.

## An Example of Arts (Drama) Assessment

The Senior Secondary Drama course in Western Australia has two points of curriculum focus: drama in performance and responding to drama. Both are taught through active engagement with the elements of drama. Assessment is a combination of school-based assessment weighted equally with external assessment. Assessment is of both demonstrated knowledge and understanding of practical and theoretical/written components. External assessment of the Year 12 Drama course is required to be rigorous, robust and compatible with the broader assessment regimes for all other Year 12 courses because Year 12 assessment is high stakes. Students rely on their Year 12 assessment for access to tertiary study.

The challenges faced in designing the Year 12 Drama assessments were significant and required drama teachers to engage with processes and practices of assessment – both within the school and in externally administered practical and written (theoretical) examinations. Assessment had to be consistent with principles of the Schools Curriculum and Standards Authority (SCSA http://www.scsa.wa.edu.au).

As Chief Examiner for Year 12 Drama, I have worked closely with teachers in schools to develop the approach taken. This has not been an instant achievement but has evolved since 1999 when the system was pioneered. Nor, is this approach sufficiently understood and applied by all drama teachers. However, the assessment approach has proven to be sustainable, viable and above all fair to students. It has met scrutiny and general acceptance from assessment specialists.

There have been a number of necessary assumptions in the approach taken:
1. Not everything can or should be assessed.
2. There are limits to the judgments that can (or should) be made. Russell (2003) drew our attention to the sorts of useful judgments that can be made in assessment: breadth, depth, frequency, accuracy, independence. Further, he argued that ultimately the judgments that can be made are limited to: does the student show:
   - the same as (=)
   - more than (>)
   - less than (<)
3. All forms of representations of assessment are proxies for student learning – they are not the actual learning. Whether a numerical score, percentage, letter grade or descriptive criterion is used, they are all symbols for our understanding of student learning. Nothing more and nothing less.
4. Whatever approaches taken there is a need to recognise overall principles of assessment (for example, in common with many systems, the Schools Curriculum and Assessment Authority of Western Australia identifies that: 1) Assessment should be an integral part of Teaching and Learning; 2) Assessment should be educative; 3) Assessment should be fair; 4) Assessments should be designed to meet their specific purposes; 5) Assessment should lead to informative reporting; and, 6) Assessment should lead to school-wide evaluation processes (http:// k10outline.scsa.wa.edu.au/Curriculum_k-10/Guiding Principles/Principles)).

5. All quantitative judgments (or judgments that we consider to meet quantitative standards) are still essentially qualitative and dependent on context, observer/teacher and student/participant.

As a consequence, the features of the approach taken to assessing drama include:
- explicit statement of expectations: the knowledge, understandings, skills, techniques and processes of drama based on articulated progressions of learning over time and development
- authentic tasks
- identification of assessable criteria: description of observable characteristics of learning in those tasks (bearing in mind the limitations described above)
- analytical marking keys[1]
- scaffolded use of tasks and marking keys

This assessment process can be graphically summarised:

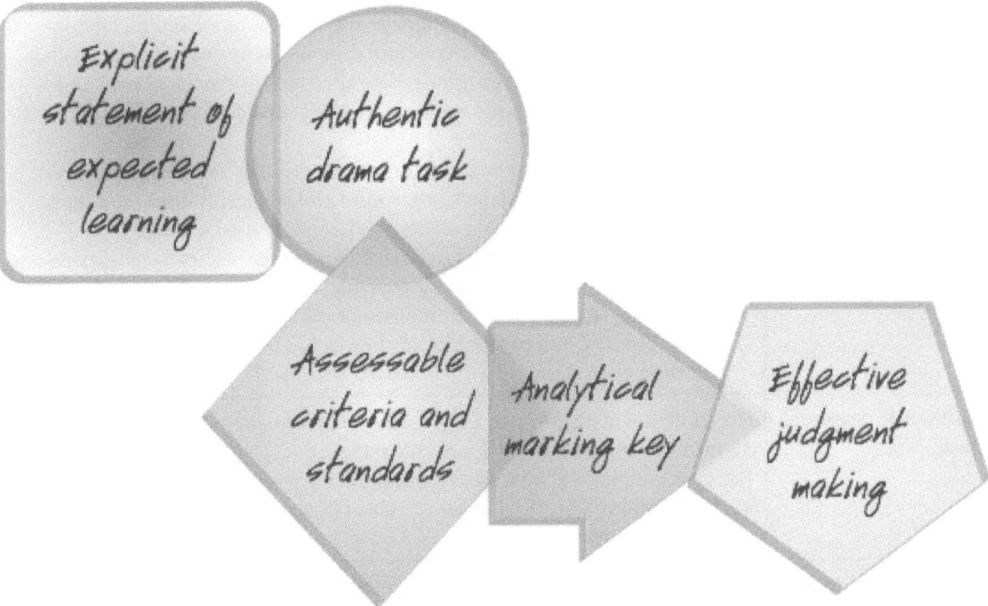

Figure 1: Features of Western Australian Year 12 Drama approach

---

1   See Andrich (2006) for discussion of analytic marking keys with particular reference to drama. An analytic marking key specifies scores against identified criteria and is contrasted with holistic ratings which assigns one score that takes account of multiple criteria simultaneously.

The following samples from the Western Australian Year 12 Drama Course (http://www.scsa.wa.edu.au/internet/Senior_Secondary/Courses/WACE_Courses/Drama) illustrate aspects of this approach.

Table 1:   Examples from the WACE Drama course

| **Explicit expectations**<br><br>*Excerpt from WACE Drama Year 12* | • Students create, interpret, explore, develop and present drama ideas.<br>• Students apply drama skills, techniques, processes, conventions and technologies.<br><br>In the context of drama in performance and responding to drama, students know, understand and apply<br><br>**Drama processes and the elements of drama**<br>• Strategies and approaches to performance refinement processes such as contemporary theatre approaches and experimental approaches developed by drama practitioners.<br>• The elements of drama (role, character and relationships, situation, voice, movement, space and time, language and texts, symbol and metaphor, mood and atmosphere, audience and dramatic tension) focusing on characterisation to develop an appropriate approach to contemporary and devised drama taking into account the performance event, space and audience.<br>• The elements of drama to create dramatic action by exploring choices about varying light and darkness, sound and silence, stillness and movement, colour and space in contemporary and devised drama.<br>• The elements of drama used in strategies and approaches to rehearsing and directing such as improvisation, systematic corrective rehearsal, shaping and pacing, selective themes and theoretical approaches and the combination of physical and psychological approaches to the interpretation of role and dramatic action. |
|---|---|
| **Authentic drama task** | The student will perform an Original Solo Performance (OSP) portraying a character journey of one or more characters.<br>The performance will be 4.00 to 6 minutes.<br>Students will initiate, develop, write, rehearse and perform their OSP for their practical examination. |
| **Assessable criteria** | **Criteria for Original Solo Performance**<br>• voice<br>• movement and non-verbal communication<br>• characterisation for audience impact and engagement<br>• structure for performance impact<br>• design/technical elements/space of performance |

| | | |
|---|---|---|
| **Analytical Marking key for criteria** | Performs a sensitively credible characterisation that has impact for the audience. A range of identifiable physical and/or psychological character qualities is sustained in a focused detailed performance that engages an audience. | 7–8 |
| *Excerpt from WACE Drama Year 12* *Marking key for* **characterisation for audience impact and engagement** | Performs a credible characterisation. Identifiable physical and/or psychological character qualities are sustained in a focused performance and directed to engaging an audience. | 6 |
| | Performs a characterisation. Physical and/or psychological aspects of the character are mostly sustained in performance and directed to engaging an audience. | 5 |
| | Performs an identifiable characterisation or stereotype. Physical aspects of the character or stereotype are mostly sustained in a performance that generally engages an audience. | 4 |
| | Performs an identifiable stereotype that is inconsistently sustained for an audience. | 3 |
| | Performs a stereotype that is not identifiable or sustained that lacks audience impact. | 1–2 |

A key factor is the scaffolding of use to support teachers making effective judgments. This approach does not deny subjectivity, in fact it recognises and celebrates it though supports its use through the use of multiple markers – allowing for different viewpoints and diversity of interpretations that is moderated by social construction of standards – collaborative processes of identifying the agreed meanings of the criteria.

Dunn, Morgan, O'Reilly and Parry (2004) offer a critique of analytical marking key approaches as reductive, prescriptive and stifling of student creativity. On the other hand they are also openly accountable (where holistic marking often is not), diagnostic and support comparability across markers and efficiency in being able to be used and re-used.

I argue, based on experience as Chief Examiner for Year 12 Drama, that this approach has been successful.
1. It has satisfied the requirements of assessment specialists
2. Over time, it has proven to be stable though subject to incremental improvement
3. It has built confidence in teachers, markers and students. Firstly, it has built the confidence of arts educators in backing their judgments about performance of learning in drama. Consequentially, it has begun to build confidence about assessment of drama amongst principals, parents and decision makers.

In the process of working with this approach, there has been a concerted effort to see assessment as a) understanding student's learning and thinking in drama (not just the products of that learning); b) focusing on the moment; c) managing the split focus of considering drama in performance – being both in the moment and out of the moment metaxically; and, d) attending to students use of specific elements (role, character, situation, voice, movement, space, time, language and audience) and dimensions such as light and darkness, sound and silence, stillness and movement, colour and space.

But it is important to also acknowledge limitations: summarised in three questions and answers:
- Is the approach defensible? Yes.
- Are there causes for concern? Yes.
- Are there viable alternatives in the current context? None that are politically, socially and morally defensible.

## Conclusion

In this short paper I have set out to provoke discussion about assessment.

As I remind my teacher education students assessment is both complex and easy. Sometimes, as teachers we overcomplicate the process.

Firstly, we need to say as clearly and honestly as possible what we are looking for in student learning. Second, as we work beside and with our students we need to look and listen carefully, deeply, knowingly (Eisner (1985) would say *connoisseurship*). Finally, we need to report what we experience honestly acknowledging our limitations but striving for aesthetic distance.

## References

Andrich, D. (2006). *A report to the Curriculum Council of Western Australia regarding assessment for tertiary selection.* Perth, Western Australia: Curriculum, Council of Western Australia.

Dunn, L., Morgan, C., O'Reilly, M., & Parry, S. (2004). *The student assessment handbook: New directions in traditional and online assessment.* London: RoutledgeFalmer.

Eisner, E.W. (1985). *The Art of Educational Evaluation: A Personal View.* London: Falmer.

Hatton, C. (2007). AGQTP Implementing the Curriculum Planning and Assessment Frameworks – Creative Arts and COGs State of New South Wales through the NSW Department of Education and Training.

Pascoe, R. (2006). Drama, Theatre and Assessment: Finding Common Ground. In L. McCammon & D. McLauchlan (Eds.), *Universal Mosaic of Drama and Theatre: The IDEA 2004 Dialogues.* Brisbane, Queensland: IDEA Publications.

Russell, S. (2003). *Getting Assessment Right Drama Grades 9-10.* Barrie, Ontario: Data Based Directions Quality Resources for Educators.

Van Damme, D. (2013). *A Skills Perspective to Arts Education.* Paper presented at the World Summit on Arts Education – Polylogue II, Munich and Wildbad Kreuth, Germany. http://worldsummit2013.bkj.de/fileadmin/user_upload/documents/Kulturelle_Bildung_International/World_Summit_2013/Keynote_Van_Damme.pdf

Diederik W. Schönau
# Self-Assessment for Learning in Visual Arts Education

## Introduction

As educators we have to make choices about what we want students to learn. These choices become more critical in school, as that is the place where society expects all students to learn what is considered essential for later life. The arts are traditionally part of our schooling systems, which has recently been reconfirmed by UNESCO's Learning Metrics Task Force. But being part of compulsory education, the arts have to confirm to the expectations of society and to show that they do contribute to those expectations. As a result, this confirmation is, among other things, sought by the introduction of standards and the use of assessment systems. The formats used to formulate standards and to assess results often reflect those used in most other school subjects. However, these general formats may be counter-productive to the essence and the effectiveness of learning in the arts. This specifically counts for the making of art.

## The Making of Art

By concentrating on the skills to *make* visual, auditory and performative products, students learn to manipulate the symbol systems (music, images, body movement, etc.) and the media (instruments, techniques, materials) of the arts.[1] It is the heart of what art is all about. In some arts (music, dance) much learning is based on the development of repertoire, basic skills and the reproduction of works composed by others. In the visual arts, and to a lesser extent in theatre, the work made by students is less reproductive. Most works of visual art, especially in the Western tradition, are highly unpredictable and unique. There we also encourage students to develop their own style and personal points of view on reality. Actually, it seems the issue of repertoire development in visual art education has almost become a non-issue. But how can we assess individual works that are more often than not supposed to be unique, creative and personal, and how do we appreciate the divergent character of the artistic development of students? These questions are especially critical in visual arts education.

It may be said that all works of art are unique. But this should not mean that one cannot say something about their quality or the process underlying their production. First the central issue must be rephrased into the question: does the work made by stu-

---
[1] See for symbol systems in art: Goodman, N. (1976). *Languages of Art. An Approach to a Theory of Symbols*. Indianapolis: Hackett Publishing Company.

dents in visual art education fulfil the criteria of artistic skills and learning? Although the artistic products can be very diverse and even unique, we do teach our students aspects of process that, to a certain extent, are common to all works made within an art discipline. Thus we can and must bring the issue of assessment of practical work in arts education back to the question: what are the common or main characteristics of artistic learning, the artistic working process and the works of art made by students in school?

## Three Types of Skills in Art Production

In all forms of education in and through the arts, when it comes to the production of a work of art, traditionally three general skills play a role: the skills to make use of material and techniques, of artistic elements and principles, and of aspects of content.

The most practical skill in a literal sense, is the skill to apply a material, a technique, a medium or an instrument, being it paint, classical ballet, the human voice, or a musical instrument. These skills are as essential as linguistics skills or the skills to use mathematical symbols and procedures: they relate to the basic symbol systems of human culture. But where in foundational education very much time is devoted to improve these latter two skills, in the art subjects mastery of technical skills is often seen as less relevant. For instance, in the Netherlands in most schools we do not teach students in primary education the first steps in musical notation. In the visual arts, the suggestion to remake a work of art that was not so successful is often seen as outrageous. There, normally preference is given to introduce a new technique in the next assignment. As a result students will actually have few opportunities to master or improve a basic technical skill.

When discussing elements and principles, we must think of these in terms of a skill as well: the skill to apply these in an effective way. How to make skilful use of movement, sounds, colours, space, rhythm, composition, illusions, dynamics, and harmonies?

The third skill is related to content. A work of art is about something. This content can be representational in character, as a reference to what is seen or sensed in reality or in fantasy. For music and dance this representational reference is often much more abstract or even non-existent, like in non-figurative visual art. Therefore content can also relate to more abstract feelings and experiences. But content as such is not a skill. When we want to define content in terms of skill, it would be helpful to talk about the skill to *thematise* content.[2] By this is meant that the content – being it a reality, an idea, a feeling or an experience – is investigated from different angles. These angles can be cultural, aesthetic, personal, historical or social. The skill to thematise content is to purposefully select, research and interpret, in a personal way, aspects of reality, ideas, stories, feelings, and experiences. What is the feeling, the idea, the experience or the thought students wish to convey, and for what purpose? This question should guide the thinking of

---

2   For an example of content and research-based student assessment, see the example of the Dutch final examination at lower-vocational level, in the Appendix of: Schönau, D.W. (2013). Developmental self-assessment in art education, in: A. Kárpáti and E. Gaul (Eds.), *From Child Art to Visual Language of Youth. New Models and Tools for Assessment of Learning and Creation in Art Education.* Bristol/Chicago: Intellect, pp. 145-174.

the students about the meaning they want to communicate. When making new works of art, students in arts education have to investigate what meaning they want to convey, and how they can put this meaning into form.

This personal, thematic research introduces the most fundamental question in art: how can I best give form to the meaning and the intentions I have in mind? In order to make the public understand or experience the meaning of what one wants to convey, the maker has to produce a work that intrigues the senses, the curiosity and the knowledge of the beholder. To arrive at this goal the maker has to use all three supportive skills. From here, choices can be made with regard to the instruments, techniques or materials, the elements and principles, and the aspects of content as references to (a) reality. It is therefore a central issue in the art subjects that students have to learn to define their goals, and think about how content, medium, and elements and principles can contribute to the materialization of the intended meaning.

## Assessing Individual Learning

What does this mean for assessment in the arts?

First of all assessment should concentrate on the relationship between the meaning of work made by a student and the skills used to give form to or express this meaning. But more importantly from a pedagogical and learning perspective is the need to look at the importance given by the student to the issues at hand, being these issues of purpose, means or learning. When we involve students actively in defining their own (learning) goals, choosing their own issues, designing their own assignments, and selecting the means that best fit their momentary needs and ambitions, the making of a work of art will become a part of an authentic and relevant learning process. At the same time learning and assessment will become the two sides of the same coin.[3] As part of the assessment it is helpful to ask students to articulate in writing their choices and approaches beforehand. They can formulate these into criteria on which they wish to assess their own work. When finished they can then better compare the result with their intentions and use the criteria to judge their working process and the result. From this perspective, the student becomes the first person to assess her or his work, through self-assessment. The teacher will act as an external advisor, discussing the choices, the work process, the product and the self-assessment of the student. Both self-assessment and external assessment will concentrate on questions that focus on what the student did to arrive at meaning and what choices she or he made to communicate this meaning in the most successful way. What went right and what went wrong, and why? And, most importantly: what will be the next step or challenge?

This way of working can start from early age onwards, as already young children have their own stories, feelings and ideas. Preferably this learning process takes place from grade 1 to 12, in varying art disciplines. Students can also discover what art form(s) best

---

3 On the improvement of the relationship between assessment and learning see: Masters, G.N. (2013). *Reforming Educational Asessment: Imperatives, principles and challenges.* Camberwell: ACER.

fit(s) their temperament and interest. We need to give students the opportunities and the time to discover their artistic interests, to develop skills, to improve their learning and thus to become master of their own artistic learning process.

## Research Questions

Based on what is discussed above, a shift should be made to research on self-directed learning in the arts. What are the best moments to develop the skills as discussed, what techniques are best fit at what age, and how does artistic understanding develop over time? How can we organize the artistic learning process in such a way, that students can follow their individual development and interests? Research is needed to get a better insight in how students in compulsory education, from age 4 to 18, with the help of their teachers can learn to develop and improve their artistic skills themselves, and how they can learn to actively structure and monitor their own artistic learning process.

# Arts Education and Education for Sustainable Development

Samuel Leong and Ernst Wagner

# UNESCO & Arts Education for Sustainable Development – An Introduction

## Introduction

UNESCO is the lead agency for the UN Decade of Education for Sustainable Development (ESD) (2005-2014). To mark the end of the Decade of ESD, a UNESCO World Conference on ESD will be held in Aichi-Nagoya, Japan, from 10-12 November 2014, with four themes/objectives serving as the bases for its monitoring and evaluation effort:
1. Celebrating a Decade of Action
2. Reorienting Education to Build a Better Future for All
3. Accelerating Action for Sustainable Development
4. Setting the Agenda for ESD beyond 2014.

At first glance ESD and arts education seem to come from two quite different domains: the sphere of normative values (the realm of ethics) and of political/economic rationality on the one hand and the domain of self formation in and through the "artes liberales", the non-functionalized, free arts (aesthetics) on the other. Both fields follow different patterns of thinking. To bring them together and to understand the tension between them as a fruitful base for a productive development of both realms, seems to be the main challenge for the future – in practice, in policies as well as in research.

## What does ESD entail?

*ESD is a vision of education that seeks to balance human and economic well-being with cultural traditions and respect for the earth's natural resources. ESD applies transdisciplinary educational methods and approaches to develop an ethic for lifelong learning; fosters respect for human needs that are compatible with sustainable use of natural resources and the needs of the planet; and nurtures a sense of global solidarity.* (UNESCO Decade of ESD, 2005-2014)

This important international initiative aims to allow every human being to acquire the knowledge, skills, attitudes and values necessary to shape a sustainable future. ESD means including key sustainable development issues into teaching and learning; for example, climate change, disaster risk reduction, biodiversity, poverty reduction, and sustainable consumption. Other topics include international understanding, gender, human rights, poverty, welfare and peace. ESD also requires participatory teaching and learning methods that motivate and empower learners to change their behaviour and take action for sustainable development. ESD consequently promotes competencies like critical thinking, imagining future scenarios and making decisions in a collaborative way. ESD requires far-reaching changes in the way education is often practised today and it touches on every aspect of education, including planning, policy development, program implementation, finance, curricula, teaching, learning, assessment, administration, etc.

ESD is also about learning to:
- respect, value and preserve the achievements of the past;
- affirm and foster intercultural understanding of cultural diversity and cultural peace;
- appreciate the wonders and the peoples of the Earth;
- live in a world where all people have sufficient food for a healthy and productive life;
- assess, care for and restore the state of our planet;
- create and enjoy a better, safer, more just world;
- be caring citizens who exercise their rights and responsibilities locally, nationally and globally.

## ESD, Education and Pedagogy

For a community or a nation, implementing ESD into the formal and the non-formal educational sector (e.g., nature centers, non-governmental organizations, public health educators, and agricultural extension agents, local television, newspaper, and radio) is a huge task. Because ESD is a lifelong process, UNESCO claims that the formal, non-formal, and informal educational sectors should work together to accomplish local and regional sustainability goals. In an ideal world, the three sectors would divide the enormous task of ESD for the entire population by identifying target audiences from the general public as well as themes of sustainability. They would then work within their mutually agreed upon realms. This division of effort would reach a broader spectrum of people and prevent redundant efforts.

ESD draws on pedagogies, not just content, from a wide variety of disciplines. Examples include:
- applying arts education principles and practices to contribute to resolving the social and cultural challenges facing today's world;
- inquiry from science;
- spatial analysis from geography;
- communication skills from language and the arts;
- creative thinking and expression from the arts;
- higher-order thinking skills from a variety of disciplines.

## The Arts and ESD

ESD is embedded in the Seoul Agenda's (2010), especially, Goal 3 of its developmental goals for arts education: "Apply arts education principles and practices to contribute to resolving the social and cultural challenges facing the world today". This includes a focus on the therapeutic and health dimensions of arts education, the potential of arts education to develop and conserve identity and heritage as well as to promote diversity and dialogue among cultures, the restorative dimensions of arts education in post-conflict and post-disaster situations, and fostering people's capacity to respond to major global challenges, from peace to sustainability through arts education.

Concrete examples of practice have to be explored and discussed in respect to these considerations. So this is just a starting point.

Yeon-hee Jung
# Expanding Sustainable Thinking through Arts Education

In December 2002, the 57th session of the UN General Assembly adopted the resolution proclaiming the UN Decade of Education for Sustainable Development (ESD), which called for governments to strengthen their efforts to achieve sustainability through education. Accordingly, UNESCO developed the *ESD International Implementation Scheme* at the international level and, subsequently, Germany, Australia and other developed countries developed national strategies and educational frameworks for implementing ESD. Compared to their efforts, the implementation of ESD in Korea has been piecemeal, due to the political situation and other priorities of Korean society.

Since successfully hosting the UNESCO Second World Forum on Arts Education in 2010 there has been increasing social and political emphasis on promoting arts education in Korea. The *Seoul Agenda: Goals for the Development of Arts Education*, adopted during the World Forum and then unanimously adopted by the UNESCO General Conference in 2011, has been especially influential in focusing attention and resources on arts education. The *Seoul Agenda* calls on governments to ensure access to high quality arts education and contribute to resolving our common global challenges through arts education. As the host of the Second World Forum, the Korean government has shown strong resolve in supporting the *Agenda*.

Given that the implementation of ESD has become UNESCO's primary agenda in the education sector it seems advisable to explore how the development of arts education can be related to ESD and how "sustainable development" can be integrated into the arts education curriculum.

This paper reviews Korea's response to UNESCO's ESD agenda. In particular, it examines how arts education is evolving with respect to ESD in the context of the *Seoul Agenda*. In addition, this paper shows how arts education can contribute to the expansion of sustainable thinking and how the inherent principles and external values of ESD can be integrated into arts education practice.

## The Goal and Focus of Education for Sustainable Development (ESD)

Because ESD is a life-long process, formal, non-formal, and informal educational sectors should work together to accomplish national and local sustainability goals (McKeown, 2002). If ESD is to be more than merely delivering knowledge related to environmental, economic and social issues, it must also develop skills, perspectives, and values for sustainable living and participation in a democratic society. In this context, the goal of ESD, as the Australian Department of the Environment and Heritage (2007, p. 4) explained, is to "equip individuals, organizations and communities to deal effectively with the complex and inter-related social, economic and environmental challenges they encounter in their personal and working lives, in a way that protects the interest of future generations."

To achieve this aim, the focus of education must shift to nurturing imagination and strengthening critical thinking which enable learners to understand the pending challenges, and fostering cooperation so people can work together with others in decision-making and resolving problems (Tilbury & Wortman, 2004). In addition, ESD can achieve its purpose only when the learners practice the specific values of sustainability in their local communities and/or homes. Therefore, the blueprint for sustainable development *(Agenda 21,* adopted during the UN Rio Summit in 1992) emphasizes mainstreaming the values of ESD into the overall education system by 1) improving basic education, 2) reorienting existing education, 3) developing public understanding and awareness, and 4) training.

Sustainable development, as a common key value of ESD, involves a combination of environmental, economic and social concerns. By considering the different dimensions that factor in sustainable development, ESD addresses different issue areas with the overarching goal of nurturing key competencies required for sustainable living. Through ESD, students acquire and develop ecological literacy, creative imagination, data collection and analysis, critical thinking, communication skills, capacities for participation and partnership, and decision-making capabilities. In developing these competencies, ESD utilizes pedagogies of collaborative learning, project-based learning, and service learning.

## Goals for the Development of Arts Education and ESD

The UNESCO Second World Forum on Arts Education, held in Seoul in 2010, has been instrumental in providing a framework for systematically and comprehensively addressing the challenges facing arts education today. The *Seoul Agenda: Goals for the Development of Arts Education* is the major outcome of the four day conference. The *Seoul Agenda* emphasizes that increasing access to arts education and improving the quality of arts education can play an important role in resolving the global challenges. In other words, the *Seoul Agenda* calls for continued efforts, in both the public and private sectors, to promote arts education as a means of reinforcing the creative and innovative capacities of society and enhancing social and cultural well-being. In this sense, the *Seoul Agenda* intrinsically embraces the vision and principles of ESD and implements the ESD goals in the development of arts education.

The *Seoul Agenda* enunciates three Goals, three or four Strategies for each goal, and 39 Action Items. Goal 3 of the *Seoul Agenda* calls for capacity building through arts education as a means to reinforce the creative and innovative capacity of society; enhance social and cultural well-being; promote social responsibility, social cohesion, cultural diversity, and intercultural dialogue; and develop the capacity to respond effectively to major global challenges. These strategies go beyond the traditional belief that arts education concentrates on the emotional development of individuals. The *Seoul Agenda* emphasizes the role of arts education as a practice to ensure quality living for individuals and communities. In short, by embracing the goals and standards of the *Seoul Agenda*, arts education promotes the critical value of sustainable thinking in its policies and practices.

## Restoring the Inherent Principles and Expanding the External Values of Arts Education

The third goal of the *Seoul Agenda* "Apply arts education principles and practices to contribute to resolving the social and cultural challenges facing our world today" internalizes the principles of ESD within the framework of arts education. In the past, arts education focused on the arts, isolated from tradition and the learners' lives, and emphasized western aesthetic values. This resulted in the loss of public support for arts education. Therefore, the expansion of ESD through arts education must begin with a reflection on arts education in general. As a first step, arts education must restore its inherent principles, which are based on 1) the relationship between life, nature and tradition; 2) a process-orientation toward life; 3) the importance of cultural diversity; and 4) the totality of the meaning structure.

In addition, arts education needs to expand its external values. In the past, arts education focused on capacity building in individuals as an aspect of social development. Although arts education has been concerned with social aspects, the emphasis has been on the economic value of arts education. Now, with globalization and the advent of the Information Age, arts education must expand its scope to address the environmental, social and economic challenges of today's world. The ESD vision of creating a sustainable future cannot be achieved solely by pursuing economic development. Environmental, cultural and social values must be factored into the equation, and arts education needs to establish its relevance in terms of these external values.

By adopting the *Seoul Agenda*, the arts education community broke away from its narrow focus on the individual and economic concerns and expressed its engagement with broad social and cultural issues. This means the arts education community began to confirm the potential for arts education to perform a central role in developing the competencies for creating a sustainable future. In performing this role, the external values of arts education can be established by restoring the inherent principles of arts education; that is, by promoting 1) arts education for communication and cohesion and 2) arts education for participation and practice.

In responding to the changing educational environment, arts education should restore its inherent principles and expand its external values, starting with reflection on existing educational practices. As the adoption of the *Seoul Agenda* indicates, the arts education community supports this intention.

## Improving Arts Education Curriculum to Expand Sustainability Thinking

ESD promotes thinking about sustainability. Arts education can expand sustainability thinking through restoring its inherent principles and expanding its external values. By integrating these principles and values into the curriculum, arts education can contribute to delivering the ESD's fundamental value, which is to create a sustainable future. How can the goals, focus, criteria and pedagogy of arts education be improved and adjusted to align with sustainability thinking?

First, the goals of arts education need to be reformulated with the intention of expanding sustainability thinking. Here, the *Seoul Agenda: Goals for the Development of Arts Education* provides a framework for modifying and adjusting the present goals of arts education to accommodate the changing educational environment.

To respond flexibly to the rapidly changing social environment and its demands arts education curriculum should focus more on why problems involving values and objectives arise. In turn, this requires arts education curriculum to provide a more philosophical and fundamental direction, which will help integrate the value judgment criteria of sustainable development into the educational contents and methods.

The arts education community has striven to overcome the perception that it focuses entirely on emotional development and has used Discipline-Based Art Education (DBAE) and other methods to reinforce the legitimacy of arts education as an academic discipline. In order to integrate interdisciplinary core values, such as sustainable development, into mainstream arts education curriculum, the curriculum needs to foster a practice-based environment focused on "education for life".

Along these lines, the contents of arts education should focus on: 1) **artistic creation** based on understanding the relationship between tradition, nature and life; 2) **artistic experience** based on the practices of cultural diversity and social cohesion; and 3) **artistic knowledge** based on the totality of life and its meaning structure. In addition, the pedagogy of arts education should emphasize 1) **participatory education** which engages directly with the real world; 2) **practical education** which seeks to contribute to resolving global challenges; and 3) **process-oriented learning** which treats education itself as a part of cultural life. All of these elements are aligned with the principles of ESD (Nolet, 2010). Applying such content and pedagogy in arts education will lead to the outcome of arts education contributing to the expansion of sustainability thinking.

Furthermore, this new focus for arts education can be developed as part of an integrated education program for expanding sustainability thinking in keeping with the values and criteria of ESD. And for arts education to incorporate the values of "education for life", the arts education curriculum should consider participation and practice as important components and the critical interdisciplinary value of sustainability must be imbedded in the education curriculum. In this author's opinion, the education system should not restrict and limit the vision and passion of future generations by focusing solely on aimless knowledge acquisition.

In conclusion, the new curriculum design of arts education for sustainable thinking should incorporate the above-mentioned principles and standards. Implementing the new curriculum can be supported by: 1) programs using nature as a context in arts education; 2) programs that bring artists to teach in schools and 3) service learning programs that utilize local community resources in the learning process.

## References

Australian Government Department of the Environment and Heritage (2007). *Caring for Our Future*. [Available at: http://aries.mq.edu.au/pdf/caring.pdf.]
Jacobs, M. (1995). *Reflections on the discourse and politics of sustainable development: Part I—Faultlines of contestation and the radical model*. Lancaster: Centre for the Study of Environmental Change, University of Lancaster.
McKeowon, R. (2002). *Education Sustainable Development Toolkit*. [Available at: http://www.esdtoolkit.org.]
Nolet, V. (2010). Education for Sustainability in Washington State: A Whole Systems Approach. *Journal of Sustainability Education*. [Available at: http://www.journalofsustainabilityeducation.org/wordpress.]
Tilbury, D. & Wortman, D. (2004). *Engaging People in Sustainability*. IUCN: Cambridge.
UNESCO (2009). From the margins into the center: Establishing ESD in education plans and curricula. UNESCO World Conference on Education for Sustainable Development. Bonn, Germany.

Gerd Michelsen
# Education for Sustainable Development: Status Quo and Perspectives

Sustainable development involves comprehensive and far-reaching societal transformations and fundamental changes in perspectives, especially regarding humanity's relationship to nature. Such a fundamental re-orientation also requires an extensive change in consciousness on the part of individuals in society. Learning processes play an important role in initiating the corresponding changes in attitudes and should thus become an established part of the educational system.

## 1. Sustainability as a Challenge

Since the 1990s after the adoption of Agenda 21 (1992), political and academic discussions have been increasingly focused on problems arising from non-sustainable development, globalization and the concept of sustainable development. "Sustainable development" is in danger of becoming however a political battle cry, above all heard in the standard speeches of politicians.

The notion of sustainable development is influenced by societal discussions, each with its own different concerns about such issues as justice between present and future generations, liberty and autonomy, human welfare or our responsibility towards the future. Governments, businesses, non-governmental organizations, and communities at both national and international conferences have, in spite of differing interests, emphasized the importance of sustainability as a goal of development. Nevertheless, talk of sustainable development frequently refers to the concept put forward in the Brundtland Report (1987), which focuses on satisfying the needs of the present without risking that future generations will not be able to satisfy theirs, making justice a key element. In Agenda 21 – which was reaffirmed in the final document "The Future We Want" at the Rio+20 Conference in 2012 – the specific changes needed were identified and it was emphasized that both the environment and development are part of a common perspective of the northern and southern hemispheres.

Alongside the dimensions of ecology, economics and society that were recognized in the Brundtland Report, the discussion has centered on the cultural, institutional and political aspects of sustainability in developing countries, with the cultural dimension being given an overriding importance. A definition of culture would include everything that human beings create while interacting with the natural world during a given period of time and within a defined region: for example, language, religion, ethics, institutions, law, technology, science, art, and music but also the processes giving rise to specific cultural artifacts and models including individual and social types of behavior. Thus culture consists of cultural values, worldviews, norms and traditions that characterize our uses of nature, social interaction and economic activity. It has to do with economic systems that structure individual and social practice (cf. Holz and Stoltenberg 2011), with culture being understood less in a theoretical and more in an operative sense, including the process of reflecting on sustainable ethical values as a part of culture. This is the starting point for demands for a culture of sustainability (cf. Stoltenberg and Michelsen 1999). Culture in this sense plays a crucial role in attaining a sustainable society and is a separate dimension to the extent that the vision of sustainability implies that our ways of living, values, our educational and economic systems, or our technological development are a cultural background that must be critically reflected upon and if necessary changed (cf. Stoltenberg 2000).

While by means of the Brundtland Report and Agenda 21 the notion of sustainable development has found its way into the political arena, sustainability and sustainable development are only able to enter the awareness of the general public with difficulty. On the other hand, fundamental principles of sustainability such as justice, fair trade between poor and rich countries or the responsible use of natural resources are approved of by most people, indicating that there is a basis in society for a politics oriented towards sustainable development and for the corresponding approaches to education. Discussions about sustainable development and its close relationship to cultural patterns of thinking and acting (e.g. the question of justice and equality) have made it clear that the vision of sustainability is closely related to different concepts of modernization and development that require greater engagement on the part of individuals. Participation is thus often seen as a new challenge for political culture and closely related to sustainable development.

Education is a crucial component of the sustainability process; indeed its contribution is explicitly called for in Chapter 36 of the Agenda 21: education is critical for promoting sustainable development and improving the capacity of people to address environmental and development issues. Without learning processes, sustainable development would be impossible (cf. Vare and Scott 2007). Education should create awareness for problems related to sustainability issues, enable the acquisition of knowledge about these problems and develop the necessary competencies for successfully working on their solution.

## 2. Education for a Sustainable Development

If education is to meet these demands, then sustainable development must be seen as an interdisciplinary task. This understanding formed the background in the 1990s as the concept of education for sustainable development was first put forward (cf. BLK 1998; de Haan and Harenberg 1999).

Since then a wide variety of efforts have been undertaken to integrate elements of education for sustainable development in all – formal, non-formal, and informal[1] – educational sectors (cf. Barth 2007; Michelsen 2006). At an international level, the United Nations proclaimed a Decade of Education for Sustainable Development in 2005 (cf. UNESCO 2005). The United Nations Economic Commission for Europe (UNECE) drew up a strategy for the implementation of education for sustainable development (UNECE 2005). In Germany an important federal initiative involved integrating education for sustainable development in school education by means of Program 21 and Transfer 21 (Programme Transfer 21 2008). In the informal sector there have also been a great many activities promoting education for sustainable development (cf. Rode et al. 2011).

The concept of education for sustainable development combines approaches found in educational programs focusing on the environment and development as well as peace, health, and politics. The contents and goals of each of these approaches are related to each other from the perspective of a sustainable development. Education for sustainable development thus attempts to make a contribution to an understanding of complex interrelationships that cannot be dealt with by environmental or development education alone.

The UNECE has articulated its understanding of education for sustainable development in its strategy as follows: "Education for sustainable development develops and strengthens the capacity of individuals, groups, communities, organizations and countries to make judgements and choices in favour of sustainable development. It can promote a shift in people's mindsets and in so doing enable them to make our world safer, healthier and more prosperous, thereby improving the quality of life. Education for sustainable development can provide critical reflection and greater awareness and empowerment so that new visions and concepts can be explored and new methods and tools developed" (UNECE 2005, p. 1). Education for sustainable development is meant to empower individuals to become involved in sustainable development and critically reflect on their own actions in this effort (cf. Künzli David 2007). This requires individual competencies that learners should be able to acquire in education for sustainable development (cf. Barth 2007; de Haan et al. 2008; Michelsen 2009; Stoltenberg 2009; Rieckmann 2010).

In addition to the development of sustainability-related competencies, Stoltenberg (2009) identifies further goals for education for sustainable development: alongside orientative knowledge and action-oriented knowledge, future-oriented knowledge plays just as important a role as the critical reflection on values that are part of a vision of sustainable development (especially as related to the preservation of natural resources, human dignity, and justice). Furthermore, this involves gaining the experiences and knowledge that one can participate together with others in shaping one's own life and by taking action today can protect future generations.

---

1  Formal education takes place in official educational or training institutions (preschool, school, colleges and universities etc.), while non-formal education includes all organized educational programs outside the formal education system (e.g. in adult education or environmental education centers). Informal learning takes place daily outside the curricula of formal and non-formal educational institutions and programs (e.g. at work, at home, during leisure time etc.) (cf. Overwien 2005).

## 3. *Gestaltungskompetenz* as an Educational Goal

The increasing complexity, uncertainty, and dynamics of social change places high demands on the individual, whether at the workplace or as an engaged volunteer or in everyday life. These changed conditions make it necessary to be able to take creative, independent action (cf. Erpenbeck 2001; Rychen 2004). Competencies describe what individuals require in order to take action in a variety of complex situations. They are individual dispositions that include cognitive, emotional, volitive, and motivational elements and are developed on the basis of reflecting on practical experiences (cf. Weinert 2001; Rychen 2003). In contrast to domain-specific competencies, key competencies are seen as multifunctional and transferable competencies that are especially relevant for attaining important societal goals, are important for all individuals, and require a high degree of reflexivity. Sustainable development can be seen as a normative framework for the selection of such key competencies.

In recent years a number of different concepts has been developed which define and identify which key competencies should be acquired as an essential part of education for sustainable development. In the German context work in education for sustainable development centers on the concept of *gestaltungskompetenz* (cf. de Haan et al. 2008). Gestaltungskompetenz describes the capabilities needed to recognize problems of non-sustainable development and effectively apply knowledge about sustainable development. It includes a number of sub-competencies, which have been repeatedly modified and supplemented. There are now twelve sub-competencies (Fig. 1).

- *Competency in perspective-taking*: being open-minded and learning by integrating new perspectives
- *Competency in anticipatory thinking*: being able to analyze and evaluate developments before they take place
- *Competency in interdisciplinary learning*: being able to acquire and use interdisciplinary knowledge
- *Competency in handling incomplete and overly complex information*: being able to recognize and evaluate risks, dangers and uncertainties
- *Competency in cooperation*: being able to plan and act together with others
- *Competency in coping with individual dilemmas in decision-making*: being able to account for goal conflicts when reflecting on action strategies
- *Competency in participation*: being able to take part in collective decision-making processes
- *Competency in motivation*: being able to motivate oneself and others to take action
- *Competency in reflection on ideals*: being able to reflect on one's own ideals and those of others
- *Competency in taking moral action*: being able to use ideas of justice as a basis for making decisions and taking action
- *Competency in taking independent action*: being able to independently plan and take action
- *Competency in supporting others*: being able to show empathy for others

Figure 1: Subcompetencies of *gestaltungskompetenz* (de Haan et al. 2008)

The concept of gestaltungskompetenz is especially characterized by subcompetencies that enable an individual to shape sustainable development in a future-oriented and autonomous way. It emphasizes in particular the fact that sustainable development entails the necessity of fundamental societal changes. At an international level the German discourse on gestaltungskompetenz can be compared to the discussion surrounding competency building by education for sustainable development, for example the concept of "sustainability literacy" (cf. Parkin et al. 2004; Wiek et al. 2011) or "social learning" (cf. Wals 2007). The key competencies found in different national discourses are comparable; however there is often a different ranking of their importance, as can be seen in a comparison between key competencies in Europe and Latin America (Rieckmann 2010).

## 4. The UN Decade of Education for Sustainable Development

Following the recommendation of the World Summit for Sustainable Development in Johannesburg (2002), the General Assembly of the United Nations proclaimed a World Decade of Education for Sustainable Development for the period 2005-2014 to be coordinated by the UNESCO. Its goal is to develop educational measures to contribute to the implementation of the Agenda 21, which was adopted at the 1992 Rio Summit and then reaffirmed at the 2002 Johannesburg Summit, and anchor the principles of sustainable development in national educational systems around the world. All member nations of the United Nations are called on to develop national and international educational activities that will show pathways to preserving and enhancing the living conditions and chances of survival for both existing and future generations.

As a result of the UN World Decade there have been many initiatives and activities that have shown what education for sustainable development is about. This includes major conferences and publications as well as concrete initiatives. For example, in China education for sustainable development was integrated in the medium and long term planning for national educational reform (2010-2020) and over 1000 experimental schools for education for sustainable development were established. In India a campaign "$CO_2$ Pick Right" was started in over 70,000 schools. In Japan education for sustainable development was codified in the national curriculum guidelines. In Asia and Africa, Sweden is supporting the training and education of teachers in education for sustainable development. The MESA program by UNEP has introduced education for sustainable development and sustainable development in over 80 universities in 40 African countries. Alongside numerous European initiatives (cf. Stoltenberg and Holz 2012), Sweden has passed legislation requiring all universities to take up education for sustainable development and sustainable development. In Canada all schools in the province of Manitoba are required to prioritize sustainable development. The United Nations University has been able to establish over 100 Regional Centers for Expertise (RCE) around the world that focus on education for sustainable development on a regional level. Research programs on education for sustainable development (for example in Germany) are beginning to take shape.

Among the most important recent international conferences focusing on education for sustainable development, the following should be mentioned: the 36th General Assembly Meeting of the UN in 2011, where 68 countries referred in their statements to the importance of education for sustainable development; the Bonn Conference on "Moving into the Second Half of the World Decade" in 2009, with its Bonn Declaration; and the Rio+20 Conference in 2012, with its final document once again emphasizing the importance of education for sustainable development. And finally UNESCO-supported networks should also be mentioned as exemplary in this context: the Global University Network for Innovation (GUNI), the "Network for Reorienting Teacher Education to Sustainability" and the global network of the UNESCO schools.

In the German-speaking countries of Austria, Switzerland and Germany, a number of structures have been firmly established for activities that are part of the UN World Decade of Education for Sustainable Development (see Table 1).

Table 1: Structures implementing the UN World Decade of Education for Sustainable Development

| Country | Structures and Activities |
| --- | --- |
| Germany | • National Committee with UN Decade Office<br>• Round Table with over 100 stakeholders<br>• Working Groups of the Round Table<br>• Decade Project Awards (over 1,700 to date)<br>• Research programme in Education for Sustainable Development<br>• Federal states with own specific activities<br>• Establishment of RCEs |
| Switzerland | • Swiss Coordination Conference: Education for Sustainable Development 2007-2014<br>• Policy Plan for Measures Promoting Education for Sustainable Development<br>• Decade Project Awards<br>• Sustainable Development in Universities Programme 2013-2017 |
| Austria | • Austrian Strategy on Education for Sustainable Development<br>• UN Decade Office<br>• Decade Project Awards<br>• Sustainability Award for Austrian Universities<br>• Establishment of RCEs |

At the Conference on the UN World Decade of Education for Sustainable Development in Bonn in 2009 – with over 900 participants from around the world – it became clear that a framework must be found for the time after the World Decade, one that would enable the continuation of the many activities around the world that are helping to establish education for sustainable development in all areas of education. The final document "The Future We Want" of the Rio+20 Conference in the summer of 2012 emphasizes the importance of continuing the activities of the World Decade after 2014. In autumn 2013 the Executive Council of the UNESCO finally adopted at its annual meeting a recommendation to the General Assembly of the UNESCO that would enable the activities of the Decade to be continued in the form of a global framework program that would promote education for sustainable development as a central element in the implementation of sustainable development in as many countries around the world as possible.

A Framework Program Education for Sustainable Development was created to continue a variety of activities in all areas of education. In contrast to a UN World Decade, a Framework Program does not have a limited time period. In such a framework, activities that were begun in the Decade can be worked out in greater detail and established on a broader footing. But it is also possible to set longer-term goals, ones that cannot be reached in ten years. For a global Framework Program Education for Sustainable Development, a new concept, a new label must be created, just as new mechanisms and structures for its implementation must be found. There is no doubt that the UNESCO will play a central role in implementing this Program Framework, just as it will be necessary for countries to provide as much support as possible (UNESCO 2012).

These structures can also serve in a post-Decade period and they will enable us to follow-up activities in modified form but also to initiate further developments, exchange experiences and critically reflect on an international level while giving fresh impetus to new activities and establishment processes on a national level. This depends however on support – also financial support – for these activities from the necessary political committees and ministries.

## 5. Conclusion

In the course of the UN World Decade, education for sustainable development has become a concept that gives us a completely new understanding of education and new opportunities for improving the quality of education. Education for sustainable development has however – in spite of uncountable initiatives, activities and projects – still not become part of the mainstream. And that is why further efforts must be made so that in the time after the UN World Decade of Education for Sustainable Development a continuation of activities as a World Program Education for Sustainable Development is meaningful and necessary, one that will be supported by countries around the world under the leadership of the UNESCO. This open-ended world program should provide impulses both on both a national and an international level for new initiatives to help establish and critically reflect on education for sustainable development.

## References

Barth, M. (2007). *Gestaltungskompetenz durch Neue Medien? Die Rolle des Lernens mit Neuen Medien in der Bildung für nachhaltige Entwicklung.* Berlin.
BLK – Bund-Länder-Kommission für Bildungsplanung und Forschungsförderung (1998). *Bildung für nachhaltige Entwicklung. Orientierungsrahmen.* Bonn.
de Haan, G. & Harenberg, D. (1999). *Gutachten zum Programm Bildung für nachhaltige Entwicklung. Bund-Länder-Kommission für Bildungsplanung und Forschungsförderung.* Bonn.
de Haan, G., Kamp, G., Lerch, A., Martignon, L., Müller-Christ, G. & Nutzinger, H.-G. (Eds.) (2008). *Nachhaltigkeit und Gerechtigkeit. Grundlagen und schulpraktische Konsequenzen.* Berlin, Heidelberg.

Erpenbeck, J. (2001). Wissensmanagement als Kompetenzmanagement. In: Franke, G. (Ed.): *Komplexität und Kompetenz. Ausgewählte Fragen der Kompetenzforschung.* Bielefeld, 102–120.

Holz, V. & Stoltenberg, U. (2011). Mit dem kulturellen Blick auf den Weg zu einer nachhaltigen Entwicklung. In: Sorgo, G. (Ed.): *Die unsichtbare Dimension. Bildung für nachhaltige Entwicklung im kulturellen Prozess* (pp. 15-34). Wien: Forum Umweltbildung.

Künzli David, C. (2007). *Zukunft mitgestalten. Bildung für nachhaltige Entwicklung – Didaktisches Konzept und Umsetzung in der Grundschule.* Bern.

Michelsen, G. (2006). Bildung für nachhaltige Entwicklung. Meilensteine auf einem langen Weg. In: Tiemeyer, E. & Wilbers, K. (Eds.): *Berufliche Bildung für nachhaltiges Wirtschaften. Konzepte – Curricula – Methoden – Beispiele.* Bielefeld, 17–32.

Michelsen, G. (2009). Kompetenzen und Bildung für nachhaltige Entwicklung. In: Overwien, B. & Rathenow, H.-F. (Eds.): *Globalisierung fordert politische Bildung. Politisches Lernen im globalen Kontext.* Opladen, Farmington Hills, 75–86.

Michelsen, G. (2013). Bildung für Nachhaltige Entwicklung in der Postdekade. In: *Bildung für nachhaltige Entwicklung.* Jahrbuch 2013. Wien, 10-15.

Overwien, B. (2005). Stichwort: Informelles Lernen. In: *Zeitschrift für Erziehungswissenschaft 8* (3), 339–355.

Parkin, S., Johnston, A., Buckland, H., Brookes, F. & White, E. (2004). *Learning and Skills for Sustainable Development. Developing a sustainability literate society. Guidance for Higher Education Institutions.* London. Online: http://www.forumforthefuture.org.uk/files/learningandskills.pdf.

Programm Transfer-21 (2008). *Programm Transfer-21: Bildung für nachhaltige Entwicklung.* Abschlussbericht des Programmträgers 1. August 2004 bis 31. Juli 2008. Online: http://www.transfer-21.de/daten/T21_Abschluss.pdf.

Rieckmann, M. (2010). *Die globale Perspektive der Bildung für nachhaltige Entwicklung. Eine europäisch-lateinamerikanische Studie zu Schlüsselkompetenzen für Denken und Handeln in der Weltgesellschaft.* Berlin.

Rode, H. (2005). *Motivation, Transfer und Gestaltungskompetenz. Ergebnisse der Abschlussevaluation des BLK-Programms „21" 1999-2004.* Berlin. Online unter: http://www.transfer-21.de/daten/evaluation/Abschlusserhebung.pdf.

Rychen, D. S. (2003). Key competencies: Meeting important challenges in life. In: Rychen, D. S. & Salganik, L. H. (Eds.): *Key competencies for a successful life and well-functioning society.* Cambridge/MA., Toronto, Bern, Göttingen, 63–107.

Rychen, D. S. (2004): Key competencies for all: an overarching conceptual frame of reference. In: Rychen, D. S. & Tiana, A. (Eds.): *Developing Key Competencies in Education: Some Lessons from International and National Experience.* Paris, 5–34.

Stoltenberg, U. (2000). Lebenswelt Hochschule als Erfahrungsraum für Nachhaltigkeit. In Michelsen, G. (Ed.). *Sustainable University. Auf dem Weg zu einem universitären Agendaprozess.* Frankfurt/Main: VAS. 90-116.

Stoltenberg, U. (2009). *Mensch und Wald. Theorie und Praxis einer Bildung für nachhaltige Entwicklung am Beispiel des Themenfeldes Wald.* München.

Stoltenberg, U. & Holz, V. (Eds.) (2012). *Education for Sustainable Development – European Approaches.* Bad Homburg: VAS.

Stoltenberg, U. & Michelsen, G. (1999). Lernen nach der Agenda 21: Überlegungen zu einem Bildungskonzept für eine nachhaltige Entwicklung. In Stoltenberg, U., Michelsen, G., Schreiner, J. (Eds.): *Umweltbildung den Möglichkeitssinn wecken.* NNA-Berichte, 12. Jg., H. 1, 45-54.

UNESCO – United Nations Educational, Scientific and Cultural Organization (2005). *United Nations Decade of Education for Sustainable Development (2005-2014): International Implementation Scheme.* Paris.

UNESCO Executive Board (2012). *190 EX/9: United Nations Decade of Education for Sustainable Development: Looking Beyond 2014.* Paris.

Vare, P. & Scott, W. (2007). Learning for a Change: Exploring the Relationship Between Education and Sustainable Development. In: *Journal of Education for Sustainable Development 1* (2), 191–198.

Wals, A. E. J., (Ed.) (2007). *Social learning towards a sustainable world: Principles, perspectives, and praxis.* Wageningen Academic Publishers, Wageningen.

Weinert, F. E. (2001). Concept of Competence: A Conceptual Clarification. In: Rychen, D. S. & Salganik, L. H. (Eds.). *Defining and Selecting Key Competencies.* Seattle, Toronto, Bern, Göttingen, 45–65.

Wiek, A., Withycombe, L. & Redman, C. L. (2011). Key competencies in sustainability: a reference framework for academic program development. In: *Sustainability Science 6* (2), 203–218.

Ernst Wagner

# Arts Education and Education for Sustainable Development
## Suggestions for Possible Bridges between Two Worlds

Arts Education (AE) and Education for Sustainable Development (ESD) appertain to two different worlds. An alliance between both sectors is hard to bring about without complications. Therefore, it is advisable, if not necessary, to analyse possible difficulties, to consider, to systemise, and to discuss existing approaches, and to identify potentially productive links between both fields. This is the purpose of the following considerations.

Educational researcher Jürgen Baumert, in the context of a publication on PISA-results in 2000, convincingly makes use of a distinction that is also relevant for the concerns discussed here: a distinction among four ways of accessing the world.[1] These four accesses are founded in general anthropological conditions, but they also remain culture-specific. They are essentially human "modes of encountering the world" and simultaneously follow culturally coded rationalities.

The dominant logic (in education and socio-political discourse, at least in a European context) relies on a cognitive-instrumental approach towards the world. This is the domain of subjects such as mathematics, natural sciences, or technology. This logic models the world differently than is the case with other approaches, such as, for instance, the sort of approach that is performed through the arts. Fine arts, literature, music, and dance follow their own language: they are realised within the specific rationality of an aesthetic-expressive logic. A third logic, the evaluative-normative logic, emerges through the concerns that are raised by legislation, economy, and the larger frameworks of society. Eventually, questions that aim for ultimate explanation – questions about the origin, destination, and purpose of human life – require an entirely different, a fourth, mode of accessing the world. These four central modes are embodied in the canon of school subjects as well as in the variety of academic disciplines. They are constitutive elements of education, and define our sense of general education. Each of them – and this is important – gives access to a unique and independent horizon of understanding. They are not exchangeable. And they are not subjected to any sort of hierarchy. Only the influence of all four accesses on our educational system conveys the necessary insight into the complexity of understanding: there is not only one access to the world that emerges in our minds; but instead, there is a whole variety of worlds, depending on the approaches we take.

The manner in which our understanding of the world emerges from and depends on different perspectives necessarily leads to problems once two perspectives are asked

---

1  Baumert 2002, p. 113 – PISA follows a similar concept, cf. PISA 2000, p. 21.

to cooperate – and the dialogue between Arts Education (AE) and Education for Sustainable Development (ESD) illustrates these complications. ESD primarily appertains to the social-economic sector. As a cross-cutting issue, ESD, however, also touches on ethical questions that are negotiated with respect to more fundamental concerns of self-location: what are our origins? What is our purpose in life? And what is our destination? Moreover, ESD also enters into conversation with instrumental and scientific aspects – sustainability, after all, needs to be practically generated and technically workable. At first glance, the aesthetic-expressive approach towards the world does not really fit into this context.

The problem becomes tangible, if we consider German definitions for arts education.[2] According to the prevalent concept, arts education is concerned with the reception and production of artistic ("non-functional") forms of expression that enrich individual lives. Arts education, according to this definition, is not occupied with creations that follow normative frameworks or are determined by any outward purpose. Instead, arts education's only obligations are towards the individual, to the (felicity of) individual lives. It is thus looking for individual solutions: every work of art is unique.

ESD, by contrast, enhances the capacity of appraising the impact individual actions exert on future generations and other regions of the world.[3] The focus, therefore, is not on the (artistic) act and the present moment, as is, for instance, the case with a drama or a dance performance or with the process of painting. The scope of ESD is situated within an entirely different period, as it aims at the well-being of future generations. Simultaneously, the concept of responsibility bears different connotations in this context, as it is not a responsibility towards a specific work of art but instead a responsibility towards the entire world. (There can hardly be a bigger scope than this). In ESD, individual actions are thus determined by specific intentions, they are not an end in themselves, but instead performed with a greater purpose in mind.

This clarification of the differences between both approaches helps in differentiating between workable links and less practical connections, but, at the same time, easily belies the structural similarities between Arts Education and Educations for Sustainable Development. The important aspects that unite both fields are: an orientation along concepts of action, the insecurities about what is right and what is wrong, the relevance of creativity, and the central role of empathy. Nevertheless, ESD and AE appertain to different rationalities; this becomes particularly clear if we consider the form of judgement that is associated with each field. Judgements that are guided by taste are categorically different from judgements that are formed on a basis of sustainability. In the first case, we are concerned with the beauty or aesthetic integrity of an object; in the second case we consider the sustainability of this object. Depending on the sphere in which I am thinking and acting and on the approach towards the world on which I rely, in a specific moment, my judgement will vary (consider the example of different bags in fig. 1).

---

2 Fischer 2014.
3 The UNESCO-website lists the following fields of responsibility for ESD: Biodiversity, climate change, reduction of risks for catastrophes, cultural diversity, poverty, equality of gender, health, sustainable lifestyles, peace and safety, water, sustainable urban development. (www.unesco.org/new/en/education/themes/leading-the-international-agenda/education-for-sustainable-development/).

Fig. 1:    Bags

On the basis of these differences, the following paragraphs explore how an alliance between ESD and AE can be conceptualised. I consider approaches that rely on the domination of one field by the other as well as attempts that depend on a more balanced form of dialogue and in which both fields aspire towards one goal.

## 1. Materials, Contents, Goals, and Ideas Appertain to ESD, AE Adopts them for its own Projects

There is a myriad of practical projects, for which ESD literally provides the "material." Fig. 2 represents an obvious example.[4] We are dealing with a work of the genre "Sculpture in public space"; in order to convince in a context of art and culture such a work needs to be aesthetically coherent, in other words: it needs to be beautiful. Such a sculpture can be perceived as beautiful: because it is adequately placed within its environment, because it has the right size, because the choice of material is coherent, or because its composition articulates, interprets, and accentuates the surrounding space in an interesting manner. Whether these aspects are successfully performed determines the quality of the work. In the case of this particular sculpture, ESD enters the game and provides the material: the sculpture is made from recycling material and it is equipped with solar cells. In this and other cases, ESD introduces new materials into artistic projects; examples range from a use of healthy and recyclable paint to self-made instruments.[5] It becomes obvious that in such cases, ESD influences not only the choice of materials but also shapes a new sensitivity towards the handling or resources. (Thus, it also prepares the scene for future sustainable business in the creative industries.)

Further contemplation affirms the suspicion that the sculpture not only "borrows" its materials, but also its central ideas and contents. It certainly had to be a flower: a flower as a symbol of life, of a beautiful life, which emerged from a marriage between waste

---

4   „UN-Dekade Bildung für nachhaltige Entwicklung": Deutsche UNESCO-Kommission (Ed.), UNESCO heute, 1.2006, Bonn 2006.
5   Schäfer in: BKJ 2012, p. 27.

Fig. 2 / Fig. 3: Illustrations in the brochure "UN-Dekade Bildung für nachhaltige Entwicklung" (see footnote 4).

and renewable energy. The specification of contents through ESD is a frequent feature in similar arts education projects. In such cases, we encounter a form of AE that is concerned with self-legitimisation, as it contributes towards a generally accepted goal. Examples are manifold: adolescents perform a drama about sustainability; children craft a picture about the topic or write a short story; a globe is manufactured, for a school party, and then delivered into the hands of children (cf. fig. 3) – an important metaphor to which I return later on.

## 2. AE Provides the Pictures or Other Formats of Sensually Accessible Presentations for ESD or AE Critically Analyses the Corporate Design of ESD

ESD needs a creative and appealing corporate design and it also needs images in order to operate effectively. And there is no better associate when it comes to the design of logos, public performances, events, and images than AE. Even if we are apparently only dealing with the decoration of brochures or websites, these aspects matter. And they are the sort of message that children or adolescents can design by themselves. If they participate in such a project, they experience two diverse learning processes: one that relates to the contents of AE and is concerned with essential aspects of communication design, and another one that relates to ESD and comprises an intensive encounter with the interests of ESD (as a basis for the creative process).

AE is, however, more than creative design; it also contains the equally important aspect of analytical reception. Arts education, therefore, also contributes to a mode of appraisal of visual representation that is central to ESD. The focus of this appraisal is on logos as well as on frequently-used visual motifs. These forms of representation provide a condensation of the metaphors that make the world view on which ESD depends accessible.

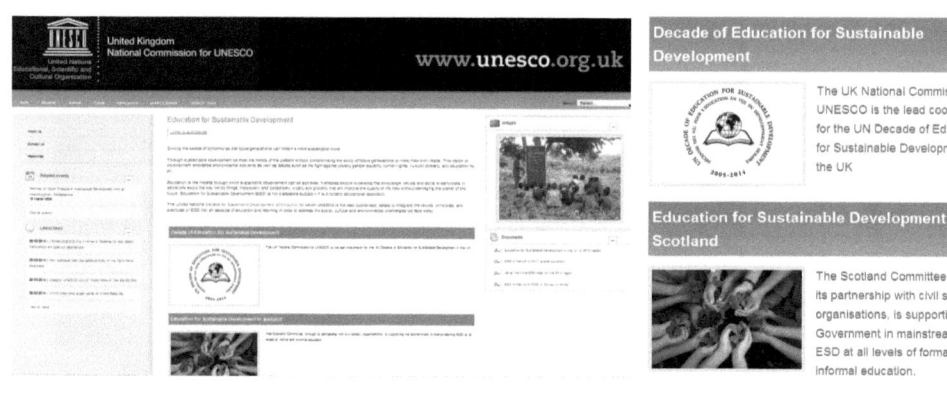

Fig. 4: www.unesco.org.uk/education_for_sustainable_development – Overview (Screenshot) and details

Fig. 5: Illustrations in the brochure "UN-Dekade Bildung für nachhaltige Entwicklung" (see footnote 4).

A first exploration of the visual worlds of ESD demonstrates that the designers apparently found it difficult to come up with a concise and expressive logo (cf. fig. 4). With respect to the illustrations (or decorative complements) – which, in this case, are much more successful with their communications – we can differentiate between two types (cf. fig. 4 and fig 5): on the one hand, there are images of destroyed nature (pictures of catastrophe) and, on the other hand, as a positively-connoted counter-image, there is the picture of hands that are carrying something. They are mostly children's hands, and they are often depicted from above; thus evoking the impression that we are seeing them from the perspective of the child. These hands are carrying plants, fruit, or the globe (representations of the nature that we are asked to preserve). While the children, in these pictures, embody the "future generation"; the gestures that are performed by their hands signal an appeal towards our empathy, or, in other words, a call to action: "Preserve! Protect!" A clipping from a Google image search[6] covers a wider field, as it is not limited to the official websites. The general impression is, however, a similar one: a variety of the typical combination of protective hands and globes.

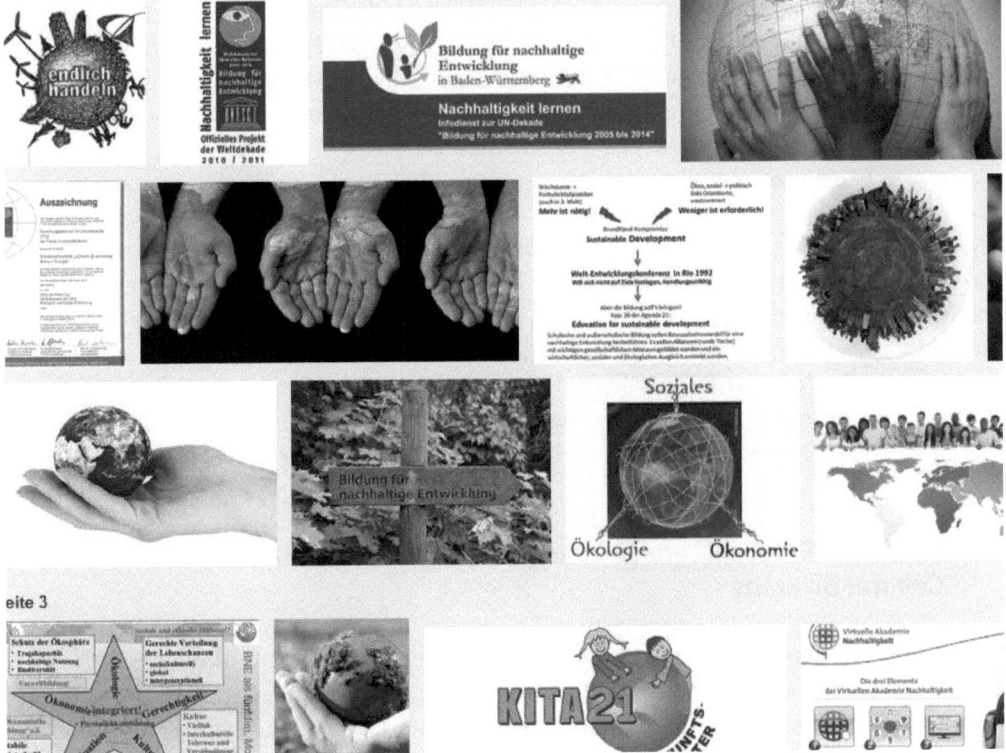

Fig. 6:   Google image search: "Bildung fuer nachhaltige Entwicklung (Education for sustainable Development)" – Clipping (19.03.2014)

---

6   Google-search for keyword „education for sustainable development", 24.11.2013.

Such an appraisal of images is to be understood within the overarching framework through which AE critically reflects the premises on which ESD relies.[7] In this context, the following questions are raised: What are the concepts of nature ESD depends on, and how are they symbolically (and often unconsciously) represented in verbal and visual communication? Which concepts are at the foundation of powerful metaphors such as "sustainability", "development", "diversity", or "growth"?[8] And what kind of imagination unfolds through these concepts, if we understand them in terms of a historically-grown cultural imagery?

## 3. Uses for and Transfer of Creative Skills for ESD

AE offers a special value for ESD projects, because it can provide things that ESD lacks: relishing in activities that involve all the senses, unrestricted possibilities of testing out new forms of presentation, variety, a plurality of perspectives, a form of doing that directly addresses our emotions.[9] AE trains unorthodox thinking and creative potential and thus generates highly attractive qualifications: skills, knowledge, and attitudes that are of great interest for ESD. The hope behind many conceptual considerations is that creatively-schooled individuals can transfer their skills to the challenges of ESD. ESD is concerned with developing things that do not exist yet (such as for instance new lifestyles); therefore, this potential has a great significance.[10]

Research on transferability, however, signals that some caution is necessary when claiming these skills.[11] The reason for this is not only that art and artistic experiences are functionalised if applied in the domain of ESD, but rather that, in many cases, the desired transfer simply does not take place: listening to Mozart does not automatically increase a child's intelligence, and, similarly, painting does not automatically equip individuals with sensitivity towards the goals of ESD. Transfer can only be achieved successfully if the possibility of transfer is reflected on a meta-cognitive level by the learners themselves. Transfer should, therefore, be regarded as a specific achievement within the learning process itself, an achievement that has to be enabled, prepared for, and shaped.

## 4. ESD and AE Collaborate on Issues such as Lifestyle, Urban Development, or Cultural Diversity

Lifestyle and urban development are domains which, according to the UNESCO agenda, fall under the responsibility of ESD. Both fields, however, overlap with the aims and contents of AE, as they are products of the "applied arts". These are, in opposition to the "liberal arts", to a certain degree, functional, as they fulfil specific tasks. Beyond this,

---

7   Eva Leipprand, in: BKJ 2012, p. 6; cf. Michael Wimmer, in: Leicht, Plum, 2007, p. 31.
8   For growth cf. Eva Leiprand in: BKJ 2012, p. 4; cf. Max Fuchs, in: Leicht, Plum, 2007 p. 16.
9   Fischer, in: BKJ 2012, p. 9.
10  de Haan; in: Leicht, Plum 2007, p. 9; also includes a reference to empathy, and the adaptation of intercultural perspectives.
11  Winner, Goldstein, Vincent-Lancrin, 2013

they are also the symbolic expression of views and values, for instance, when the design of a car reveals not only something about a society's attitude towards mobility, but also about issues of gender, resources, nature, or general values. Fashion tells us something about the habitus of human beings; product design, houses, apartments, and urban spaces are legible as manifestations of their inhabitants' attitudes towards life, towards nature, towards their environment; and similar messages are inscribed into the design of sport events, parties, or folklore. Tattoos, as an example of contemporary everyday aesthetics, show the relationships of human beings to their bodies. In all these examples, if we translate them as manifestations of ideas about life, we see how specific values and mindsets are visualised. They are shaped by the interplay between individual life designs and the value systems that are sustained by a society. As such, they directly influence the way in which human beings perceive themselves and in which they interact with others and with the environment.

These social codes are, however, not only quasi-neutral enunciations within a neutral space. Instead, they condense into a direct expression of identity designs within a social sphere (where they also exert their influence on others) and, therefore, they get close to each of us: to the agent (that is: the producer, purchaser, or consumer) and to the recipient or observer.

AE has the skills that are necessary in order to explore and evaluate the communication of values through products. Beyond this, AE also offers the possibility of testing out our own designs, of imagining, developing, and crafting things (such as fashion, design, houses), which act as vehicles for attitudes, mindsets, and values. AE thus not only accomplishes a receptive-analytical reflection of models, but also enhances the productive-creative competencies that allow us to act on our own accord.[12]

## 5. Conflict as a Chance for Learning – Negotiation as a Principle

As a conclusion, I offer a last observation that is based on the initially-sketched potential for conflict between AE and ESD – an observation of a fundamental nature, for that matter. It assumes that conflict is an instigator of educational processes. As an illustration, I want to return to the example of different bag designs that was invoked at the beginning of this text. Let us imagine an Arts Education project in which adolescents are asked to design bags that are then really produced. The choice of material in this example is – with respect to sustainability – of vital importance, but it is equally relevant with regard to the product's beauty: sustainable jute and ecological dye limit the possibilities of design; they are not combinable with particular aesthetics, perhaps they also contradict the specific aesthetics that appeal to adolescents. Conflict (at least in some cases) is unavoidable. The designer has to decide which path to take.

This unpreventable and implicit conflict makes the dilemma pedagogically productive. The fundamental dilemma is that, as human beings, we cannot live without destruction. The question, whether we want a plastic bag or a jute bag, is the perfect example for raising this issue. It also is the perfect example for discussing what we need in

---

12 de Haan, in: Leicht, Plum, 2007, p. 26.

order to live with this dilemma. But this is not only about living with it – there is more at stake: how can we productively cope with the contradictions? Conflict can turn into a point of departure for processes of negotiation and of reflection. These are negotiations between the non-functional and the functional, the local and the global, the present moment and long-term perspectives, between a focus on the individual or on the collective.

## References

Baumert, J. (2002). Deutschland im internationalen Bildungsvergleich; in: N. Kilius et al. (Eds.), *Die Zukunft der Bildung,* Frankfurt a. Main.
BKJ (Ed.) (2012). *Kulturelle Bildung für nachhaltige Entwicklung, (Reflexionen. Argumente. Impulse),* Jg. 2012, Nr. 9, Remscheid.
Deutsche UNESCO-Kommission (Ed.) (2006). *UNESCO heute, 1.2006,* Bonn.
Fischer, B. (2014). *Internes Arbeitspapier der AG Kulturelle Bildung am „Runden Tisch für Nachhaltige Entwicklung",* Remscheid.
Leicht, A. & Plum, L. J. (Eds.) (2007). *Kulturelle Bildung und nachhaltige Entwicklung,* Sankt Augustin.
PISA (2000). *Basiskompetenzen von Schülerinnen und Schülern im internationalen Vergleich,* Opladen.
Winner, E., Goldstein, T. R. & Vincent-Lancrin, S. (2013). *Art for Art's Sake – The Impact of Arts Education,* Paris (OECD).

# Arts Education and Peace Education

Cynthia Cohen

# Linking Arts Education with the Field of Peacebuilding and the Arts

## Introduction

The field of Peacebuilding and the Arts draws on the most ancient of wisdom and the most current of creative innovations to support communities working towards social, economic, political and cultural arrangements that are more just, less violent and more generative of life. This essay describes the breadth of the peace building/arts field, and suggests that questions of epistemology are at the core of its relationship with the field of arts education.

## The Breadth of the Field of Peacebuilding and the Arts

The practices embraced within the wide umbrella of 'peacebuilding and the arts' are extremely varied, reflecting different cultures and embodying diverse theories of change. The field embraces collectivities' expressive forms, such as ritual and folk traditions, as well as all of the different arts, including visual arts, architecture, music, dance, theatre, film, literature, spoken word, digital arts, artfully constructed monuments and memorials, urban design, etc. Practitioners and producers of peacebuilding/arts initiatives balance aesthetic and socio-political imperatives in very different ways, ranging from projects whose messages are pre-determined by commissioning governments or ngos to those that allow the content of works to emerge from embodied engagement in aesthetic processes. Well-designed peacebuilding/arts initiatives lead to changes in beliefs, attitudes and actions in individual participants and members of audiences, as well as to transformations in relationships, communities (both local and global), and institutional, governmental and intergovernmental policies.

Both artist-based and community-based productions can be crafted to contribute to the creative transformation of conflict. Such peacebuilding/arts initiatives take place in schools, theatres, museums, television studios, as well as in in public plazas and projected onto the walls of buildings. They emerge in contexts marked by direct and/or structural violence as well as in the aftermath of gross violations of human rights. In relatively peaceful societies, they strengthen a culture of peace and address global injustices and threats to human life such as climate change. In contexts of government repression, truths can sometimes be told through the arts in coded messages that elude military censors and other forms of surveillance.

## The Educational Dimension of Peacebuilding and the Arts

In all such instances, peacebuilding/arts initiatives are educational, in the sense that they create spaces for expression and reflection and, often, for experiencing interdependence. They function to enhance metacognitive awareness, as participants and audience members witness themselves seeing, become aware of the quality of their listening, and interrogate the symbols and narratives through which they construct meaning.

Peacebuilding/arts activities serve to cultivate the creative, intellectual and moral capacities required to live peacefully and responsibly. But, of course, not all artistic expression can be considered as peacebuilding. In fact, the expressive forms we associate with the arts notoriously have been used to instill sentiments of over-reaching national pride, to motivate military expeditions, and even to torture. In addition, the relations inherent in cultural production can function to replicate and exacerbate, rather than challenge, unequal power dynamics (along divides of ethnicity, class, race, gender, etc.). All too often, the expressive forms of subjugated peoples are appropriated for the benefit of the dominant community. Even very beautiful works, executed with political and aesthetic sensitivity, can be appropriated to serve governmental or agency agendas in ways that put communities at risk, exacerbate tensions, or offer cover for repressive policies and regimes.

## Distinguishing Peacebuilding Arts Practices from Other Kinds of Engagement with the Arts

So how, then, are we to distinguish peacebuilding/arts from other kinds of art-making efforts? The peacebuilding scholar/practitioner John Paul Lederach, in *The Moral Imagination: The Art and Soul of Building Peace,* suggests that in the "simplicity that can be found on the far side of complexity," peacebuilding processes are characterized by the moral imagination, i.e. the ability to stay grounded in the real world (with its suffering, its injustices, its violence) and <u>at the same time</u> imagine and work toward a less violent, more just, more vibrant order. His proposes that moral imagination requires the practice of four disciplines: creating spaces of creativity, for both oneself and others; taking risks to reach out and make oneself vulnerable to one's enemies and adversaries; always acting with an awareness of interdependence, knowing that our own and each person's wellbeing is contingent on the wellbeing of others; and embracing what he refers to as "paradoxical curiosity," an eagerness to identify how multiple narratives and seemingly mutually truths, can in fact coexist. Artistic practices that are animated by these commitments and values are likely to contribute to the creative transformation of conflict; those that are motivated by other commitments – for instance to celebrity or profit or cultural pride to the exclusion of respect for others – are likely to fall short of peacebuilding standards; in fact, they often cause harms.

## Epistemological Links between Arts Education and Peacebuilding and the Arts

The cultivation of the moral imagination and other capacities and sensibilities required for peacebuilding is one of the main areas of overlap between the fields of arts education and peacebuilding and the arts. The arts are uniquely well-suited to cultivate such capacities by virtue of the strong alignment between the ways of understanding the world that are cultivated through the arts and the ways of knowing, understanding and meaning-making required to transform violence in the direction of a culture of peace.

As the Quaker educator Parker Palmer notes, embedded within every epistemology is a moral trajectory. Peacebuilding requires modes of knowing that engage both heart and mind. It requires certain qualities of presence – such as heartfelt awareness, alert calmness and engaged detachment – qualities that are precisely those cultivated by aesthetic engagement. This in part due to the linking of cognitive, sensory, emotional and spiritual faculties that take place in aesthetic transactions. Also, in the arts, the collaborative process of meaning-construction between the viewer or listener and the work, both reflects and engenders respect and reciprocity essential to the creative transformation of conflict.

## Documentation and Assessment in the Field of Peacebuilding and the Arts

Evaluating such rich, fluid and often ephemeral experiences remain a challenge for both the Arts in Education and Peacebuilding and the Arts fields. The American lesbian feminist poet Adrienne Rich suggests that the true impacts of artistic engagement cannot be known; she argues that there is a 'permeable membrane' between art and society, a continuous inter-animation of social concerns and cultural productions (as 'tides brine the estuary and the rivers enter the sea'). While acknowledging that attempts to <u>measure</u> the changes elicited through the arts are often counterproductive and can actually interfere with aesthetic processes themselves, the field of peacebuilding/arts does recognize that we have a responsibility to document our practice so we and others can learn from it, and to seek to understand the impact of our work on communities and to understand at least whether our initiatives may have caused any harm. Arts educators face a parallel challenge: while acknowledging that the full range of effects of education in the arts cannot be measured, there remains an obligation to document whether and how students are leaning.

Artists and peacebuilders, both scholars and practitioners, working on *Acting Together on the World Stage*, a multi-year project documenting the contributions of performance to the creative transformation of conflict, devised a framework that acknowledges BOTH the socio-political conditions before and after arts interventions AND the aesthetic (and therefore potentially transformative) quality of the artwork itself. The framework is designed to assist artists (whose primary concerns tend to be aesthetic) to attend to the social and political conditions outside of the creative space, and to assist peacebuilders and policy-makers, whose focus typically is on socio-political conditions, to open themselves to aesthetic experiences and to value aesthetic quality as significant in itself. The framework is based on the idea that, in instances where arts contribute to the creative transformation of conflict, the permeable membrane between art and society is animated by the aesthetic and ethical sensibilities of the moral imagination. This framework suggests a set of questions that can be used to document and assess peacebuilding/arts:

- Does the initiative, institution, or project animate untapped sources of resilience from within the community?
- Does it allow untold stories, suppressed truths, unmourned losses, unacknowledged complicities, unfulfilled yearnings, etc., to enter into the space of creativity?
- How robust is the moral imagination that animates the work? Could artists' and cultural workers' capacities be enhanced?
- Are non-conscious channels of expression honored as well as conscious (goal-oriented) agendas?
- What new ideas, feelings, possibilities, hopes, acknowledgements, images, relationships, etc., emerge in those who participate and witnesss?
- Have artists and cultural leaders engaged the resources of their craft with sensitivity, skill and imagination? Does the work resonate deeply with those who participate and witness?
- Are the transformations achieved within the creative space propelled broadly, deeply and strategically back into society? Are both broad audiences and key people being reached? How could the reach and effectiveness be enhanced?
- Has care been taken to minimize risks of doing harm?

Perhaps the framework of the moral imagination, the permeable membrane between arts and society, and the questions that emerge from them can be of use to the arts education field as well, as it addresses the key questions of documentation, evaluation and assessment.

## The Ideas in this Essay are Elaborated Further in the Following Resources:

*Acting Together on the World Stage* documentary and toolkit. Co-created by Cynthia Cohen and Allison Lund. (The toolkit includes worksheets on the moral imagination, minimizing risks of doing harm, and guidelines for planning and documenting peacebuilding/performance initiatives. The documentary is available with subtitles in Arabic, Hebrew, Japanese, Sinhala, Spanish and Tamil.) http://www.recastinc.org.

Cohen, C., Varea, R. & Walker, P. (2011). *Acting Together: Performance and the Creative Transformation of Conflict. Volume I: Resistance and Reconciliation in Regions of Violence;* and *Volume II: Building Just and Inclusive Communities.* New Village Press. (Volume II Chapter 6 lays out the framework of the permeable membrane and peacebuilding performance.) http://www.newvillagepress.net/catalog.

Lederach, J. P. (2005). *The Moral Imagination: The Art and Soul of Building Peace.* Oxford University Press.

Palmer, P. "Community, Conflict and Ways of Knowing." http://www.couragerenewal.org/parker/writings/community-conflict.

Rich, A. (2006). "Permeable Membrane" in The Virginia Quarterly, Spring 2006. http://www.vqronline.org/articles/2006/spring/rich-permeable-membrane/.

Thompson, J. (2011). *Performance Affects: Applied Theatre and the End of Effect.* Palgrave MacMillan. Reprint edition.

## Additional Key Resources from the Peacebuilding and the Arts Field

### Links:
Arts and Peace Commission of the International Peace Research Association. http://ipra2014.org

Barefooot Artists. www.barefootartists.org/

International Theatre Institute – UNESCO. www.iti-worldwide.org.

"Peacebuilding and the Arts Now" e-newsletter. http://www.brandeis.edu/ethics/peacebuildingarts/news/newsletter.html

Peacebuilding and the Arts online Resource Library. http://www.brandeis.edu/ethics/peacebuildingarts/library/index.html

Playback Theatre. http://www.playbackcentre.org

### Books:
Balfour, M. (Ed.) (2012). *Refugee Performance*. University of Chicago Press.

Cleveland, W. (2008). *Art and Upheaval: Artists on the World's Frontlines*. New Village Press.

Jackson, N. & Shapiro-Phim, T. (Eds.) (2008). *Dance, Human Rights and Social Justice: Dignity in Motion*. Scarecrow Press.

Laurence, F. & Urbain, O. (Eds.) (2011). *Music and Solidarity: Questions of Universality, Consciousness and Connections*. Transaction Publishers.

LeBaron, M., MacLeod, C., & Acland, A. (Eds.) (2013). *The Choreography of Resolution: Conflict, Movement, and Neuroscience*. American Bar Association.

Thompson, J., Hughes, J. & Balfour, M. (2009). *Performance in Place of War*. Seagull Books.

Urbain, O. (Ed.) (2008). *Music and Conflict Transformation: Harmonies and Dissonances in Geopolitics*. I. B. Tauris.

Van Erven, E. (2001). *Community Theatre: Global Perspectives*. Routledge.

Eugène van Erven

# Exploring the Peace Building Potential of Community Arts

Community Arts is a contested term, also in the Netherlands from where I write this. For lack of a better label and to avoid getting caught in a web of endless discussions, most Dutch professionals in the field have by now embraced it, albeit reluctantanly. They use it to refer to a great variety of art practices. In our country, these range from site-specific events that involve local villagers in hybrid participatory performances (including music, drama, visual arts, and film) about disappearing communities in rural areas, to massive urban parades with hundreds of participants and small-scale dance projects with at-risk youth in low income neighborhoods. They include any imaginable art discipline and can literally be found in all regions of our country. While focus, methodology, location, artistic quality, and a host of additional factors obviously vary, the quintessential aspect that unifies this practice in the Netherlands and elsewhere is arguably the relationship between trained artists and a group of people that normally speaking has no direct involvement in art making. Dialogue is at the very heart of this dynamic that yields extraordinary art in unusual places (churchyards, pubs, abandoned factory halls, and, yes, even in theatres). Simply put, it generates conversations that would not otherwise take place. And therein lies precisely its peace building potential. On Dutch turf, where sustained large-scale violent political or ethnic conflicts have been virtually absent since World War II, the peace building aspect of community arts could be considered preventative rather than conciliatory and operates predominantly within the dynamics of cross-cultural relations. Through their active involvement in arts activities and working together towards a public manifestation, people productively explore differences and, in addition to expanding their creative, cognitive, and organizational abilities, learn particularly to communicate inter- and intraculturally.

If we expand our perspective beyond the borders of our small country, gradually a more complex picture of a rapidly growing field emerges. Immediately to our south, our Belgian community arts colleagues are every bit as active and diverse, although still largely linguistically separate. In the French-speaking provinces, their enterprises have a more activist orientation (*art d'action*) than in the Netherlands. In Flanders they have even coined a term of their own: *sociaal-artistieke praktijk*, which loosely translates as 'social art'. An de Bischop, the director of Demos, a Brussels-based agency that promotes this kind of work, explains: 'We define two principles behind the concept of community arts. One is making art more inclusive, accessible, diverse and thereby democratizing it. The other is from welfare to well-being, which is a more competence-based approach for people with the power and will to change, to create, and become free spirits' (Cohen-Cruz and van Erven 2013, 161). But that is the theory. The reality, as de Bischop hastens to add, is that many community arts enterprises in Belgium are funded by the welfare sector because they regard them as a cheaper form of social work. 'Economic power dominates everything in policy,' she sighs (ibid.). And wherever you find community arts, which is literally all over the globe, similar tensions exist; not in the least in that specialized area of community arts specifically engaging in peace building.

Powerful examples of peace building through participation in the arts can be found in all corners of the world. Two recent publications provide broad overviews of the different kinds of work being done in this field. Thus, *Acting Together: Performance and the Creative Transformation of Conflict* contains case studies (and video documentation) about projects in former Yugoslavia, Uganda, Sri Lanka, Palestine, Israel, Argentina, Peru, India, Cambodia, Aboriginal Australia, South Africa, and an intercultural community theatre project in the Netherlands, which I contributed (Cohen et al., 2011, 9–41). In my piece I analyze a year-long play-development process in a troubled neighbourhood of the Hague. It was based on personal narratives of thirteen fathers from Dutch, Sudanese, Iraqi, Turkish, Kurdish, Moroccan, Antillean and Surinamese backgrounds. The resulting play, which was performed twenty times for well over 1000 neighbours, friends, and relatives, was the condensed, aesthetically shaped culmination of highly sophisticated inter- and intracultural dialogues that took place in the relatively safe environment of weekly rehearsals. Facilitated by a female Dutch theatre director, these were sometimes quite confrontational and addressed delicate subjects such as sexuality among Muslim men, incest, female circumcision, and domestic violence perpetrated by fathers on their sons. What prompted these men to continue these conversations was curiosity about each others' lives and the surprise of realizing that their stories mattered to others as well, the joy of creating a powerful work of art together with support from a professional team of artists and technicians, and the anticipation of performing their show before a general public. The immediate effect of the performances was more heated talks, this time between actors and spectators. Thus, multiple dialogues that would never have happened without this play-making process took place between the thirteen participants, between them and their audiences, and, significantly, within their larger families. 'There has been a lot of discussion in their homes,' confirms social worker Anita Schwab, 'including about the consequences of saying all these delicate things on stage' (ibid., 12)

The model represented by the fathers play is by no means the only one available for this kind of work, nor is theatre necessarily the most effective art form. I could cite equally impressive examples involving music that temporarily connected Turkish and Greek communities across the demilitarized zone in Nicosia, Cyprus; a visual arts enterprise in Israel involving Jews and Arabs that resulted in the world's largest sock mosaic; or hip hop dance in Cambodia that provides young gang members an alternative to a life of crime and drug abuse. The relational and dialogical dimensions in all these projects are one cause for their potential usefulness in peace building. The way they can stimulate people's imagination and their capacity of reclaiming public space, are two others.

The *Acting Together* anthology (2011) focuses predominantly on professional theatre productions catering to higher educated audiences in former war zones and in the U.S. It is intended as an advocacy and teaching tool (it includes classroom exercises), but because most of the case studies are written by the practitioners themselves, the book lacks critical distance. This is certainly not the case in *Theatre in Place of War*, which provides a kaleidoscopic – and critical overview – of a variety of grass-roots visual arts and performance practices in Africa, Asia and in the U.K. (including art with refugees and in Northern Ireland). Thick descriptions are alternated with personal statements by practitioners and sharp ethical commentary by the three nominal authors. They applaud arts initiatives that, instead of cultivating victimhood, carve out places for play and fantasy during actual warfare, or that 'open spaces for debate where the events of the recent past can be remembered and the consequences of war can be explored' (Thompson et al. 2009, 6). They also favourable mention the work of artists who believe in creating beauty in response to the extreme ugliness of a physically devastated warzone and helping people through art to imagine a different reality as a step towards actually constructing one (ibid., 27-8). But in the same breath they also warn artists to always remain aware of the bigger picture, of the biases in their own ideologies and cultural preferences, and of their unavoidable entanglement in issues of individual, local, national and international power. If they fail to investigate the geopolitical dynamics at the macro level, myopic artists may cause more harm than good in a micro context, as Thompson himself found out to his great shock in Sri Lanka (2009, 116-124).

From visual art gardens for former child soldiers to ludic parades in downtown Guatemala City and from forum theatre involving Palestinians and Israelis to high tech Aboriginal performance in the Australian national parliament in Canberra, the types, styles, methods, and forms of community arts for peace building are sheer endless. With the notable exception of Boal's work and to a lesser degree the Playback approach, very few other methodologies have entered western and non-western professional arts colleges. As a result, training young artists for working in community settings – both in terms of techniques, intercultural social skills, and critical reflection – still leaves much to be desired. Much the same goes for bringing arts for peace building into classrooms at all educational levels. It will require shifts in curricula and staff of arts and teachers colleges, which for many countries (including my own) is unfortunately still wishful thinking. A first step might be to concoct intercontinental collaborations between artists from different countries for the co-creation of new work. The increasing availability of smart phones and advanced communication technology even in the poorest and most remote areas of this planet make such ventures quite feasible. But more than anything, in order to train artists and teachers for this work, the rapidly expanding practice in the field needs to be meticulously and attractively documented. Only then can we extract methodologies from it and can we critically reflect on the material to nourish a truly international discourse that includes voices from north and south and diverse ideological positions.

## References

Cohen, C., Gutiérrez Varea, R. & Walker, P. O. (Eds.) (2011). *Acting Together: Performance and the Creative Transformation of Conflict*. Oakland, California: New Village Press.

Cohen-Cruz, J. & van Erven, E. (2013). 'A Field Ready to Leave Home'. In E. van Erven (Ed.) *Community, Art, Power*. Rotterdam, RWT.

Thompson, J. (2009). 'The Ends of Applied Theatre: Incidents of Cutting and Chopping', in T. Prentki and S. Preston (Eds.), *The Applied Theatre Reader*. London: Routledge.

Thompson, J., Hughes, J. & Balfour, M. (2009). *Performance in Place of War*. Calcutta: Seagull Press.

Wolfgang Dietrich
# Education for the Arts and the Peace"s"

If it comes to the question of arts, peace and education one cannot but begin with Brazilian liberation educationalist Paolo Freire, who was likely the first to combine these three terms to produce an effective and inspiring model that has become popular under the title 'pedagogy of the oppressed'. Freire wrote his groundbreaking work during his stay at Harvard University in 1968. The practice-centered methods section in Freire's main work can be understood as a precursor of "elicitive conflict transformation", the state of the art in contemporary conflict work. John Paul Lederach coined this artificial term in the 1990's and developed a respective method based on the principles of Freire's pedagogy.[1] Freire's criticism of what he called the "banking concept of education,"[2] wherein oppressors understand education as filling an initially empty student brain with static knowledge, has ensured wide recognition of his name across several generations and, regrettably, it has retained its relevance to this day. Freire, by contrast, advocated a method of problem-posing education that accepts neither a well-ordered society nor a predetermined future. For Freire, human beings do not exist outside of their day to day reality. Accordingly, every consideration takes its departure point in the present, the situation in which we find ourselves.

At the time of Freire's stay at Harvard Adam Curle was director of the Center for Studies in Education and Development. Curle[3] became the first declared peace researcher to understand and describe the relationality of conflict and peace, and understood them as processes of communication. Curle's works published in 1971 and 1973 were of decisive importance for peace research and they clearly reveal Freire's influence. They also represent an attempt to integrate his thinking on education and peace, inspired by early liberation theology, into the blossoming Human Potential Movement.[4]

Freire, Curle and Lederach built on the insights of many others, mostly humanistic psychologists and therapists who are not commonly considered peace researchers, but who articulated the ancient wisdom of Sufism, Zen, Tao and Tantra in a new way. They all agreed that peacelessness is not so much the result of clashes of interest, but rather of people letting themselves be driven by projects, plans, and expectations throughout life, and become entangled in regret, guilt, and shame for past events and actions. Con-

---

1 Freire, Paulo (1971). *Pedagogy of the Oppressed*; New York; pp. 75–118. Lederach, John Paul (2005). *The Moral Imagination. The Art and Soul of Building Peace*; Oxford; p. 124.
2 Freire (1971, pp. 57–74)
3 Lederach, John Paul (1997). *Building Peace. Sustainable Reconciliation in Divided Societies*; Washington; p. 64.
4 Ramsbotham, Oliver; Woodhouse, Tom; Miall, Hugh (2005). *Contemporary Conflict Resolution*; Cambridge; p. 219.

flict ceases when we are conscious of life and our relations in the present. Perhaps no one expressed this in clearer terms than the mystic Jeru Kabbal: "We do not want to go to heaven, we do not want to escape hell. We simply want to be here."[5] This may be the most succinct expression of peace. It is the peace of allowing ourselves to simply be here. Each disturbance, whether from the outside or the inside, amounts to peacelessness; and the most frequent cause of peacelessness is our insatiable desire to become, rather than accept the simplicity of being.

Since such peace is an art in itself it requires a whole lot of virtues such as awareness of the self, awareness of the surrounding world, awareness of one's own fantasies, control of one's language and gestures, agility, release of muscle tension, elaborate control of breath and body and empathic resonance with potential adversaries. This is precisely the list of virtues by which Morihei Ueshiba defines aikidō as the art of peace. In its most perfected form, aikidō is not a martial art, but a relational body art; that is, an art of movement based on a harmonious unity with the energies of the other, or the others:

> The Art of Peace begins with you. Work on yourself and your appointed task in the Art of Peace. Everyone has a spirit that can be refined, a body that can be trained in some manner, a suitable path to follow. You are here for no other purpose than to realize your inner divinity and manifest your inner enlightenment. Foster peace in your own life and then apply the art to all that you encounter.[6]

It is the intention of aikidō to help people grow into thoughtful, responsible human beings, that is, beings who connect mind and body and who are capable of acting responsibly without hesitation or doubt, understanding the power exercised by the word over physical violence.

Compared to painting, music, dance, sculpturing and others aikidō may be not the most popular art, but what its highly respected founder, a member of the strictly arts-oriented Ōmoto sect in Japan, says applies for any discipline: The archaic connection between arts and peace lies in the creative spark, in the undisturbed presence in the here and now. Peace and arts unite in the here and now. Therefore both peace education and arts education have to start with the awareness of the self, of the surrounding world and of one's own imagination, fantasies and concepts of the disciple in the here and now. This requires quite some practice in stressful modern contexts.[7]

And it requires on the side of the teachers a clear epistemology that grounds their methodological approaches. In this context it may be crucial to point out that Darwin's interpretation that the natural process of selection would be a struggle of all against all is not proven in the sense of the common natural scientific methods. Factual claims based on systematically produced evidence purport the contrary about the origin of species and the human being. Selection and adaptation do not necessarily imply combat and annihilation of the other. Life takes place, because everything is connected to everything

---

5   Kabbal, Jeru (2006). *Finding Clarity. A Guide to the Deeper Levels of Your Being*; Berkeley/Cal.; p. 35.
6   Ueshiba, Morihei (2007). *The Art of Peace*; Boston, London; p. 141.
7   Ibid. pp. 3 and 8.

else. Interdependence demands the capacity for cooperation rather than superiority. That is of crucial importance for peace education, because it is about the human species' fundamental peaceableness. While Darwin's doctrines led into the great wars of annihilation of the twentieth century[8] neurobiology confirmed at the end of the same century the principal orientation of the human brain towards cooperation. Rationality empowers, yet dooms, the sane human being to see things from the perspective of others and to perceive the mutual enrichment that arises from all differences. Rationality affirms the plurality of perspectives and does not subject them to abstract questions about uniformity.

An education, hence, that aspires making the student fit for life, for society, for the world will be necessarily peace education. It will increase the students' creativity and their ability to cooperate. It will teach them the layers of human nature they can resonate with. Resonance is an art in itself that works with a multitude of tools and methods. Arts education is about expression, communication, resonance and addressing the human nature in all its layers.

The Innsbruck school of Peace Studies[9] developed along the line of its principles resonance, correspondence and homeostasis an 'Elicitive Conflict Map' that shall help the conflict worker finding orientation within this multitude of human properties. We call them layers and presume that beyond the surface of any conflict narration we find the sexual-familial layer, further the emotional-communal, the mental-societal, the spiritual-policitary and further subtle layers that feed the superficial episode of conflict with deeper meaning, reasoning and energy. That is, a human conflict is rarely what it seems to be on the surface of the narration.[10] The art and the science of conflict transformation therefore require in the ability of the conflict worker to resonate with the parties on all these layers and thus contribute to the homeostatic flow of life energy. This is rather different to the emphasis on strictly rational and factual conflict resolution as advocated in conventional approaches. Elicitive conflict transformation is an art in itself.

The knowledge about this holistic approach to education is neither a secret nor an exclusive method of conflict transformation. It applies to education in general. It invites to turn away from the modern myth of healthy competition that has been destroying the motivation, the trust and creativity of generations for the sake of large scale production. It rediscovers the human and humanistic virtue of cooperation and promotes joyful creativity, the beginning of any kind of arts. There is no difference between education for arts and education for peace. It is the same. It is inherently human and a common goal for all of us, if we believe in what UNESCO states in the preamble to its constitution: Since wars begin in the minds of human beings, it is in the minds of human beings where peace has to be defended.[11]

---

8  Weikart, Richard (2004). *From Darwin to Hitler. Evolutionary Ethics, Eugenics and Racism in Germany*; New York.
9  http://www.uibk.ac.at/peacestudies (16.03.2014)
10  Dietrich, Wolfgang (2013). *Elicitive Conflict Transformation and the Transrational Shift in Peace Politics*; London; pp. 200-224.
11  UNESCO: *UNESCO Constitution;* 16th November 1945: http://portal.unesco.org/en/ev.php-URL_ID=15244&URL_DO=DO_TOPIC&URL_SECTION=201.html (09.10.2013). I update this quote with Hansa Mehta's important contribution to the Universal Declaration of Human Rights 1948: I say "human beings" instead of "men".

Anne Bamford and Matt Qvortrup

# Politics of the Soul: The Contribution of the Arts to Social Cohesion and Peace

## Introduction

In her book, *Homo Aestheticus*[1], the anthropologist Ellen Dissanayake describes an Amazonian tribe which releases its strongest men for several months from the day-to-day business of hunting for survival. The men work on the elaborate carving of a giant tree trunk. The work is laborious and takes several months to complete. At the end of the process, there is a celebration event and the trunk is burnt leaving little more than charred remains. Why would a tribe of people choose to release the young men to do this? The answer is relatively simple. Through the collaborative arts making process, social cohesion is forged. The young men work closely together and this reduces violent behaviour both within the tribe and with neighbouring tribes. In effect, the arts activity increases the survival of the tribe by creating a more empathetic and less violent society. Arguably, at the local and global level society needs to work to create a more cohesive and peaceful society. Can arts contribute to this peace?

## Definitions of Peace

Peace, of course is many things. At the extreme, peace can simply be seen as the absence of violence and war. For example, in the United Nations Charter (1945), peace is not explicitly defined. Instead, it is implicitly a negative definition of peace – that is, peace as being the lack of war. But others might want a more positive definition. One could argue that peace can be seen as an environment that is conducive to human growth and flourishing; a state under which human beings can realise their true potential and achieve what Aristotle called their *ergon*; their true inner nature. Such a definition would arguable be more cogent with United Nations' General Assembly's *Declaration and Programme of Action on a Culture of Peace*[2]. In Article 2, this declaration talks about the "development of a culture of peace comes about through values, attitudes, modes of behaviour and ways of life conducive to the promotion of peace among individuals, groups and nations".

---

1  Dissanayake, E. (1995). *Homo Aestheticus: Where Art Comes from and why*. University of Washington Press.
2  53/243, http://cpnn-world.org/resolutions/resA-53-243A.html, accessed 13 October 2013.

## Definitions of the Arts

Art as a term covers a diverse range of human activities and the products of those activities. If used in the European context, the word 'art' tends to imply the inclusion of visual arts (including crafts) music, theatre, film, dance, and other performing arts, as well as literature, and other media such as interactive media. In other places though, the arts can include a range of actives such as mediation, festivals, hair braiding and even stilt walking. So the most of appropriate one might be a very inclusive definition any skilled activity where aesthetic considerations are paramount including the products of such activity. Under this definition, arts can also be expanded to include popular culture. Culture represents the artefacts of society – both tangible and intangible – including the distinct ways that people live, represent their experiences and act creatively. Mulcahy (2006: p. 325) argues for a *latitudinarium* approach to the definitions of arts and culture that is open both to institutionalised culture and the arts and the more populist models. This view addresses the more postmodernist call for allowing both government and the individual to define the arts on their own terms.

The broad definitions of both peace and the arts and culture are used as the basis for this chapter.

## The Growth of Empathy

There are many things about human experience that exceed the representational capacity of verbal language or intellectual analysis but yield themselves to us through art. All human societies throughout history have given a special place to the arts and so it can be presupposed that a human appetite or need is being met through artistic activity. Intrinsic impact of the arts can include dimensions such as captivation, pleasure, imagination, meaning-making, and empathy (Mc Carthy et al. 2004).

Arguably, empathy for the natural world and for each other regardless of cultural, religious and ethnic division could be seen to be a factor leading to a more peaceful and sustainable society. Empathy requires imagination and this is the realm of creativity. In this way, art establishes an empathetic link between the artist and the viewer by embodying experiences in a way that is simultaneously available to the individual and to the broader global society. Art can provide access through simulation to personal histories and personal connections. These resonances evident within art pieces activate the so-called mirroring neurons[3] in the brain, meaning that individuals can vicariously feel the emotional intent of the artwork through direct experiential understanding of objects and the inner world of others. In this way, art becomes an active mirror, holding up to humans the deepest aspects of humanity enabling the individual and society to make sense of the actions, emotions or sensations in other people through embodied simulation.

White (2008: p. viii) argues that there art works can build empathy by making a connection between the circumstances of the individual and more general human condi-

---

3  Rizzolatti G., Craighero L. (2004). "The Mirror-Neuron System". *Annual Rev. Neurosci.* 27, 169-92.

tions. Through discourse with the art work (or performance) and communication with others, perception and sensation is heightened. This creates resonance for the community or the individual flowing from an artistic or creative encounter. In particular, White (2008: p. 172) argues that this encounter can develop a personal sense of well-being and greater collective empathy because of the ability of artistic moments to provide:
- Respite (temporary relief from the everyday);
- Catharsis (purging of emotions); and
- Enrichment (adding greater significance to life).

## Social Cohesion and Art

That social harmony leads to greater peace is not in dispute. Social capital, although contested, refers to "the ability of actors to secure benefits by virtue of membership in social networks or other social structures" (Portes 1998: p. 6). At the heart of social capital theory is the assertion that "relationships matter". Given that, art may have a positive impact on community cohesion and mutual understanding. Cultural competence begins from the understanding that we are all influenced by the different social, educational and organisational cultures in which we live and participate. Art provides an expressive form that recognises that ours is not the only way of seeing or doing things and therefore opens us to learning about other perspectives. Exploring differences as well as similarities in our cultural expectations improves our capacity to understand and relate to others and helps to build social cohesion.

This is why the arts have so much to contribute to wider social issues. From neighbourhood renewal to health, and from the criminal justice system to employment, the arts have something to offer. There are some who argue that the arts used covertly to meet social cohesion goals may lead to a 'dumbing down' of the artistic experience. These same people insist that quality art cannot possibly come out of programmes with social aims. But looking back through history, there are numerous examples of the arts emerging out of vivid (and often violent) social contexts that demonstrate excellence. Given that quality of the arts and social purpose are more often complementary than mutually exclusive.

The arts make a contribution to social cohesion, and ultimately peace, through the communication of ideas, information and values. Kelly and Kelly (2000) contend that the arts can contribute to social cohesion through improving people's understanding of different cultures and lifestyles and through partnership building. This can enhance the likelihood of a peaceful society by developing a sense of community identity, social cohesion, recreational opportunities, development of local enterprise, improvement of public facilities and amenities, and help to convey history and heritage of an area.

While Kelly and Kelly highlight the social impact of the arts on building cohesion within a nation, area, community or population, the arts may also be a resource for peace by building resilience within individuals within a society. For example, creating art, especially within a collaborative or social context, can lead to the individual trying new experiences, and thereby increasing his or her confidence and self-esteem. Participation in the arts can promote positive inter-group attitudes and more cross-group friendships. This in turn can create individual social capital through communication, sharing of memories and an enhanced cultural awareness. The arts can challenge social exclusion and challenge or change negative perceptions and attitudes (Jermyn 2001; Matarasso 1997; Mills and Brown 2004). Intercultural competence enables individuals to interact effectively and in a way that is acceptable to others when from different cultural backgrounds.

Despite the research indicating that the arts may enhance the possibility of peace through building social cohesion, there are some studies that question the positive impact claimed. For example, Andries van den Broek conducted a study in 2007-08 to determine whether the arts had greater or lesser impact on cultural participation and social cohesion amongst people within multi-ethnic Holland, as opposed (or as compared to) sport. This extensive study showed only limited differences between arts and culture and sport. But the research adds considerably to providing some guidelines for conducting such research in the future. Van der Broek (2008) defines social cohesion as being comprised on identification; trust, sentiment, respect and interethnic leisure (2008: p. 2). This echoes the work of Putnam (2000) that makes a distinction in social research between 'bonding with' the "other" and 'bridging between' groups.

The research found that there was not a causal link between arts and cultural activity and social cohesion, but that people who possessed an "open-minded and outgoing take on life" (Van der Broek 2008: p. 8) were more likely to experience greater social cohesion and take up offers in both cultural and sport. While van der Broek appropriately stops short of implying any causality, it could be suggested that increasing the arts and cultural activities within a multi-ethnic community could assist in boosting the sort of disposition that might promote on-going engagement with bot the arts and sport. Interestingly, one pattern in the findings of van der Broek was that popular culture was much more successful than other forms of culture at encouraging social cohesion.

The way the connection between participation and social cohesion might operate is quite complex, with at least four possibilities offered by van der Broek. He suggests there are four interpretations of the relations between cultural participation and social cohesion:
- Cultural participation influences social cohesion
- Cohesion influences cultural participation
- Cultural participation and social cohesion influence one another
- A third factor influences both cultural participation and social cohesion

Fillis (2004: p. 136) argued it is "important to realise that art continually impacts on society and changes the way we think." The arts can initiate social change and public awareness by changing people' attitudes on political, ethnical, religious and moral issues. If the arts can powerfully change people's attitudes it is important to also consider the negative aspects of arts impact. Matarasso (1997: p. 3) cautions:

> A more balanced understanding of the role and worth of the arts in our society – one which simultaneously embraces their [intrinsic], aesthetic, cultural, economic and social [impact] and allows for the different judgements inevitable in a pluralistic society. We need to understand that the arts produce impacts as complex as the human beings who create and enjoy them.

It has been argued that the arts have favoured the socioeconomically privileged and have reinforced nationalist conceptions of a dominant culture. The perception that arts and culture therefore acts more as a cradle for social division and unrest, however, appears to be unfounded.

## The Arts' Non-Violence

According to Thomas Hobbes' *Leviathan* in the 17$^{th}$ Century, peace can be defined as the absence of physical threats. In this context we will focus on absence of criminal threats – that is the absence of assaults and the absence of threats from political violence, such as fatal terrorist attacks. As these threats are particularly acute in post-conflict societies (societies that have recently experienced prolonged civil or international war) it is particularly interesting to look at factors that have proved to be conducive to reducing threats to peace. The hypothesis is that the arts can contribute to protecting citizens from criminal and political violence.

"There are three kinds of lies", Benjamin Disareli, the Victorian Statesman quipped, "Lies, God damn lies and statistics". Undoubtedly, figures and numerical data can be abused and can reduce complex relationships to over simplification. While the nature of the arts and cultural activity is complex, equally complex are the forms of violence that afflict society. Given that limitation, it is still worthwhile to explore the statistical evidence in relation to the arts and non-violence, or at least a reduction in violent crimes. One such statistical relationship is that between figures for crime and terrorism on the one side and on the other spending on the arts.

To measure the strength of a statistical relationship statisticians use a measure called Pearson correlation coefficient, also known as R. A perfect positive correlation has the value R=1, no correlation has the value R=0. Generally in the social sciences a correlation coefficient of over 0.3 is considered to be a relatively strong correlation, or in other words as being statistically significant.

One of the hypotheses in recent cultural policy is that more spending on the arts not only has an intrinsic value but that such spending also – albeit indirectly – can have a positive effect on lower levels of violence and terror.

But is this hypothesis supported statistically and by hard data?

Using figures from the Arts Council of England and Wales and figures by criminologists and political scientists it is possible to test this relationship.

If we correlate the average amount of money spent on each citizen in the developed countries for which we have figures with the number of assaults we find that there is a relatively *negative* strong correlation of R=-.42 (statistically significant at the 10 per cent level)[4].

Now it could be argued that assaults are the result of many other factors. For example that longer prison sentences all other things being equal would deter would-be criminals from committing violent crimes. In fact, the correlation between assaults and prison population is not statistically significant (there is a margin of error of 33 per cent!)

---

4   This means that there is a 10 per cent margin of error.

and the relationship is positive R=.17. In other words put simply, more prisons, more assaults! Conversely, based on the statistical evidence the assault rate is more likely to be lowered if we give people an opportunity to participate and enjoy arts and culture.

But, of course, assaults are but one form of social strife. Would these results be the same if we correlated the presence of fatal terrorist attacks with the spending on the arts?

Interestingly, there is a negative correlation between the average arts spending per citizen and the measure of fatal terrorist attacks of R=-.54, and this relationship is statistically significant at the 0.05 level, meaning that the margin of error is a mere 5 per cent. So in the case of terrorism, more spending on the arts leads to less fatal terrorist attacks.

| Country | Per Capita AS | Fatal Terror | | Assaults Per Year |
|---|---|---|---|---|
| Finland | 59.2 | 0.47 | 0 | 586 |
| Germany | 56.5 | 0.36 | 0 | 619 |
| France | 37.8 | 0.26 | 1 | 180 |
| Sweden | 37.5 | 0.29 | 0 | 845 |
| Netherlands | £30.3 | 0.21 | 0 | 351 |
| Canada | 29.9 | 0.21 | 1 | 737 |
| UK | 16.6 | 0.14 | 1 | 1365 |
| Australia | 16.4 | 0.14 | 0 | 797 |
| US | 3.8 | 0.02 | 1 | 786 |

Figure 1: Spending on the Arts and Crime Statistics[5]

Of course, statistical figures can be deceiving and the real world is always more complex than the mathematician. Still, the evidence clearly suggests that spending on the arts – in addition to its aesthetic benefits – also is associated with lower levels of violence and lower levels of terrorism.

## Building Culturally-Rich Citizenship

The arts, in all their rich variety, belong to everyone, regardless of race, class, culture, age, sex, disability or sexuality. The arts can offer innovative solutions, build bridges and express differences positively. They can break boundaries. According to Vargo (2008) the community could be considered to be co-creators of value. They argue that rather than value *per se*, it is better to think about a *value network* – where organisations and individuals are part of the arts and culture offering itself. Mulcahy (2006: p. 324) argues that there needs to be a shift from, "Top-down to bottom-up policy: that is, the governments

---

5  Correlational table created based on information derived from Sources: Arts Council of England, Policy Research and Planning Department, Research Report Number 13, International Data on Public Spending on the Arts in Eleven Countries, March 1998. Harrendorf, S., Heiskanen, M., & Malby, S. (2010). *International Statistics on Crime and Justice*, Vienna, UNODC. Qvortrup, M. H. (2012). 'Terrorism and Political Science'. *The British Journal of Politics & International Relations*, 14(4), 503-517.

responsible to provide equal opportunities for citizens to be culturally active on their own terms."

Such a statement proposes more open and democratic definitions of the arts. If a country is going to build a more peaceful citizen there is the need for greater dialogue with their participants (existing and future) and use of this knowledge to be more responsive to the citizens' arts and cultural needs (Colbert 2003; Knell 2006; Rentschler 2004; Rentschler, Hede and White 2007).

## Conclusions

The arts are at the heart of what it means to be human, and humane. Humanity is shaped by things we care about. Peace comes about through values, attitudes, modes of behaviour and ways of life conducive to the promotion of peace among individuals, groups and nations. The value of the arts to the peace process may be that it provides a space to think and to act as a means of bringing some sense to bear on the current world. It is worth considering that the arts might offer a different set of possible actions within a conflict zone. Peace may be achieved by a form of politics less about power and force and more about a politic of the soul. The arts may build sustainable and peaceful communities by enhancing personal development, social cohesion, community empowerment and self-determination. The arts can build a local image and identity while at the same time acknowledging the relevance of cultural diversity and cultural identity.

There is a possible link between culture and development. Arts and culture can drive peace-building by promoting openness and the right to difference and respect for 'otherness.'

## References

Colbert, F. (2003). "Entrepreneurship and leadership in Marketing the Arts". *International Journal of Arts Management*. Vol. 6, No. 1, Fall.
Dissanayake, E. (1995). *Homo Aestheticus: Where Art Comes from and why*. University of Washington Press.
Fillis, I. (2004). "The Entrepreneurial Artist as Marketer: Drawing from the smaller-firm literature". *International Journal of Arts Management*. Vol. 7, No. 1, Fall.
Jermyn, H. (2001). *The Arts and Social Exclusion: a review prepared for the Arts Council of England*. London: Arts Council England.
Kelly, A. & Kelly, A. (2000). *Impact and Values, Assessing the Arts and Creative Industries in the South West*. Bristol: Bristol Cultural Development Partnership.
Knell, J. (2006). *Whose art is it anyway?* London: Arts Council, England.
Matarasso, F. (1997). *The social impact of participation in the arts*. London: Comedia.
Mc Carthy, et al. (2004). Millers Triangle of clinical competence in G.E. Miller, 'The assessment of clinical skills/competence/performance'. *Acad Med* 65 (1990), 563-567.
Mc Carthy, K. F. & Jinnett, K. (2001). *A New Framework for Building Participation in the Arts* Santa Monica: Rand.
Mills, D. & Brown, P. (2004). *Art and Wellbeing: A guide to the connections between community cultural development and health, ecologically sustainable development and public housing*. Sydney, Australia Council.

Mulcahy, K. (2006). "Cultural Policy: Definitions and Theoretical Approaches". *The Journal of Arts Management, Law, and Society*, Vol. 35, No. 4.

Putnam, R. (2000). *Bowling alone: The collapse and revival of American community*. New York: Simon and Schuster.

Rentschler (2004). *Museum marketing: understanding different types of audiences.* London: Taylor & Francis.

Rentschler, R., Hede. A-M. & White, T. (2007). "Museum pricing: challenges to theory development and practice". *International Journal of Nonprofit and Voluntary Sector Marketing.* Vol. 12, No. 2, 163-173.

Rizzolatti, G. & Craighero, L. (2004). "The Mirror-Neuron System". *Annual Rev. Neurosci.* Vol. 27, 169-92.

Van der Broek, A. (2008). "Arts and culture and the public sphere". A paper presented at the *ESA Research Network for the Sociology of Culture Conference* Venice, November 4-8, 2008.

Vargo, S. L. (2008). "Customer Integration and Value Creation: Paradigmatic Traps and Perspectives". *Journal of Service Research,* November 2008, Vol. 11 No. 2.

Peter Harris

# 'Playing' with 'Others' in a 'Neutral Zone':
# *Intergroup Contact in the Aesthetic[1] Space*

In considering "Arts for Peace", it is my firm conviction, that the way to peace must be paved with intimate interpersonal and intergroup contact, aimed at dismantling prejudiced misconceptions and de-demonizing the "other". This process can best happen through collaborative dramatic action set on an equal footing in a space which Augusto Boal, has termed the "aesthetic space" (Boal, 1992), where willing suspension of disbelief in the form of Stanislavsky's *"as-if"* (Stanislavski, 1936 ) or Landy's *"to be and not to be"* (Landy, 1993) paradigms enable "players" to bypass prejudice, take a deep look at their own fears and demons and see others for their uniqueness.

The "theatre aspect" in the model I will describe, functions as a catalyst, dismantling stereotypes which shroud the meeting between socially and ideologically polarized others. The model, which I have developed over some twelve years in bi-cultural and multicultural community theatre projects subsequently became the subject of my Ph.D. dissertation – "Intergroup contact in the aesthetic space" (Harris, 2013).

The process I will attempt to describe purports to changing perceptions of reality through the meeting of two (or more) socially polarized groups in the theatrical arena. The participant – players in this process attain "equal status" within the creative space, thus redefining themselves as part of a new "one group" under a 'chosen' status – "actors". It is this acquired status which enables re-definition, of "self image" and the perception of "other".

The theoretical innovation in this work focuses on *"how"* the *"intergroup contact in the aesthetic space"* praxis, accelerates what Pettigrew (Pettigrew, 1998) has termed a longitudinal categorization model (de-categorization, salient categorization, and re-categorization) which is generally tested in conventional, short term, limited laboratory controlled experiments focusing on the end result, the *"what"*, and have neglected to investigate long term processes.

Analysis of dramatic materials produced by participants, in my working model, which combines group-dynamics and a theatrical process, both of which occur in; parallel, reciprocal and synergetic syntax, has shown that introduction of the "theatre aspect" over an extended period of time, upgrades and deepens *attitude change* by activating creative and emotional (affect) responses – the *"how"*.

---

1  In its Greek root 'aesthtic' means 'of or pertaining to things perceptible by the senses'. (Boal 1995: p. 18).

The main objective of my research therefore was to investigate the effectiveness of *the process* (workshop and production) in this specific Community Based Theatre (CBT) model, which had been developed intuitively as an experiential learning module for theatre arts students; 'Participatory Theatre in the community'. The objective of this learning module was to provide a first step in understanding the role of the Community Theatre practitioner as an agent for change by enabling students to deconstruct and reconstruct attitudes and biases toward society, crime, punishment, ethnicity etc. and to reevaluate their own value systems through meeting with polarized 'others' in the 'Aesthetic space'.

The Interdisciplinary model "Intergroup contact in the Aesthetic space" draws on knowledge from the field of CBT (Community based theatre), Boals' (Boal 1995) definitions of the properties of the aesthetic space; having oneiric[2] qualities and liberating memory and imagination, and Social Identity Theory, in particular theories based on Allports' Contact Hypothesis (Allport 1954; Gaertner & Dovidio 2005) and Pettigrews' Intergroup Contact Theory (Pettigrew 1998; Tropp & Pettigrew 2005).

My research paradigm recognizes the potential of the aesthetic space to enable 'actors' to reframe their constructions of reality (Berger & Luckman, 1991) and that of the "theatre aspect" as a catalyst which challenges 'actors' to deconstruct and later reconstruct attitudes and identities. This process bridges gaps based in prejudiced ideas and allows 'actors' to modify their conceptions of 'self' and 'other' through becoming 'mutually significant others'.

The efficacy of the model was examined in relation to its two stages, **process** (the workshop) and **product** (the theatrical event) in light of three questions:
1. How do the processes unique to this CBT model, consequences of the quality of dialogue the 'actor' conducts with 'others' in familiar and unfamiliar environments, contribute to changes in ones' awareness and behavior?
2. How does the creative experience and the challenge of performance in front of an audience, serve as a catalyst in the participants' personal development?
3. Can **long term** participation in a process based on CBT disciplines, in a group made up of polarized entities; bring a marked change in the individuals' biased perceptions of 'super ordinate' values? And induce change in attitudes, behavior, values and points of view in both in the short term, and over time?

Over a period of twelve years, the model was implemented and honed with a variety of populations: Jewish theatre arts students and Arab peers, Theatre arts students and rehabilitating substance abusers, Culturally contrasted Theatre arts students on campus in the U.S., diverse culture M.A. human rights student cohorts from the Asia-pacific region at Sydney University, M.A. Social work students at the University of Southern California, Theatre arts students and incarcerated men and women, Theatre arts students and blind and partially sighted counterparts and Theatre arts students and senior citizens.

The *inter-group contact in the aesthetic space* placed participants in creative-psychodynamic processes, from which selected narratives, improvised and performed texts and personal accounts and interviews, served as research material. Analysis of these materi-

---

2  Oneiric – of or belonging to dreams (Boal, 1995: p. 18).

als shows an activation of dramaturgic strategies spontaneously devised in the process which express the following dual-relations in the liminal expanse:

1. **The 'double identity' phenomena (Brown & Hewstone 2005: p. 264-267) as expressed in the actor – character binary.**

Ruby participated in a student-prisoner CBT project in 2002, Ruby's monologue demonstrates how the mask provided by the 'theatre' is peeled off (or not) at the actors' chosen pace moving step by step form being camouflaged, under the pretext of the 'acting' mode, to exposure in the 'non acting' mode (Kirby 1972; Landy 1993). Ruby, serving a life sentence for a double murder relates his discovery of the double identity binary in a 'self disclosing' monologue, using the 'mask' as a prop and a metaphor to convey his experience:

"[Face masked] ... And so **I devised a performance,** where I take centre stage and remove a mask and a layer of armor and retreat. I recall saying earlier, that I want to portray characters, like... Anger, maybe that will help me...But I found that maybe to remove the masks is what I need, then, without masks I will be able to play all the roles, with all the fear... the pain... *I wanted to tell you who I really am* (removes his mask) this has been holding me back... *I am here because I have done a terrible thing* ..."

Ruby's monologue clearly illustrates the potential of the *intergroup contact in the aesthetic space* experience to provide a learning experience, synergistically enhanced by the masking and exposing properties of the 'playing' space.

2. **The use of the expanse between fiction and non-fiction to express the dissonance between social, ethical and moral expressions and interpersonal friendship.**

Cliff and Shila, theatre students at Drew University in New Jersey, participated in an *intergroup contact in the aesthetic space* workshop in 2009. Cliff, (a white homosexual man) and Shila's (an African American woman) close friendship was tested by confrontational exercises. Moving from non-fiction to fiction, from workshop and discussion to a staged performance, enabled the two 'actors' to contest their conflicted ideologies and finally to maintain their friendship.

Shila: (Emotions for the Unspoken) "Yeah, I guess I never told you. I never thought it had anything to do with my friendship with you. Now you're talking about a bunch of laws I don't think I understand or never heard of before. You claim that you don't understand how I want you to be happy if I would take away your right to be married. You can't seem to face the fact that me wanting happiness for you runs deeper than your sexual preference or gay marriage."

Cliff: "Wait! I didn't even know you were that religious. I mean you always think you'll hear stuff like, 'I think you're going to hell!' from some old Midwest cowboy minister – you know the kind that runs around screaming "GOD HATES FAGS!" – But that's not you [...] Just two days ago you were teaching me how to make my booty clap."

The surreal framing of the scene which culminates in the two "protagonists" hugging each other in the presence of an audience shows the "antagonist" witnessing the others' monologue while standing in the background. This positioning depicts 'aware-reconciliation', indicating that the interpersonal can allow both sides to "agree to disagree", or in Shilas' words; "Understand me as you want me to understand you."

**In concluding**, 'playing' with 'others' in a 'neutral zone' creates building blocks for an honest dialogue in a mutually respecting binary situation. The reflection of *self* in the *other* evokes a *reversed 'therapeutic' process* wherein the *player* gains awareness through the gradual return from 'playing' to reflecting, from acting to not acting, from 'portrayal' to 'being' and from *make belief* to the *real world*. This transition allows participants on either side of a conflicted equation to be aware of their biases in relation to the other and become sensitive to the potential secreted in one another's and their united, strengths.

## References

Allport, G. W. (1954). *The Nature of Prejudice*. New York: Doubleday Anchor Books.
Berger, P., & Luckmann, T. (1991). *The Social Construction of Reality*. London: Penguin Books.
Boal, A. (1992). *Games for Actors and Non Actors*. London & New York: Routledge.
Boal, A. (1995). *The Rainbow of Desire*. New York: Routledge.
Brown, R., & Hewstone, M. (2005). "An Integrative Theory of Intergroup Contact." *Advances in Experimental Social Psychology*, 37, 255-343.
Gaertner, S. L., & Dovidio, J. F. (2005). "Categorization, Recateogrization and Intergroup Bias." In: Dovidio, J.F., Glick, P., & Rudman, L. (Eds.), *On the Nature of Prejudice: Fifty Years after Allport*. (pp. 71-88). Philadelphia: Psychology Press.
Harris, P. (2013). *"Inter-group Contact in the Aesthetic Space" – Changing Perceptions of Reality through the Meeting of Two Socially Polarized Groups in the Theatrical Arena*. PhD Thesis, Submitted to the Senate of Tel-Aviv University.
Kirby, M. (March 1972). "On Acting and Not-Acting". *The Drama Review: TDR, 16*(1), 3-15.
Landy, R. (1993). *Persona and Performance*. New York: The Guilford press.
Pettigrew, T.F. (1998). "Intergroup Contact Theory." *Annual Review of Psychology*, 49, 65-85.
Stanislavski, C. (1982 [1936]). *An Actor Prepares*. New York: Theatre Arts Books.
Thompson, J. (2006). *Applied Theatre Bewilderment and Beyond*. Bern: Peter Lang.
Tropp, L.R., & Pettigrew, T.F. (2005). "Relationships Between Intergroup Contact and Prejudice Among Minority and Majority Status Groups." *Psychological Science, 16*(12), 951-957.

Vedat Özsoy
# Arts Education and Violence in Schools

## Abstract

School violence is a serious and global issue and authorities strive to solve this problem. Public awareness and intolerance of school violence has greatly increased over the last 10 years, and some governments have put this issue on their political agendas. Also new institutions have been established and campaigns have been organized in some countries in order to overcome the problem. In Turkey, a parliamentary commission responsible for the investigation of the situation in the country was established in 2006, and a symposium about "Arts Education and Violence" was organized in 2007. The commission prepared a comprehensive report and published it. Scholars and researchers from various institutions held presentations about their views and investigation results on the subject during the symposium. They all shared the idea that the arts education to prevent violence in schools plays an incontrovertible role. Speaking in the symposium, the head of the parliamentary commission stated that if interests of children or youth could be canalized towards any form of the arts either as a hobby or a professional activity, they would not choose to participate in any activities of violence in or out of their schools. Arts educators believe that the arts education will be effective in decreasing violence in schools through its spiritual, creative, and practical characteristics if it is provided well-programmed and applied within primary school education by well-trained teachers.
Keywords: children and violence, violence in school, school shootings, arts education.

## Introduction

Violence in schools is a global problem. Many countries suffer from different type of violence in schools. There might be many reasons behind it, such as a history of childhood abuse, unsuitable family environment, violence in childhood, dominant mothers, absent fathers, media influence, drugs, Internet usage, parental neglect, etc. (Elliot, Hamburg, Williams, 1998; Kimmel & Mehler, 2003). It is certain that school violence is a serious issue worldwide.

The Council of Europe (2011) prepared an action program indicating that;

> "Violence in schools is one of the most visible forms of violence against children. But the widespread belief that it is on the increase is not fully supported by statistics. Public fear that schools are unsafe is partly fuelled by sensational media reporting, backed up by little or no analysis. However, public awareness and intolerance of school violence has greatly increased over the last 10 years, and most European governments have put school violence on their political agendas. Schools cannot fulfill their role as places of learning and socialization if children and young people are not in an environment free of bullying, intimidation and repression." (CE Human Rights and Rule of Law).

Although public fear about violence in schools might be partly fuelled by sensational media reporting, it is clear today that many countries in the world have been still suffering from this sort of violence (CDC, 2012 ). It is known that new institutions are established and campaigns are organized in some countries in order to overcome violence in schools. Among these, the Prevention Institution in Oakland (PIO, 2014), the Protsahan India Foundation (PIF, 2014), the Media Database's campaign etc. (MD, 2014) can be given as examples.

Contributions of arts to a human being's life is incontrovertible. Nevertheless, arts courses in schools' curricula are neglected and not enough time is allocated to these courses in many countries. However, it should be remembered that with properly designed arts courses students will not only gain artistic talents and aesthetic behaviors but also will have an opportunity to discharge, pour out their feelings and share their thoughts, emotions, and even problems with others. So the conclusion is that for a student that deals with an art practice, it would be difficult to say that he or she will be involved in activities of violent nature.

This paper studies positive effects of arts education in Turkey to prevent violence in schools. Since school violence is still a problem in Turkey and there have been examples of it as given in the paper, it is expected that the paper may help to understand the contributions of arts education to decrease violence in schools.

In 2006, violence in primary and secondary schools in Turkey increased remarkably. In the first two months of this year 9 students died, 35 teachers and students were injured as a result of these incidents. According to İstanbul Police Department's 2005 data, only in İstanbul, 868 girls and 379 boys between the age of 0-11 years, and 1369 girls and 12656 boys between the age of 12-18 years committed a crime in 2005. It was stated that 63 percent of convicted children studied in primary schools, and 12 percent attended secondary schools. The incidents had a great repercussion in printed and visual media. Families felt uneasy about the news. In order to investigate the situation the Turkish National Grand Assembly established a commission called "The Parliamentary Investigation Commission for determining through research the precautions against the increasing tendency of children and youth towards violence and related cases in schools" (TBMM, 2007).

The Commission prepared a comprehensive report consisting 6 parts and 497 pages without appendices after a two-year investigation and research covering 2006 and 2007.

Let us begin describing this report with taking a glance at interview records made with two important names.

## Opinions of Authorities and Experts

In 2006, Minister of National Education of that time, Hüseyin Çelik presented his opinion on preventing violence in schools. Minister stated that he was preparing a five-year strategic and action plan between 2006-2011 in order to prevent violence and decrease act of violence in educational environments and they were trying hard on parents within the framework of "Protect Your Life" Project. Minister specified that they signed a protocol with The Ministry of Culture and Tourism regarding cultural and arts education and the cooperation was continuing intensively. However, he did not point out what the studies were specifically. Moreover, Minister Çelik said that MOBESE (Central Camera Control System) system was used in Istanbul that frequently faced act of violence and this system aimed to control over the entrance and exits of schools against malicious people; however he stated if this system was used in all parts of schools, this would not be pedagogical.

One of the important interviews made by the commission was the one with Lua Pieters who is the Program Coordinator in UNICEF. Pieters initially pointed out that the commission was founded in the right time because United Nations (UN) started a global study on the subject of violence towards children. Pieters said that violence was not specific to Turkey, but it was a global one. The worst part of this problem was normalizing it; that was the act of violence in schools becomes ordinary, and this makes the problem more serious. Finally she said that the act of violence in schools increased globally. Pieters emphasized the fact that violence leads to the poverty, therefore the relations between violence and poverty should be studied. Pieters also mentioned that sport was the antidote of violence; relatively sport was cheaper and easier to do than art.

## Field Studies

A considerable part of the report consisted of field studies regarding the reasons of increasing tendency of children and youth towards violence. These studies included:
1. Detecting the Reasons Affecting the Violence and the Violence in Students Continuing on Secondary Schools in Turkey.
2. Detecting the Reasons Affecting the Violence and the Violence in Children Arrested and Convicted in Penal Institutions.
3. Inter-institutional Knowledge Sharing and Collaboration Incentive Meeting.
4. Science, Art and Media Meeting Against Violence.

The aim of these studies was to detect the factors related with the circumstances that the students would face with and/or use the violence in terms of different types of violence and according to the "changeability" of these factors, in forward studies, this aim was defined to specify the foreground of "risk groups" and to provide information into planning a "proper intervention".

The studies were made through surveys, document reviews and interviews. One of the case studies titled *"The Study on Detecting the Reasons Affecting the Violence and the Violence in Students Continuing on Secondary Schools in Turkey"* reached 29162 students from 261 high schools in 2007. According to the results of survey, the reasons of wide spread violence among students were defined as: a) unsafe neighborhood, b) disregard of moral values, c) more respect for the tough people in the society, and d) ignoring the religious values. Students also said that insufficient educational level of parents, angry behaviors of parents, negative financial situation of the family and parents' unloving attitudes towards their children were effective on wide spreading violence. Another reason expressed by the students was that they wanted to be powerful like TV and movie stars. According to the findings of the study, the following recommendations in respect of preventing violence were presented:

- Activities for youngsters such as popularizing the cultural activities and providing more attendance of youth to these activities, increasing sports opportunities and providing the youth with more chances to practice on, preventing the youth from game arcades, promoting the use of internet in schools and reducing the behavior of going to internet cafes.
- Helping students develop perspectives regarding the lifestyle of youth. They should be informed that doing exercise or attending cultural activities will develop and enhance their personalities.
- More importantly, it should be provided that the youth attend these kinds of activities and they adopt these activities as lifestyle habits. By this way, the youth understand that these positive activities will improve themselves and they can learn and adopt these behaviors through experience.

Another important field study was the one conducted in 2007 towards children arrested and convicted in 21 Penal Institutions from 19 cities in Turkey. In this study, the data was collected from 330 people via using survey forms which is peculiar to this study and face to face interview technique in a one to one application platform.

This study was conducted towards children and youth who were arrested and convicted in these penal institutions, 1420 boys and 51 girls in total 1545 children and youth were contacted. This study helped us understand better socioeconomic background information such as family, lifestyle and social environment features of the children in penal institutions in Turkey; characteristics of youth facing with violence and using violence; and factors related to violence where it was practiced According to the findings, these children's fathers and more remarkably their mothers had a low level education. 70.7 percent of their fathers and 82.7 percent of their mothers were primary school graduates or less. Mainly fathers earned a living for the family (55.4%); in each family out of five neither father nor mother had a job.

The Head of the Commission, Mrs. Halide İncekara, a Member of the Parliament, as a keynote speaker delivered a paper on the results of the research in the "Symposium on Arts Education and Violence" in Gazi University, in 2007. According to the information given by İncekara, no one was engaged in art among the family members of these children; moreover they had no relations with art. It was also reported by İncekara that the children and the youth who were dealing with art or getting training on arts education had no tendency to violence. In order to prevent children and youth from violence, the findings also provided important data such as where the programs might be found or which resources and methods could be used. For example; it was determined that before they were put in penitentiary, children frequently spent their spare time by going out with their friends, boys rarely went to the cafe/internet cafe and girls rarely read newspaper/magazine. The rates of "reading books apart from school books" or "attending cultural activities" in spare time were under the expectations. As an advice, it was stated that providing necessary environment and physical conditions, in which they could spend their free time to gain positive life skills with the help of activities on sports, arts and culture, would make a contribution to decrease acts of violence between children and youth.

While the report sorted the circumstances inviting the violence problems under various titles, it also emphasized the importance of education and activities of arts, culture and sports on preventing violence in schools. In this context, the report stated that all official and private organizations and non-governmental organizations should make an attempt in order to make every children had an interest on art, culture and sport.

## Proceedings from the Symposium on Arts Education and Violence

In the Symposium on Arts Education and Violence (Gazi University, 2007), 32 academic papers, which were directly related to this subject, were presented. In these papers, in the light of quantitative and qualitative researches, it was claimed that the children who took art classes like visual arts, music and drama, and media literacy classes both through formal and non-formal educational ways stayed away from the violence. For instance, the title of Feyzan M. Göher's paper was *"Violence Problems in Song Lyrics: A Case Study on Fifth Grade Students in Elementary Schools"* (Göher, 2007). The research, which was executed as a case study, aimed to investigate the effect of violence on children and youth, examining the reasons of violence, and by this way detecting the effects of violent expressions involved in song lyrics. In the research, 100 5th Grade students and 10 music teachers were interviewed. It was defined that the top ten music lists that students liked to listen contained violent expressions in their lyrics. In the interviews with teachers, it appeared that the students had tendencies on violence generally preferred to listen to Turkish Rap and Hip-hop music consisting lyrics with violent indications. The researcher pointed that censorship in art was unacceptable; however song writers and artists had responsibility to protect children and youth from the violence.

Another research made by Kazım Artut and Filiz Yurtal was titled *"Defining the Violence in Schools with Students' Paintings"* (Artut & Yurtal, 2007). The research showed how students expressed violence in schools in their paintings. How the children pictured the people who were exposed to violence and used the violence was examined. It was evaluated in relation to gender, violence scenes and ways of using violence. In total 66 children samples were taken at random from 36 girls and 30 boys between the ages of 12-13 years, and they were asked to paint something on the subject of "any act of violence in school that they witnessed, heard or experienced". Among the paintings which were examined through content analysis, 33 described the violence between students, 16 of them described the violence used by teachers towards students, and 6 of them described the violence used by adults towards children. Inexplicable 7 paintings were not taken into consideration. Moreover, the most popular violence scenes were the school garden with 38 paintings, classes with 14, school entrance and exit with 4, school administrative office with 3, and school corridors with 2. The ways of using violence were described in the paintings as brutal force with 38 paintings, knife with 16, verbal attack with 10, and club with 7. To sum up, researchers put forward that acts of violence took part in schools and these incidents had significant impact on children. Children who are exposed to violence go into depression or increasingly become diffident or start to perceive the act of violence as normal and ordinary, which is the worst part of this problem. If such events are not prevented on the spot, they may lead children to get psychological problems or see violence as a way of solution to the problems among themselves or lose their trust to people.

## Concluding Remark

We, as arts educators, are sure that if the arts education in schools' curricula take an important part then it will help to prevent school violence through its spiritual, creative, rich and pragmatic content and characteristics.

Thus in the US, the Obama administration launched a test program, investing 2 million dollar over two years on arts education in the nation's most poorly performing schools. Orchard Gardens is one of the eight schools participating in this program. BBC Reporter Jane O'Brien visited this pilot school in Boston and saw firsthand the transformative effect of the arts education. The reporter indicated that 90% of the students at Orchard Gardens Pilot School lives under the poverty line, and some are homeless. In fact, violence was normal at this failing school. This news is on the website of Arts to Grow and continuing to say that "Students carried weapons and teachers didn't stay for long. When Andrew Bott, Principal of Orchard Gardens Pilot School, took over, he fired the security guards and hired arts teachers. Many advised him at the time to go for a phased approach, but Bott decided to tackle a total transformation. Anyone who sees the results today, Bott's bold move appeared to be the right one" (Arts to Grow, 2014).

Although act of violence in schools is decreasing year by year in Turkey, it is difficult to say that it will be over soon. It is certain that the arts education provided from early years by well-programmed and well-trained teachers is effective in decreasing these acts which are based on different reasons. It makes sense to end this paper by referring to Parliament Member Halide İncekara's address to arts educators in the symposium on Arts Education and Violence (Gazi University, 2007) with these important words:

> "Distinguished educators, please protect your art and arts of education both in schools and as a free time activity in order to keep our children away from the violence. The children dealing with art definitely do not involve in acts of violence, we saw it in our researches. Everybody should be in cooperation with

you for increasing arts classes in schools, modernizing the curriculum of the arts education and up skilling every child a hobby in one of the art branches. For this purpose, let's work together."

We should remember these words and fulfill our duty.

## References

Arts to Grow (2014). *Arts replaced violence in school*: http://artstogrow.tumblr.com/post/49512030258/arts-replaced-violence-in-school 10.01.2014.

Artut, K. & Yurtal, F. (2007). Okulda Yaşanan Şiddetin, Öğrencilerin Yaptıkları Resimlerle Tanımlanması (Defining the Violence in Schools with Students' Paintings), *Sanat Eğitimi ve Şiddet, 3. Ulusal Sanat Eğitimi Sempozyumu Bildirileri*, Gazi Üniversitesi & Görsel Sanatlar Eğitimi Derneği & Müzik Eğitimcileri Derneği, Ankara, 19-21 Kasım 2007, s. 527-528. (*Arts Education and Violence, 3. National Arts Education Symposium Proceedings*), Gazi University & Turkish Visual Arts Education Association & Music Educators Association, Ankara, 19-21 November 2007, pp. 527-528).

CDC (2012). Centers for Disease Control and Prevention *Understanding School Violence*: http://www.cdc.gov/violenceprevention/pdf/schoolviolence_factsheet-a.pdf 10.01.2014.

Council of Europe (2011). *Tackling violence in schools*. High-Level Expert meeting co-organised by the Government of Norway, the Council of Europe and the UN Special Representative of the Secretary-General on Violence against Children, Oslo, 27-28 June 2011, Final report of the meeting http://www.coe.int/t/dg3/children/violence/OsloReport_en.pdf 19.07.2013.

Elliot, D.S., Hamburg, B.A., & Williams, K.R. (1998). *Violence in American Schools*. New York: Cambridge University Press.

Gazi University (2007). *Sanat Eğitimi ve Şiddet, 3. Ulusal Sanat Eğitimi Sempozyumu Bildirileri*, Gazi Üniversitesi & Görsel Sanatlar Eğitimi Derneği & Müzik Eğitimcileri Derneği, Gündüz Eğitim ve Yayıcılık: Ankara, 19-21 Kasım 2007. (*Arts Education and Violence, 3. National Arts Education Symposium Proceedings*), Gazi University & Turkish Visual Arts Education Association & Music Educator Association, Ankara, 19-21 November 2007.

Göher, F.M. (2007). Şarkı Sözlerindeki Şiddet'li Sorunlar: İlköğretim Beşinci Sınıf Öğrencileriyle Yapılan Bir Çalışma (Violence Problems in Song Lyrics: A Case Study on Fifth Grade Students in Elementary Schools), *Sanat Eğitimi ve Şiddet, 3. Ulusal Sanat Eğitimi Sempozyumu Bildirileri*, Gazi Üniversitesi & Görsel Sanatlar Eğitimi Derneği & Müzik Eğitimcileri Derneği, Gündüz Eğitim ve Yayıcılık: Ankara, 19-21 Kasım 2007, s. 309-320. (*Arts Education and Violence, 3. National Arts Education Symposium Proceedings*), Gazi University & Turkish Visual Arts Education Association & Music Educator Association, Ankara, 19-21 November 2007, pp. 309-320).

Kimmel, M.S. & Mehler, M. (2003). Adolescent Masculinity, Homophobia, and Violence: Random School Shootings, 1982-2001. *American Behavioral Scientist*. http://abs.sagepub.com/cgi/content/abstract/46/10/1439. 12.08.2013.

MD (2014). Medya Database's campain called "Beyond Bullets: Americans Using Media To Stop Gun Violence": http://media.gfem.org/node/12632 10.01.2014.

PIF (2014). Protsahan India Foundation, (Encouraging Creative Education And Sustainable Livelihoods Through Art, Cinema And Technology – Protsahan's Fight To End Violence) http://protsahan.wordpress.com 10.01.2014.

PIO (2014). Prevention Institute Oakland, Putting Prevention at the Center of Community Well-Being. www.PreventionInstitute.org 10.01.2014.

Taşkesen, O. (2011). *Güzel Sanatlar ve Spor Liselerinin Resim Bölümleri ile Genel Liselerde Verilen Görsel Sanatlar Eğitiminin Öğrencilerin Şiddete Yönelik Davranışlarına Etkileri Üzerine Bir Araştırma* (The Effects of Visual Arts Education on Students Violent Behaviors in Fine Arts and Sports High Schools Painting Departments and General High Schools), Yayımlanmamış Doktora Tezi (Unpublished Doctoral Dissertation), Ankara: Gazi Üniversitesi Eğitim Bilimleri Enstitüsü (Gazi University, Graduate Scgool of Education).

TBMM (2007). *Türkiye Büyük Millet Meclisi Çocuklarda ve Gençlerde Artan Şiddet Eğilimi ile Okullarda Meydana Gelen Olayların Araştırılarak Alınması Gereken Önlemlerin Belirlenmesi Amacıyla Kurulan (10/337, 343, 356, 357) Esas Numaralı Meclis Araştırması Komisyonu Raporu* (Report of the Parliamentary Investigation Commission for determining through research the precautions against the increasing tendency of children and youth towards violence and related cases in schools), Dönem: 22, Yasama Yılı: 5, (S. Sayısı: 1413).

World Summit on Arts Education – Polylogue II, 13-17 May 2013, Munich and Wildbad Kreuth, Germany. http://worldsummit2013.bkj.de/speakers/otoole-john.html 18.08.2013.

Mousumi De

# Rethinking UNESCO's Commitment to Education for Peace and International Understanding through Art: From the Bristol Seminar to the Seoul Agenda

Throughout history, various philosophers and educators have advocated for using education and art for peace amongst people from different cultures and countries in the world. Education for peace to prevent international conflicts became more pertinent with the establishment of UNESCO after the Second World War. Resolutions were also adopted to inquire into art education that led to UNESCO's seminar 'The Visual Arts in General Education' in 1951 in Bristol, UK. A significant outcome of the seminar, was applying the ideal of worldwide cooperation that animates UNESCO and the UN in the field of art education (Munro, 1954, p. 116) and establishment of the International Society for Education through Art, which recognized the necessity of representing the humanizing values of art on a global basis (Ziegfeld, 1954, p. 119).

Scholars at the seminar envisaged how art education might promote the ideal of peace and proposed approaches such as exchanging children's artworks, fostering cultural interchange and studying about art and cultures of others to promote international attitudes of understanding, respect and sympathy, thereby building a new generation of peace-loving citizens (Ziegfeld, 1954, p. 115-17). These approaches were grounded in the understanding that values, beliefs, attitudes and socio-cultural contexts of people from other cultures are inherent in their artworks, and these communicate across cultures at an intuitive and deeply emotional level, connecting people at a basic human and universal level. While the Bristol seminar provided impetus to the ideal of educating for peace and international understanding, emergent needs after the Second World War compelled scholars to consider the use of art education for intranational concerns, such as increasing movement of immigrant populations resulting in a multiracial and multicultural society, thereby steering the focus on issues such as race, cultural diversity, intercultural and multicultural understanding (e.g. Efland, Freedman, Stuhr, 1996; McFee, 1966).

Consequentially, research (and practice) in art education for peace, has comparatively remained in the margins, 'especially, on how art educators address issues of ethnic and political conflict with their students' (Cohen-Evron, 2007, p. 1032). Several studies show that art educators often ignore issues of conflict and social concern in class (e.g. Cohen-Evron, 2005, 2007; Mason, 1995; Milbrandt, 2002). A study by Cohen-Evron (2007) found that some art educators apply art therapy for victims of conflicts, and others apply a variety of approaches, all of which are grounded in multicultural art education in its various forms. Amongst these, one approach for promoting peace and tolerance towards the Other, addresses issues of social equity, cultural pluralism and tolerance by including Other's art as a legitimate part of the curriculum; an approach reminiscent of global or internationalist multicultural education. Art educators also encourage art activities dedicated to significant celebrations of the Other, and facilitate joint art activities with Others to promote mutual understanding and cooperative relations (Cohen-Evron, 2007, p. 1034-38).

In places with ongoing conflicts, art educators aim to broaden students' perception about the Other and include Others' art in the curriculum, specifically to question narrow perspectives and stereotypes, and unlearn bias and prejudice. They also seek to change binary perceptions of us/them or good/bad by inculcating analytical and critical thinking skills in students, to enable them to re-examine these concepts; an approach reminiscent of social reconstruction multicultural art education. Another approach art educators apply is deconstructing racial and political imagery to combat racism by addressing issues of power relationships and its influence on cultural and political identity construction, which is reminiscent of critical and feminist multicultural art education (ibid, p. 1038-42). Whilst acknowledging the contribution of these approaches, I reiterate Steers' (2009) concern, "can international cooperation and better understanding between peoples be furthered through art education?" (2009, p. 316).

Educating for peace is a complex endeavor because "peace" is a complex and multifaceted concept, which calls for re-thinking the grounds on which we base our curricular approaches, and our efforts to uphold UNESCO's commitment towards educating for peace and international understanding through art. Drawing from discourses in peace studies and social psychology, as well as my experiences as a practitioner using art for peace building and peace education, I explain here that art educators have not only underutilized established theoretical and curricular frameworks in peace education as precedents, but there are also significant knowledge gaps that undermine contemporary approaches in achieving their goals effectively. In the following sections, I explicate the complexities of educating for peace and suggest recommendations at different levels, with the intention of precipitating dialogue that bridges art educational discourse with peace education. While these recommendations are not absolute or exclusive, they seek to contribute towards the process of educating for peace through art.

## At Conceptual Level

Given that most approaches aimed at promoting peace are grounded in various forms of multicultural art education, it may be useful to define the concept. Multicultural education that originated in Europe and North America holds the view that "cultural variation should be represented and transmitted in (art education) in the school system in order for children to accept it in a given society" (Barry, Poortinga, Segal, & Dasen, 1992). The underlying idea, in approaches based on multicultural art education, that knowing about Others' values, beliefs, cultural similarities and dissimilarities through their art can promote mutual understanding, tolerance and peace, puts the onus on "knowledge" for promoting peace, which ignores the complex constructs of attitudes and prejudice that are inextricably intertwined in any conflict situation, especially political and ethnic conflicts and more importantly, ignores the crucial relationship between peace and conflict.

Approaches hinged on multicultural art education can be problematic for other reasons. Western concepts of multicultural art education, despite its contribution towards representing minority cultures, has been criticized as 'irrelevant to the needs of the world's aboriginal peoples' (Irwin, Rogers & Farrell, 1999) and unsuited to the needs of colonized people (Barbosa, 1999). Specifically in relation to peace, it should be noted that peace means different things for different individuals, contexts and cultures, as opposed to a perceived homologous entity. Several educational initiatives portray peace and conflict as a 'reachable and erasable thing' (Bekerman & Zembylas, 2011, p. 3). Such a concept of peace viewed as a 'universal utopia' rejects multiple representations of truth, various understandings of justice, and disregards the close connection between conflict and justice (ibid, p. 27). Thus, how we conceptualize "peace" has important implications in our ability to envision and enact appropriate pedagogies for promoting peace.

A review of literature in art education has not yielded a definition of peace that can guide our efforts in achieving this goal; at least not to my knowledge. A starting point therefore, maybe to conceive a definition of peace that can help understand, what art education for peace or peace education through art might entail. When peace is understood as absence of direct, or overt violence, it is referred as 'negative peace', and when it is understood as the presence of justice, it is referred as 'positive peace' (Galtung, 1969). To capture a broader and more dynamic meaning of peace, Galtung (1996) defined it as "what we have when creative conflict transformation can take place non-violently" (1996, p. 24-36). In the context of peace education through art, one might consider UNICEF's (1999) definition, as "the process of promoting the knowledge, skills and attitudes needed to bring about behavior changes, that will enable children, youth and adults to prevent conflict and violence, resolve conflict peacefully and create conditions conducive for peace at an intrapersonal, interpersonal, intergroup, national and international level" (Fountain, 1999, p. 6). Both these conceptions, define peace and peace education as processes, which provides a more action-centered approach, than a universally self-evident reachable thing.

Thus, art education curricula aimed at promoting peace, might do more than transmit cultural similarities and variations from multiple cultures, and promote the knowledge, skills and attitudes needed for learners to creatively resolve and prevent conflicts, and create conditions conducive for peace. A deeper understanding of what peace entails, also helps in differentiating *education in art* that seeks to promote peace, from *education through art* that seeks to promote peace, as well as curricula that only seeks to *educate about peace*.

## At Pedagogical Level

Many art pedagogies aimed at promoting peace and tolerance are based on the rationale that studying about Other's art would help to promote "attitudes" of understanding, respect, tolerance and peace. Expansion of knowledge about Others' values, beliefs and socio-cultural contexts do not necessarily translate into attitude or behavior change. Attitudes are complex constructs that often drive behavior, and are formed by processing different types of information. Depending on the accessibility and predominance of one information type over others, the focusing information establishes our attitude about it (see Petty, Briñol & DeMarree, 2007). Thus, knowledge gained through art, is only one information type, and we may have other conflicting or more influential information from our family, peers, media and the Internet, that can influence our attitude formation about the Other.

Flinders (2005) study for example, found that adolescents in the US who had various sources of information for forming their view about the Iraq War, (such as the Internet, news media, friends, teachers and parents), considered information received from their parents, to be most trustworthy and influential in forming their opinion about the war. Thus, approaches aimed at changing attitudes primarily by broadening knowledge about the Other, might not be effective, thereby undermining the process of attitude change to promote peace.

Many art pedagogies grounded in social reconstruction, critical, and feminist multicultural art education are based on the rationale that inculcating analytical and critical thinking skills in learners will enable them to deconstruct dominant discourses of power relationships, help change binary perceptions of us/them, and hence, reduce "prejudice", stereotyping and racism (Cohen-Evron, 2007, p. 1040-42). Inculcating cognitive skills however, are not sufficient to reduce prejudice or racism. While scholars agree that prejudice can be reduced (Allport, 1954), and intergroup relations improved by providing information about the group, such as educational programs (Triandis, 1975), prejudice is not just a cognitive attitudinal phenomenon, but also has affective and behavioral components. It is best understood as "any attitude, *emotion* or behavior towards members of a group that directly or indirectly implies some negativity or antipathy towards the group" (Brown, 2011, p. 7). Hence, emotions such as fear and anger can build and strengthen prejudice.

A prevalent example is prejudice against Muslims in several countries. A study by Ispas (2007) that investigated emotions amongst British non-Muslims towards Muslims, found greater fear- and anger-based emotional reactions, as well as greater avoidance towards Muslim minorities than non-Muslim minorities. Hence, art pedagogies that involve teaching Islamic art to students in order to address racist stereotypes against Muslims, after the September 11 attacks (for e.g. study by Oweis, 2002), might not be effective, because cognitive processing of information does not necessarily mitigate *emotional* causes such as fear and anger that underpin prejudice. In fact, emotional prejudice towards Muslims can be understood in terms of the perceived threat that some people perceive radical Islam (such as groups like Al Qaeda) poses at this point in history, and people over-generalize this to Muslims as a whole (Spears, Leach, van Zomeren, Ispas, Sweetman & Tausch, 2011, p. 129). Various scholars suggest that if we are to understand the power and tenacity of racism, then attending to feelings of fear, anxiety, resentment and hatred is essential (Davidson, Bondi, & Smith, 2005).

An important component missing in approaches aimed at promoting peace is teaching skills for learners to resolve and prevent conflicts peacefully. Conflict resolution skills are a 'central component' of peace education (e.g., Johnson & Johnson, 2005), that involve understanding the conflict, especially from the other's perspective, needs and goals, and most importantly reframing the conflict as a mutual problem that needs to be resolved collaboratively and, cooperatively brainstorming to create and enhance a variety of peaceful solutions (e.g. Bar-Tal & Rosen, 2009, p. 566). Thus art education curricula aimed at promoting peace, tolerance and understanding through reduction of prejudice, stereotyping and racism, might need more than inculcating cognitive capacities for critical thinking, and 'address students' critical emotions' (see Zembylas, 2012) to mitigate the emotional causes that underpin such phenomena. Most significantly, art pedagogies might find opportunities to teach conflict resolution skills that can enable learners to resolve conflicts peacefully.

A critical issue, art educators might want to consider in applying art pedagogies for promoting peace and understanding is: what are the goals of the pedagogy. For example, learning a specific art form about the Other (such as Islamic art) might be the primary goal, with the secondary goal of promoting more knowledge about the Other (such as Muslims), with the hope that it might provide an alternative view of the Other and help change attitudes. However, if the primary goal of art pedagogy is to bring about transformational changes in the learner, then we might want to consider the "domains of change" (Salomon & Kupermintz, 2002) the pedagogy aims to impact; whether, it intends to impact at a cognitive level (for e.g. cross-cultural knowledge, prejudice, empathy), or at an affective level (for e.g. prejudice, tolerance, empathy), or at volitional level (for e.g. willingness for contact, openness to accept Other's perspective) and/or at behavioral level (for e.g. conflict resolution and pro-social skills) (2002, p. 13-14). Although a sharp distinction between these domains is difficult to draw since changes occur at multiple levels, it provides a direction to determine the appropriate rationale for developing the pedagogy and instruction, as well as the appropriate assessment criteria and method.

## At Instructional Level

A common approach to promoting peace and tolerance towards the Other is by facilitating joint art activities, that provide an opportunity to meet with them and foster a sense of unity by emphasizing shared qualities of art and art making (Cohen-Evron, 2007, p. 1037-38). A few joint art activities however, are not sufficient for attitude change towards the Other, as these do not withstand the eroding forces of time and adverse events. Scholars believe that inter-group contact can change attitudes, and creating opportunities for mutual acquaintance that can enhance understanding and acceptance amongst group members, can improve relations amongst them (Allport, 1954; Miller & Brewer, 1984). However, empirical research shows that positive impact of the contact depends on certain conditions, for e.g., (a) contact should involve a balanced ratio of group members from both sides allowing a genuine acquaintance potential, (b) it should be amongst individuals who share equality of status, and most importantly, (c) contact should be *regular and frequent* (see Brewer, 1996; Stephan & Stephan, 2001). In one example, a peace education program, that was based on the assumption that attitudes towards another disliked group can be changed as a mere function of a few meetings, found *no* changes in attitudes (Tal-Or, Boninger, & Gleicher, 2002). Thus, joint art activities can be effective only when these conditions are met, especially when they are regular and frequent.

A common practice in several art pedagogies, especially in places with ongoing conflicts, is changing binary perceptions of us/them, or good/bad to provide an alternative view of the Other. This rhetoric of "us and them" or "the Other" in conflict situations is problematic, because it misrepresents the nature of conflict. It portrays *two* sides to a conflict, often divided by essentialist differences and primordial hatred, which (a) dichotomizes complex problems, (b) portrays the Other as the enemy, ignoring interconnections between various groups in the conflict, (c) misrepresents history and (d) misunderstands the malleable multiplicity of identity, that is entwined in any conflict situation (e.g. Ross, 2006, p. 9). Therefore, instructing students to understand or examine their perceptions of a homogenized 'Other', is not only a fallacy, since it portrays them as the *only* group and *central* to the conflict, but also reinforces and perpetuates prejudice against them.

Scholars in peace studies suggest avoiding an epistemology of "us versus them", as it produces a polarized view; instead, deconstructing the conflict helps in recognizing various parties, goals and issues, and thus possible solutions to different issues, which can eventually promote peace (e.g. Galtung, 2000; McGoldrick & Lynch, 2000, p. 9). Education scholars also urge that this 'paradigmatic dichotomy of us/them (or good/bad) set by Western epistemology seems to only replicate past outcomes' (Bekerman & Zembylas, 2011, p. 27). Art educators might thus, seek to avoid such a polarized view in their instruction, as it is counterproductive to the overall goal of promoting better understanding towards the Other.

A critical need in art pedagogies aimed at promoting peace and understanding is establishing assessment criteria and methods. While there are established standards for assessing *learning in the arts*, changes in students' minds, such as changed attitudes or reduced prejudice, are rarely assessed seriously. Assessments that measure changes in students' level of artistic skill and knowledge are not indicative of affective or behavioral changes since cognitive measures do not provide predictive validity for changes in emotions, dispositions, and behaviors that may or may not occur as a result of instruction. It is therefore important to note that *assessment in the arts* are distinctively different from *assessment of affective and behavioral changes,* i.e. transformations in students' minds – which is currently the least developed area in the domain of educating for peace through art.

A systematic and empirical assessment of the impact of instruction on change variables intended in the students' minds, helps determine if the instruction was successful or not and the extent to which the impact was realized, i.e. whether changes were significant, or modest or transient improvements. A starting point therefore, might be to delineate appropriate criteria for assessing change. These might include, (i) *change variable* i.e. the domains of change as a result of instruction and the (ii) *magnitude of change*, i.e. the extent to which the change was realized, which can be assessed based on a comparison between post-instruction and pre-instruction measures (iii) *robustness of change*, i.e. the extent to which the impact sustains the weakening effects of time and adverse effects for e.g. terrorist attacks. Many studies indicate that newly reinforced changes in attitudes or values tend to weaken over time, thus, longitudinal assessments provide a credible indication of whether the changes are sustainable or not; (iv) *uniformity of impact*, i.e. whether the instruction impacts all the students or only partially. This helps in understanding the extent to which initial views, attitudes, proclivities and abilities predict the magnitude, and direction of changes as a result of instruction (see Salomon & Kupermintz, 2002, p. 15-18).

An important criterion for assessing change is (v) *explicit and implicit changes*, i.e. whether changes in attitudes, prejudice, and volitional tendencies etc. are conscious changes (explicit level) or under involuntary control (at implicit level). Students might portray favorable attitudes towards Others, due to social desirability conditions, such as, it is socially inappropriate to admit or express prejudice, but students might still hold such values implicitly. Thus, implicit changes, assessed through indirect measures are regarded as more valid, than explicit measures that are assessed through self-reports or students' reflections. Apart from these, additional criteria for assessing change might include (vi) *specificity or generalizability of the impact*, i.e. if the change is highly specific or generalizable in different areas, such as, (a) transfer of learning, i.e. if one affecting measure also generalizes to another related measure. For example, in a program, White participants showed greater agreement with views about tuition for Blacks, which they initially opposed, and also changed their general views of Blacks (Leippe & Eisenstadt, 1994). (b) Generalizability over situations, i.e. if effects observed in one situation, for e.g. valuation of equality between ethnic groups also transfers to equality between socioeconomic classes. (c) An important criterion is generalizability from individuals to groups, i.e., if personal friendship for e.g. fostered through joint art activities with a member of a disliked group, also generalizes to new ways of thinking about the friend's entire group (see ibid, p. 15-18).

Thus, art education curricula aimed at promoting peace might need to clearly define learning and transformational goals that can help develop pedagogy and instruction based on appropriate rationale for achieving those goals, as well as, delineate appropriate assessment and evaluation criteria and methods, to best affect sustainable change.

## At Institutional Level

In the context of this text, institution refers to individual art education institutions, as well as art education community interested in educating for peace and international understanding through art. Given the need for more research in this area, at an institutional level, we might want to identify critical issues that need addressing, and key areas of research that can contribute towards best practices in this domain. A starting point might be to establish frameworks for curricular design, attributes, criteria for implementation and evaluation that is specific to the purpose of educating for peace through art. For example, with regard to curricular design, we might want to explore different ways art might be utilized for (i) addressing student's critical emotions related to Others, (ii) teaching about conflicts, not only as contested issues, but problems that need to be resolved peacefully, (iii) teaching about positive peace that is action-centered and has real meaning in students' lives and most significantly, (iv) promoting conflict resolution skills.

In terms of establishing frameworks for curricular attributes and criteria of implementation, we might want to consider, (i) the duration of such curricula, whether a single or a series of lessons and how often to implement (ii) quality of the rationale underlying such curricula, (iii) relationship to theory and praxis, (iv) nature of pedagogy, instruction and processes (for e.g., didactic teaching, joint art creations, experiential learning, conflict resolution skill training etc.); (v) art integration in the curriculum, i.e. how well art is integrated that promotes a balance between education in art as well as education for peace through art and (vi) the socio-political context of the curriculum, i.e. whether it is suited for an ongoing conflict, inter-group tension, majority-minority relations, post-conflict reconciliation or a peaceful situation. In terms of establishing frameworks for effective evaluation strategies, we might want to consider, how to evaluate (i) the rationale underlying a curriculum, (ii) the quality of implementation, (iii) measurable evidence of the curricular impact, and its effectiveness, (iv) the process by which measureable results have come about and (v) appropriateness within the socio-political context, in which it takes place (see Salomon & Kupermintz, 2002, p. 3-13). Establishing systematic evaluation strategies for such curricula (both summative and formative) can foster best practices in this domain.

Equally important is to foster cross-disciplinary research and shared practice between scholars in art education and peace education that can benefit art educators from understanding alternate modes of inquiry and praxis in this domain. Cross-disciplinary research on existing discourses in these fields might yield new knowledge that can augment and shape future efforts in educating for peace. For example, a study on intersections of art history and peace history found that there is more anti-war art than peace art, because it was perceived to be illusive in terms of definition (Rank, 2008). How might this be different in contemporary art practices and peace discourses, and subsequently, how might these shape our efforts to teach about and for peace? We might want to forge partnerships with peace museums that can support our efforts in out-of-school contexts. Further, fertile collaborations with scholars in social psychology and peace psychology might broaden our theoretical underpinnings and help us build upon existing research and practice in these domains, for example, applying drawing-based implicit measures for assessing changes at implicit level. Last but not the least; we might want to address the need to educate for peace at the teacher education level, so they are well prepared to address such issues with their students in classrooms.

Mason (1995) has argued that while art educators agree with UNESCO's suggestion that 'art teaching can be a pillar which supports understanding and tolerance between people from different regions and/or cultural backgrounds', the reality is that curriculum change takes place slowly and majority of art education systems are experiencing cut backs. Furthermore, art teachers are ill prepared for cultural reforms and are required to be subservient to political policies (1995, p. 15). Efforts to uphold UNESCO's commitment to educating for peace and international understanding through art, would thus require concerted efforts from art educators, to not only incorporate new pedagogies and instruction that are effective in achieving this goal, but also bring about necessary changes and support at an institutional and policy level.

## At Policy Level

Several art educators who ignore issues of social and political conflict in classrooms feel that addressing these issues are adding objectives beyond those required by the state (and/or national) curriculum, as well as fear reprisals from administrative systems if they addressed such issues in class (see Milbrandt, 2002, p. 147). Educating for peace is thus, not only a complex endeavor, but also an arduous one that might need changes at the state and national policy level, to be effective at the implementation level. Bartelds (1984) reminds us that our efforts would have real effect only when there is an attitude of 'international solidarity advocated by politicians, or by important and influential groups within society' (1984, p. 308). Thus, for raising awareness about the importance of educating for peace amongst art educators, and its effective implementation, we might need to broaden the goals of the *Seoul Agenda: Development of Arts Education*, which currently has among its goals applying arts education to contribute towards resolving social and cultural challenges facing today's world. These goals encompass – supporting and enhancing the role of arts education in (i) promotion of social cohesion, (ii) fostering democracy and peace in communities, and (iii) supporting reconstruction in post-conflict societies. It might help to expand these goals and include arts role in promoting peace education and clearly articulate objectives of how the arts might educate through peace.

Since the Second World War (1946) until 2001, there have been 225-armed conflicts worldwide (Gleditsch, Wallensteen, Eriksson, Sollenberg & Strand, 2002), and changing patterns of conflicts have considerably increased the risk for children (Raviv, Oppenheimer, & Bar-Tal, 1999). Educating for peace through art therefore remains crucial. We might want to re-think our practices at different levels in order to effectively contribute towards a 'transition from a culture of war to a culture of peace' (UN A/RES/53/243 General Assembly, 6 October, 1999, agenda item 31).

## References

Allport, G. W. (1954). *The Nature of Human Prejudice*. Basic books.
Barbosa, A.M. (1999). Cultural identity in a dependent counter: The case of Brazil. In D. Boughton & R. Mason (Eds.). *Beyond multicultural art education: International perspectives* (pp. 185-198). (Vol. 12). Waxmann.
Barry, J., Poortinga, Y., Segal, M. & Dasen, P. (1992). *Cross-cultural psychology: Research and applications*. Cambridge: Cambridge University Press
Bar-Tal, D., & Rosen, Y. (2009). Peace education in societies involved in intractable conflicts: Direct and indirect models. *Review of educational research*, 79(2), 557-575.
Bartelds, C. (1984). Peace education and solidarity. *Gandhi Marg*, 6(4/5), 306-315.
Bekerman, Z., & Zembylas, M. (2011). *Teaching contested narratives: Identity, memory and reconciliation in peace education and beyond*. Cambridge University Press.
Brewer, M. B. (1996). When contact is not enough: Social identity and intergroup cooperation. *International Journal of Intercultural Relations*, 20(3), 291-303.
Brewer, M. B., & Miller, N. (1984). *Groups in contact: The psychology of desegregation*. San Diego: Academic Press.
Brown, R. (2011). *Prejudice: Its social psychology*. John Wiley & Sons.

Cohen-Evron, N. (2005). Students Living within Violent Conflict: Should Art Educators "Play it Safe" or Face "Difficult Knowledge"?. *Studies in Art Education*, 309-322.

Cohen-Evron, N. (2007). Conflict and peace: Challenges for art educators. In L. Bresler (Ed.), *International handbook of research in art education* (pp. 1031-1054). Dordrecht, The Netherlands: Springer.

Davidson, J., Bondi, L., & Smith, M. (2005). *Emotional geographies*. Aldershot: Ashgate.

Efland, A., Freedman, K., & Stuhr, P. (1996). *Postmodern art education: An approach to curriculum*. Reston, Virginia: National Art Education Association.

Flinders, D. (2005). Adolescents talk about the Iraq war. *Phi Delta Kappan*, 87(4), 320-323

Fountain, S. (1999). *Peace Education in UNICEF*. New York: UNICEF.

Galtung, J. (1969). Violence, peace, and peace research. *Journal of peace research*, 6(3), 167-191.

Galtung, J. (1996). *Peace by peaceful means: Peace and conflict, development and civilization* (Vol. 14). Sage.

Galtung, J. (2000). *Conflict transformation by peaceful means: The Transcend method*. UN.

Gleditsch, N. P., Wallensteen, P., Eriksson, M., Sollenberg, M., & Strand, H. (2002). Armed conflict 1946-2001: A new dataset. *Journal of peace research*, 39(5), 615-637.

Irwin, R., Rogers, T., & Farrell, R. (1999). Multiculturalism denies the realities of Aboriginal artists and culture. In D. Boughton, & R. Mason (Eds.), *Beyond multicultural art education: International perspectives* (pp. 49-64). (Vol. 12). Waxmann.

Ispas, A. (2007). Prejudice and intergroup conflict: the strategic attribution of anger and fear in the context of intergroup relations. *Unpublished MPhil dissertation. Cardiff: Cardiff University.*

Johnson, D. W., & Johnson, R. T. (2005). Essential components of peace education. *Theory into Practice*, 44(4), 280-292.

Leippe, M. & Eisenstadt, D. (1994). Generalization of dissonance reduction: decreasing prejudice through induced compliance. *Journal of Personality and Social Psychology*, 67(3), 395-413.

Mason, R. (1995). *Art education and multiculturalism*. Corsham: National Society for Education in Art and Design.

McFee, J. K. (1966). Society, art and education. In E. Mattil (Ed.), *A seminar in art education for research and curriculum development: Cooperative research project* no. V-002 (pp. 122–136). University Park, PA: The Pennsylvania State University.

McGoldrick, A. & Lynch, J. (2000). *Peace Journalism: how to do it?*, TRANSCEND http://www.transcend.org/pjmanual.htm.

Milbrandt, M. K. (2002). Addressing contemporary social issues in art education: A survey of public school art educators in Georgia. *Studies in Art Education*, 43(2), 141-157.

Miller, N., & Brewer, M. B. (1984). *Groups in contact: The psychology of desegregation*. San Diego: Academic.

Munro, T. (1954). Art and International Understanding. In E. Ziegfeld (Ed.), *Education and Art: A Symposium* (pp. 116-117). Paris: UNESCO.

Oweis, F. S. (2002). Islamic art as an educational tool about teaching of Islam. *Art Education*, 55(2), 18-24.

Petty, R. E., Briñol, P., & DeMarree, K. G. (2007). The meta-cognitive model (MCM) of attitudes: Implications for attitude measurement, change, and strength. *Social Cognition*, 25, 657-686.

Rank, C. (2008). Promoting Peace through the Arts. *Proceedings of the 2008 International Peace Research Association (IPRA) Conference*, IPRA 2008. 15-19 July 2008, Leuven, Belgium.

Raviv, A., Oppenheimer, L., & Bar-Tal, D. (1999). *How children understand war and peace: A call for international peace education*. San Francisco: Jossey-Bass.

Ross, D. S. (2006). (De)Constructing Conflict: A Focused Review of War and Peace Journalism. *Conflict & Communication Online*, 5 (2). Verlag Irena Regener Berlin.

Salomon, G., & Kupermintz, H. (2002). *The Evaluation of Peace Education Programs: Main Considerations and Criteria.* University of Haifa, Israel: The Center for Research on Peace Education, 1-24.

Spears, R., Leach, C., van Zomeren, M., Ispas, A., Sweetman, J., & Tausch, N. (2011). Intergroup Emotions: More than the Sum of the Parts. In I. Nyklicek, A. Vingerhoets & M. Zeelenberg, (Eds.), *Emotion Regulation and Well-Being* (pp. 121-145). New York: Springer.

Steers, J. (2009). Some reflections on globalizing (visual) culture. In E. Delacruz, A. Arnold, A. Kuo & M. Parson (Eds.), *An Anthology: Globalization, art, and education* (pp. 314-320). Reston, VA: National Art Education Association.

Stephan, W. G., & Stephan, C. W. (2001). *Improving intergroup relations.* Sage Publications, Inc.

Tal-Or, N., Boninger, D., & Gleicher, F. (2002). Understanding the Conditions and Processes Necessary for Intergroup Contact to Reduce Prejudice. In G. Salomon & B. Nevo (Eds.), *Peace Education, The concept, Principles, and practices around the world.* Mahwah, NJ: Lawrence Erlbaum Associates Publishers.

Triandis, H.C. (1975). Culture training, cognitive complexity, and interpersonal attitudes. In R. Brislin, S. Bochner, & W. Lonner (Eds.), *Cross-cultural perspectives on learning* (pp. 39-77). Beverly Hills, CA: Sage Publications.

United Nations (1999). *Declaration and Program of Action of a Culture of Peace.* A/RES/53/243.

Zembylas, M. (2012). Critical emotional praxis for reconciliation education: emerging evidence and pedagogical implications. *Irish educational studies,* 31(1), 19-33.

Ziegfeld, E. (1954). *Education and Art: A Symposium.* Paris: UNESCO. 1953

Shifra Schonmann

# Arts for Peace Education:
# False Reflections or a Real Chance for a Change?

The body of research on *Arts for Peace Education* that has accumulated so far around the world is, metaphorically speaking, a 'fly sitting on the back of a giant'. The giant is of course the field of research *in education*; the 'fly' is the field of *research in 'arts for peace'*. The buzz that the fly is making is a misleading reflection, claiming that *research in 'arts for peace'* is a well-established field of research, and that its findings are leading to a real change.

In this short chapter I would raise a doubt, and claim that the many axioms spreading around the successful results of research in *arts for peace education* are very often no more than mantra, slogans or wishful thinking. The danger lies in believing in the effectiveness of the buzz. It can be harmful because it might lock out the possibility of opening education to a real change.

I realize that by saying this I am swimming against the current. Nevertheless I'll take the chance and be clear from the outset: I *do* follow many great thinkers such as John Dewey, Herbert Read, Nelson Goodman, Elliot Eisner and Maxine Greene in their ways of understanding that the *Arts* have a crucial function in education. However, I am against the widespread notion that gives predominance to the "by products" of works of art at the expense of their initial proposals as *arts per se*, as will be explained later, in the phrase 'Applied Arts'.

Many *peace education* projects are in operation throughout the world: there is a huge number of courses in schools and universities, thousands of centers, a sea of researchers diving to discover any possibility to enhance education for peace (see: Salomon and Cairns, 2010); and UNESCO is working constantly for the dissemination of 'A Culture of Peace' around the world. The concept of *peace education* has been growing since the middle of the twentieth century. An internet search for peace education publications in the U.S. alone comes up with millions of items. However, if one tries to find what is the share of **the arts** among the above-mentioned plethora, the findings shrink to a very low percentage. Mahatma Ghandi tried to teach what he had preached; his philosophy, *Pedagogy of Peace*, is based on principles of non-violent speech and action, openness and flexibility. His brave stand facilitated the work of implementing the curriculum of peace education into educational systems around the world. However, "in spite of this tremendous growth, in the 20$^{th}$ century, peace education has not really taken hold in school systems around the world" (Harris 2010, p. 19). In most countries peace education is carried out mostly informally in community settings and through national peace organizations. The arts are trying to be an integral part of this movement, aspiring to find their place in the main course of the educational dish, but with no success. Arts education remains marginal all over the world.

## Applied Arts

On what grounds can this phenomenon be understood and how can one connect it to the concern raised at the outset of this chapter? The answer can be looked at against the solid background of 'applied arts'.

*Peace education* is an **applied subject** that is practiced in different ways but must always be firmly based on a range of established empirical disciplines (Salomom and Cairns 2010). *Arts education* is a field of two related dimensions: one is 'pure art' or art for the sake of art while the other is **applied art.** The applied aspect relies "on the arts as a platform for social innovation and peace education, in order to inspire hope and build bridges across cultures" (http://www.arts-for-peace.or). In this and in similar expressions, the instrumental aspect of the arts is prominent.

*Arts for peace education* is relatively a new combination of **applied fields**, it envisages that the whole society will be involved in building the culture of peace: "To use the arts and intercultural learning in order to inspire a culture of peace and hope and educate for non-violent alternatives to create a sustainable, equitable, and harmonious earth society" (http://www.arts-for-peace.or). The *Peace Through Art methodology* developed by the International Child Art Foundation (ICAF, Sweden 2008) claims: "the Peace through Art methodology draws upon the creativity and imagination of young people… The methodology incorporates best **practices** from the **fields of** psychology, conflict resolution and peace education, while **employing the power of the arts for self-expression, healing and communication**" (author's emphasis) (http://en.wikipedia.org/wiki/Art_methodology).

The danger is that the applied aspect will 'swallow' the power of the artistic aspect, and will ruin it. Peace projects may lose their power to change hearts and minds because they may lose the artistic aesthetic core from which their power stems as I hope to make clear later.

As to the aspect of the arts for the sake of art, we can ask: Can any work of art, be it music, painting, or dance, have such an impact that could empower people to go out and stand up for the political cause they believe in? Take, for example, Picasso's painting, *Guernica*; it was painted in 1937, a few weeks after the Nazis had bombed Guernica. The painting is a biting demonstration against the evil they had done. The elements of pain, anguish and helplessness are seen from every single image in the painting. The impression is tremendous, and attracted world-wide responses then (as it does today), yet it did not empower people to go out, into the streets, and do something. There is an unbridgeable gap between reality and the modes of symbolization we use to represent reality, as Derrida teaches us. I do not know of any art that influences people to go and change their reality.

My point so far is that the power of arts lies not in the influence that it has on direct political change but on the influence on the mind and the spirit of the human beings in the deepest sense. This deepest sense cannot be evaluated or measured. The chance for a change depends on an ongoing education that would free the child's spirit, promote love of others as Montessori, for example, had already advocated in the early 1940s (Montessori, 1974/1946), and Eisner does nowadays (Eisner, 1998; 2002).

## Arts for Peace Education in Conflict Zones

One obvious division among *arts for peace education* programs is related to the context in which they take place. Programs that take place in a context of conflict are different from those which take place in peaceful places. Based on my experience and my research projects I have challenged the axiom that peace education via the arts is applicable to *all* stages of conflict and hostilities.

There is a determined Israeli struggle to ensure the life and security of the Jewish state, opposed by an on-going legitimate Palestinian struggle to create their own independent state. This setting serves as the modus operandi in which education is called to play its role. There are many projects in theatre/drama education, in music education, in the visual arts and in films, which have been implemented in schools in Israel. I, personally, was very much involved in this endeavor, believing in the power of arts education in developing a culture of discourse and respect for 'the other'.

However, the turn of events of September 11, 2001, as a turning point in the way in which the free world perceives terror and the murderous acts of terror in the heart of crowded cities in many places all over the world have triggered me to pause for a moment. To examine the question of **proximity between the arts (especially theatre) and life** from the viewpoint of the benefits we gain from educational arts projects for peace that involves (for example) Arabs and Jews.

My research studies in the context of the Israeli–Arab conflict (Schonmann, 2000, 2002, 2006), have taught me that the expectations from theatre-drama encounters between Arabs and Jews are not realistic. There is no such thing that working in the field of drama is working in a "safe environment". I have learned to be alert to the situation of the encounters in which we actually used "live ammunition", when we tried to use the theatre projects for a political change. The common assumption is that if the students are actively involved in arts projects, they can actually experience a situation, which is parallel to everyday life and this involvement can lead to insights which, in turn, can pave the way for personal change to resolve many conflicts.

Most of the research projects in theatre drama education do not dare to raise any doubt regarding the above sentiments and they are used like a "mantra" to justify the educational work. I was also in that stream until I reached the point where I can, regretfully, say that:

**Firstly: The proximity between life and theatre is the main danger while dealing in conflict situations.**

**And secondly: The 'contact theory' for solving problems is <u>not</u> suitable if one is in the midst of a violent conflict.**

The **instrumental function** of the arts in education, serving peace purposes in a conflict zone, based on my experience and research, resulted in failure. I can claim: **Arts should not be used as an instrument for political change because, as I have tried to argue, the arts should serve for the sake of art.**

The polar encounter between a tense life situation and a fictional situation building up, is too dangerous, and even an experienced teacher can sometimes fail to keep a very tense and potentially dangerous situation under control.

## The 'Contact Theory'

It is widely documented that many of the attitudes of Israeli Arabs and Jews toward each other are quite negative; they are rife with fear and prejudice. Contact does not always lead to positive changes in ethnic attitudes and relations (Ben-Ari and Amir, 1988). On the contrary, there is now enough research in sociology that shows that the face-to-face contact in tense conflicts can serve as a boomerang.

My claim is that most of the projects in *arts education for peace* are using the contact theory, Jews and Arabs working together in a **docu-media** model or in a **mosaic** model, or in a **kaleidoscopic** one (Schonmann, 1996). Because life in the Middle East is steeped in the culture of war and violence, arts projects cannot smooth away any real difficulties. It is too naïve to think that arts projects can facilitate a deep conflict situation. On the contrary, studies show that drama education activities can amplify the problems, and sharpen the stereotypes that one group has of the other; and that the mental images become even extreme (Schonmann, 2002, 2006). My point is that we have to admit that ethnic and national conflicts are usually prolonged, sometimes over decades; a solution to the clash between Israel and the Arabs is a long-term process that goes beyond the encounters of children's drama or theatre. The chance for a change, in this case, is beyond the power of any applied art.

## Closing Note

Back to the opening, I *do* follow many great thinkers such as John Dewey, Herbert Read, Nelson Goodman, Elliot Eisner and Maxine Greene in their ways of understanding that the *Arts* have a crucial function in education. They meant *arts per se*, not 'a tool for', but 'essence of'. Enhancing the artistic aesthetic dimension of the arts may enable each of us to polish the stars inside us as human beings. This is a real chance for a change.

## Note

In the above chapter I mentioned four works of mine which I consider to be the hard core of my research into Arts for Peace Education in Zones of Conflict.
- **JewishArab encounters in the drama/theatre classroom battlefield (1996)** was the first comprehensive study calling for dramatic representation as a meeting ground for oppositional forces in society, using Jewish-Arab encounters as an authentic mode

for deliberate reflections on the peace process in the Middle East in the shadow of war and hostility. The study investigated three projects, drawing conclusions, deriving models from the projects, and formulating hypotheses which are still to be tested.
- **Playing Peace: School Performance as an Aesthetic Mode of Knowing (2000)** analyzed a theatre project in two Israeli junior high schools, one in an Arab village and the other in a Jewish town. The study explored the meaning of "living" in an era of peace while preparing for a school performance celebrating peace.
- **The Quest for Peace: Some Reservations on Peace Education via Drama (2002)** re-examined the value of drama projects aimed at peace education in light of the renewed outburst of war between Israelis and Palestinians. The study criticizes the 'contact model' of solving problems, and points out its dangers and pitfalls.
- **Theatre as a Medium for Children and Young People: Images and Observations (2006)** is a book in which two chapters are devoted to school culture, questioning the power of arts in education. It reports on Arts for Peace projects and their power to build or to ruin a school's environment.

## References

Ben-Ari, R. & Amir, Y. (1988). Promoting relations between Arabs and Jewish youth. In Hoffman, J.H. et al. *Arab-Jewish relations in Israel: A quest in human understanding*. Bristol: Wyndham Hall Press.
Eisner, E. W. (1998). *The Kind of Schools We Need: Personal Essays*. Portsmouth, USA: Heinemann.
Eisner, E. (2002). *The Arts and the Creation of Mind*. New Haven: Yale University Press.
Harris, I. (2010). History of Peace Education. In: Salomon, G. and Cairns, E. (Eds.). *Handbook on Peace Education* (pp. 13-20). New York: Taylor and Francis Group, LLC.
Montessori, M. (1974). *Education for a New World*. Thiruvanmiyur, India: Kalashetra Press (original work published 1946).
Salomon, G. & Cairns, E. (2010). Peace education: Setting the Scene. In: Salomon, G. and Cairns, E. (Eds.). *Handbook on Peace Education* (pp. 1-7). New York: Taylor and Francis Group, LLC.
Salomon, G. & Cairns, E. (Eds.) (2010). *Handbook on Peace Education*. New York: Taylor and Francis Group, LLC.
Schonmann, S. (1996). JewishArab encounters in the drama/theatre classroom battlefield. *Research in Drama Education, 1(2)*, 175-188.
Schonmann, S. (2000). Playing peace: School performance as an aesthetic mode of knowing. *Contemporary Theatre Review, 10(2)*, 45-60.
Schonmann, S. (2002). The Quest for Peace: Some reservations on peace education via drama. *Drama Australia Journal 26(1)*, 15-26.
Schonmann, S. (2006). *Theatre as a Medium for Children and Young People: Images and Observations*. New York: Springer.

# Presentations given at The World Summit on Arts Education, Polylogue II, Wildbad Kreuth/Munich, Germany, May 2013

Nicole Pereira and Ralph Buck

# Building Community Well-Being: Global and Local Policy Intersections

The need for further research into arts education practices in New Zealand has been identified by the New Zealand Centre for Education Research (Ministry of Culture), with a particular focus on how arts education impacts on New Zealand's future social, economic and cultural prosperity (Bolstad, 2011). Within this context our pilot research project investigated how Auckland City Council's policies and practices intersected with UNESCO's global policies for the development of arts education.

This research project focused on how Auckland Council currently supports dance teaching and learning in the community. Mapping Auckland policy against UNESCO expectations may help in building a stronger understanding of how to foster the sustainability and growth of arts in urban community contexts. We acknowledge that the New Zealand National Curriculum (www.tki.org.nz) addresses dance education in formal education contexts and future study would be required to understand the interface between 'in' school and 'out' of school dance education.

This qualitative study began by acknowledging our perspectives as dance education and community dance research advocates (Bogdan & Biklen, 2007; Fraleigh & Hanstein, 1999; Marshall & Rossman, 2006; Robson & Foster, 1989). Our methodology focused upon comparative analysis (Hewitt-Taylor, 2001; Thorne, 2000) of the UNESCO Seoul Agenda (UNESCO, 2010) the UNESCO Road Map for Arts Education (UNESCO, 2006) and the Auckland City Council's current Auckland Plan for Arts and Culture (Auckland Council, 2013). This analysis was followed by semi-structured interviews (DiCicco-Bloom & Crabtree, 2006; Wengraf, 2001) with key policy staff in Auckland City Council. A comparative analysis of the data revealed the dominant themes in respect to policy differences.

This research was concerned with comparing and connecting global policies with local policies and actions in Auckland. It was evident through this research that there were some philosophical similarities between global trends on arts education and local policy and practices. The strongest intersection between the policies was in terms of a centralized focus on using arts as a vehicle to promote and foster the building of communities and enhancing social well-being. A key distinction that surfaced in the findings was Auckland Council's focus on arts as opposed to arts education. Interviews with policy officers at Auckland Council revealed the view that, "the council's role is not arts education" and the educational aspects should be left for formal education institutions (Raewyn Stone, personal communication, March 13, 2013). However, upon examining meanings around arts education and Auckland Councils' aims concerning the well-being of communities, we believe arts education certainly falls into their remit.

The significance of this research may be found in the potential for Auckland Council value adding to their current arts funding investment by making explicit connections with community based arts education practices. Our research found that Auckland Council may better fulfill their policy vision statements by systematically including arts education criteria and outcomes within project funding conditions. By adjusting policy they could more specifically address issues concerning building communities and fostering social well-being. This action may find a stronger alignment between UNESCO policy and local policy.

Our study also found that irrespective of the considerable international profile and energy invested in to the development of global UNESCO policies, the local Auckland Council policy officers had no knowledge of the UNESCO Seoul Agenda or the Road map. The Policy Officers were extremely interested in these documents and were very grateful that our research raised their awareness of these documents. However, it is clear much work needs to be done in making stronger connections between global and local policy, as everyone would benefit from sharing local and international perspectives.

This research was located in Auckland, New Zealand. It has been an interesting pilot study that may have value in being replicated in other cities. Making stronger connections between grass roots practice, needs, policy and global advocacy documents such as the Seoul Agenda is very important if arts education is indeed going to help build communities and develop social well-being.

## References

Auckland Council. (2013). *The Auckland Plan*. Retrieved from: http://theplan.theaucklandplan.govt.nz/

Bogdan R. C., & Biklen, S. K. (2007). *Qualitative research for education: An introduction to theories and models* (5th Ed.). Boston: Pearson Education.

Bolstad, R. (2011). *The contributions of learning in the arts to educational, social and economic outcomes*. Wellington: Ministry of Culture and Heritage.

DiCicco-Bloom, B., & Crabtree, B. F. (2006). The qualitative research interview. *Medical education, 40*(4), 314-321.

Fraleigh, S. H. & Hanstein, P. (1999). *Researching dance: Evolving modes of inquiry*. Pittsburgh: University of Pittsburgh Press.

Hewitt-Taylor, J. (2001). Use of constant comparative analysis in qualitative research. *Nursing Standard (Royal College of Nursing (Great Britain): 1987), 15*(42), 39.

Marshall, C. & Rossman, G. (2006). *Designing qualitative research*. Thousand Oaks, CA: Sage.

Robson, S. & Foster, A. (1989). Qualitative research in action. London: Edward Arnold.

Thorne, S. (2000). Data analysis in qualitative research. *Evidence Based Nursing, 3*(3), 68-70.

UNESCO. (2006). *Road Map for Arts Education* [The World Conference on Arts Education: Building Creative Capacities for the 21st century, Lisbon]. Retrieved from: http://www.unesco.org/new/fileadmin/MULTIMEDIA/HQ/CLT/CLT/pdf/Arts_Edu_RoadMap_en.pdf

UNESCO. (2010). *Seoul Agenda: Goals for the Development of Arts Education* [The Second World Conference on Arts Education]. Retrieved from: http://www.unesco.org/new/fileadmin/MULTIMEDIA/HQ/CLT/CLT/pdf/Seoul_Agenda_EN.pdf

Wengraf, T. (2001). *Qualitative research interviewing: Biographic narrative and semi-structured methods*. Sage.

Nicholas Rowe

# What Challenges face Students, Teachers and Researchers of Community Dance, within Cross-Cultural and Cross-Educational Contexts? A Sino-Kiwi Experience

Between the 18th-20th April, 2013 academic staff from the Beijing Dance Academy and University of Auckland Dance Studies Programme met in Beijing, China, for the *New Pathways and Meanings: Community Dance and Dance Education Symposium*. The aim of the meeting was to consider how our two institutions might collaborate to advance research and learning on community dance and dance in education in China. As the leading tertiary dance academy in China and the leading dance research institute in the Asia Pacific, our two institutions shared common goals yet came from very different educational and cultural backgrounds. The aim of the symposium was to investigate some of these differences, so that we might learn from each other and begin to re-construct common understandings, to move forward in partnership.

This investigation revealed three core differences, associated with the meanings of community, the relationship between community and dance and pedagogic philosophy.

The first distinction, over the meanings of 'community', can be traced to when the term was first introduced to China from English in the 1930s and transliterated into a compound of the words 'people' and 'place' (Rui, 2013). Community dance therefore came to be associated with the particular dances of particular regions, or what is considered in English to be folk dances, and the subsequent reconfiguration of folk dances into a performed spectacle (Hoerburger, 1968). By contrast, the English meaning of the term 'community' transformed throughout the 20th century into a socially constructed association that maintains no discrete boundaries or locations, but instead reflects a sense of belonging (Clarke, 1973; Williams, 1976; Anderson, 1991; Bhabha, 1994; Foley, 1995). This distinguished the very notion of community as a location that defines a group of people, to a way of being that people realize together.

The second distinction related to the function of dance in a community, and queried whether a community should serve a dance, or if dance should serve a community? We noted within this our alignment with different UNESCO mandates associated with dance and communities. For scholars from the BDA, the UNESCO *Convention on the Safeguarding of Intangible Cultural Heritage* emphasized how communities have responsibilities towards "...the production, safeguarding, maintenance and re-creation of the intangible cultural heritage" (UNESCO, 2003, para. 7). By contrast, the University of Auckland scholars sought to address the UNESCO *Seoul Agenda for Arts Education*, which calls upon communities to engage in dance education

"...to positively renew educational systems, to achieve crucial social and cultural objectives, and ultimately to benefit children, youth and lifelong learners of all ages." (UNESCO, 2011, p. 2)

This contrasted an approach that sought to work with communities to preserve dance heritage, with one that sought to use dance to sustain communities.

The third distinction noted differences in our pedagogic philosophies and approaches to teaching dance in higher education. These distinctions can be noted in the generic differences between Beijing Dance Academy's conservatory approach to dance education (Yuan, 1999; Jin, 2008) and the liberal arts approach of the University of Auckland Dance Studies Programme (Glyer & Weeks, 1998). This dance education might be further understood within the Beijing Dance Academy's cultural environment of Confucian education (Confucius, 1938), which requires dance students to recognize the pre-eminence of the knowledge of their teachers (Lv, 2000; Xiong, 2004; Zhao, 1989), with a dance education system informed by Freire (1972) and Dewey (1916), which requires that students co-construct with teachers and other students the dance knowledge that is relevant to them (Buck, 2006).

Despite the different scholarly histories we brought to the forum, the scholars from both institutions recognized in each other a mutual desire to use dance to enable people to belong and feel part of a larger collective, to feel both significance and solidarity. The above issues, and our pathways of understanding, are probed further within a forthcoming full-length journal article (Rowe, Buck, Martin & Lee, TBA).

## References

Anderson, B. (1991). *Imagined communities: reflections on the origins and spread of nationalism.* New York: Verso.
Bhabha, H. (1994). *The location of culture.* London: Routledge.
Buck, R. (2006). Teaching dance in the curriculum. In *Handbook of Physical Education*, ed. D. Kirk, D. McDonald and M. O'Sullivan, (703-719). London: Sage.
Clarke, D. B. (1973). The concept of community: A re-examination. *Sociological Review* 21, no. 3, 32-37.
Clifford, J. (1987). Of Other Peoples: Beyond the 'Salvage' Paradigm. In *Discussions in Contemporary Culture*, ed. H. Foster, (120-130). Seattle, WA: Bay Press.
Confucius. (1938). *The analects of Confucius* (A. Waley Trans.). London: G. Allen & Unwin.
Dewey, J. (1916). *Democracy and education.* New York, NY: Macmillan.
Foley, D. E. (1995). *The heartland chronicles.* Philadelphia: University of Pennsylvania Press.
Freire, P. (1972). *Pedagogy of the oppressed.* Harmondsworth, U.K.: Penguin.
Glyer, D., & Weeks, D. (1998). Liberal education: Initiating the conversation. In *The liberal arts in higher education*, ed. D. Glyer and D. Weeks, (ix-xxix). New York, NY: University Press of America.
Hoerburger, F. (1968). Once Again the Concept of Folk Dance. *The Journal of International Folk Music Council, 20*, (30-31).
Jin, Y. (2008). *Dance pedagogy at the Beijing Dance Academy: The learner's perspective.* Unpublished Master's Thesis, Dance Studies, The University of Auckland.
Lv, Y. (2000). *Chinese art education encyclopedia, dance volume: Dance education.* Shanghai: SMPH.

Rowe, N., Buck, R., Martin R. & Lee, P. (TBA). "The gaze or the groove? The future of community dance in China".
Rui, X. (2013). The modern transform of awareness and space of community in Chinese traditional dance. Paper presented at the *New meanings, new pathways: Community dance and dance education symposium*, Beijing, China, 18th–20th April, 2013.
UNESCO. (2003). *Text of the Convention for the Safeguarding of Intangible Cultural Heritage*. Retrieved on May 21 2013, from: http://www.unesco.org/culture/ich/index.php?lg=en&pg=00022
UNESCO. (2011). *Seoul Agenda: Goals for the Development of Arts Education*. Retrieved on May 24 2013, from: http://www.unesco.org/new/en/culture/themes/creativity/arts-education/official-texts/development-goals/
Williams, R. (1976). *Keywords: a vocabulary of culture and society*. Oxford: Oxford University Press.
Xi, X. (2009). *Constructing and challenging my personal meanings of dance education*. Unpublished Master's Thesis, Dance Studies, The University of Auckland.
Xiong, J. (2004). *Basic teaching materials and methodology in Chinese classical dance*. Shanghai: SMPH.
Yuan, H. (1999). *Chinese dance*. Shanghai: Shanghai wai yu jiao yu chu ban she.
Zhao, G. (1989). *Dance teaching psychology*. Beijing: Zhong Guo Wu Dao Chu Ban She.

Naomi Faik-Simet

# Undertaking Research for Dance Education
## A Collaborative Work between the Institute of Papua New Guinea Studies and the Port Moresby Grammar School

The Institute of Papua New Guinea Studies is a government cultural research institute established in 1974 with the primary aim to conduct research on Papua New Guinea's diverse cultures and traditions. Functioning at present, are three departments: Music and Dance, Ethnology and Literature. Maintaining the largest collection of Papua New Guinea's traditional music in the world, the Institute continues to function as the only research institute in the country responsible in the research and dissemination of cultural information.

The research method used by the Institute to collect data is mainly qualitative which involves the recording of traditional music/songs, dance and oral history. Interviews are carried out with informants who possess the knowledge of these practices. Ethnographic accounts of the various aspects of Papua New Guinea dance and music are published in books while music recordings are published in cassettes and compact discs. These materials are kept in the archive and are further used for research and educational purposes.

More recently, the Institute is exploring new methods of research in the area of dance education. This is to meet the growing needs of young people in formal and non-formal sectors who have developed an interest in learning and performing a traditional dance. An observational study was trialed in April this year at the Port Moresby Grammar School on a certain dance called *libung* – a traditional Tolai dance performed by the East New Britain people. The dance was performed by some female students during the school's Foundation Day celebrations. The school has made it compulsory for all students to participate in traditional dancing as a way of promoting cultural development as part of their curriculum. Traditional dance teachers/choreographers are engaged by the school to teach dance to students as one way of addressing the issue of cultural competency in schools.

Results from this work has been used by the Institute of Papua New Guinea Studies (PNG Studies) in advocating for the need for schools to work in partnership with traditional dance teachers who possess the knowledge and skills to teach dance for cultural maintenance and awareness amongst the young. The Institute is now working closely with schools and the Education department in providing research information on the importance of dance to education such as its contribution to the current arts and culture syllabus (still in draft form) for secondary school teachers.

Cultural development has now become an area for learning from early childhood to tertiary levels of education. More collaboration work between teachers, students, parents and traditional dance/arts practitioners, stake-holders and cultural institutions to implement arts and culture education in the country. Institute of PNG Studies is challenged to take on new research methods such as the phenomenological approach aimed at getting the best results to advance the cause for dance education in the country.

Lily Chen-Hafteck

# Educating the Creative Mind Project: Bringing Arts-Based Education to Every Child

Preschool is a critical period in learning and in achieving social justice in education; as such influence can be most crucial for children from underserved populations at this stage while the gap in scholastic achievement between them and other children is still minimal. Young children naturally love the arts, as observed from their engagement in activities such as singing, drawing, dancing, and dramatizing. It is therefore vital to provide these children with ample arts experiences that will develop their life-long interest in the arts. Unfortunately, the current budget situation in American public education has led to a decrease in time for the arts in the classroom. Children have to focus on academic subjects such as Language Arts and Math as soon as they start school, without adequate opportunities for expressing themselves and creating through the arts.

The *Educating the Creative Mind* Project aims to bring a well-rounded education to children. Besides cultivating life-long interest in music and the arts that will enrich children's lives, an arts-based interdisciplinary curriculum can also help children develop an interest in learning which will in turn enhance success in school.

The project started with an international conference in 2010, featuring a renowned educator as keynote speaker and bringing government officials, school administrators, scholars, teachers together to discuss the challenges and solutions in bringing comprehensive arts-based education to public school. In June 2012, a yearlong professional development project supported by a grant from National Endowment for the Arts started. 27 teachers and 7 administrators (supervisors and principals) working in school districts of low-income families participated in the project. Music teachers worked together with visual arts teachers and general pre-kindergarten and kindergarten classroom teachers at *the Music, Arts and Interdisciplinary Institute*. It was a two-day workshop that provided professional development to incorporate creative arts in early childhood classroom, highlighting the significance of interdisciplinary curriculum and collaboration among teachers. Following the workshop, teachers implemented the newly acquired methods into their classrooms and project mentors provided support by visiting the classes and providing comments and suggestions through discussion and written observational reports. Project evaluation includes pre- and post-project questionnaires and interviews, as well as teacher and mentor reports. In May 2013, the Educating the Creative Mind Conference II was held where the participating teachers presented their work in the classroom. The grant also supported free registration for 200 schoolteachers to attend the conference so that they were able to learn about the interdisciplinary arts-based curriculum most effectively by observing how their peers (rather than experts) implement the approach. The final report of the project was published and distributed widely to school administrators and teachers for the purpose of disseminating the *Educating the Creative Mind* approach.

The project was a success. By the end of the project, the participating teachers increased their interest and commitment to the arts, and developed skills and understandings on arts-based interdisciplinary education. They implemented these learning in their teaching and became more confident with using the arts in the classroom.

Andrea Creech

# Community Opera in a Centre of Excellence: An Instrumental Case Study

## Introduction

This paper sets out an 'instrumental case study' approach to evaluation of an intergenerational community opera project. In this approach, the case study provides insight into a wider issue. The case, described in rich detail, may be accessed vicariously and contributes to a deep understanding of the broad principles and practices that it exemplifies (Stake, 1995).

The case analysed here demonstrates the principle that when individuals from mixed generations have access to quality opportunities and expert support they will collectively rise to the challenge, achieving remarkable things. In particular, the case provides an example of how an intergenerational music project supported participants of all ages in developing positive 'possible selves' (Markus & Nurius, 1986). The context is the Glyndebourne Opera House in England, where a specially commissioned community opera, entitled 'Imago', focused on the theme of ageing in a digital world. A key feature of Imago was the juxtaposition of intergenerational community singers and instrumentalists (aged 14-76) alongside young aspiring musicians on the cusp of professional careers, professional soloists, and a creative, technical, and administrative team of international stature, within a centre of artistic excellence.

## Possible Selves

The idea of 'possible selves' refers to psychologically accessible and elaborately understood ideal and hoped-for selves, as well as 'lost and found' possible selves (King & Hicks, 2007). Possible selves are not restricted to youth. We continue to develop dynamic and varied possible selves, and in some cases rediscover lost possible selves, throughout our lifetimes (Smith & Freund, 2002). The Imago project offered experiences that supported musical possible selves, as well as possible selves related to the challenges of later life.

## Evaluation Methods

The Imago project was evaluated, using mixed methods in order to capture a rich picture of personal, social, and musical processes and outcomes. Participants included Glyndebourne staff, community chorus and orchestra members, professional singers and orchestral musicians, and the creative team. Data were collected via questionnaires, interviews, focus groups, observations and email diaries.

## Key Findings

### A Context of Musical Excellence

It has been well-established that music has a powerful effect on our emotions, moods and behaviour, influencing social, emotional and cognitive outcomes. The Imago project offered a powerful context of musical excellence, within which participants had the scope to access and develop possible selves.

### Intergenerational Dynamics and Possible Selves

A special facet of Imago was its intergenerational dynamic. The story itself captured issues that were relevant to people at all stages of the life-course, from childhood through to old age.

The factor that was unanimously identified as being key to the successful intergenerational dynamic was that the different groups were united in striving towards a common, challenging goal. This in turn generated rich opportunities for mutual support, social bonding, and peer learning.

Younger adults developed positive possible selves concerned with active ageing and possibilities in life, through their interactions with the elders chorus. Through interactions with the younger groups, the elders rekindled lost possible selves as performers and valued members of a creative community.

### Professionals and Community Members: Supporting Possible Selves

Imago offered opportunities for nurturing possible musical and creative selves, at every level of the production. Community chorus members spoke of developing self-concept as performers, underpinned by the experience of progression in terms of discipline, commitment and professionalism as well as their cohesiveness as an ensemble. For aspiring professionals, Imago was a major step on a progression pathway in music, offering an opportunity to work alongside professionals within a centre of international excellence. For professionals too, there were opportunities for rich development of musicianship and artistry, as well as a renewed sense of the joy in singing.

## Conclusion

This case study demonstrates that creative arts projects may offer a rich context where intergenerational groups can together develop salient possible selves in a number of domains. A combination of factors contributed to the powerful reported outcomes of Imago.

First, the opera had the community element embedded within it as opposed to being an 'add-on'. Secondly, the project took place at a centre of international excellence, offering the opportunity for an authentic experience of excellence. Thirdly, the story line addressed issues such as ageing and the digital age, which have high relevance within our current social context and were therefore domains where possible selves were salient for individuals. Finally, the intergenerational nature of the project was inclusive, providing opportunities for cross-generational peer learning and social bonds to develop amongst individuals from diverse backgrounds.

Creative projects, supported by excellent resources, may be particularly important in contributing to an understanding of ageing amongst younger generations, while amongst older people the benefits may relate to lifelong learning and vitality. A context that offers the opportunity for community members to collaborate with professionals within an intergenerational context may be particularly powerful with regard to the potential for positive possible selves to flourish.

## References

Cross, S., & Markus, H. (1991). Possible selves across the life span. *Human Development, 34*(4), 230-255.

King, L., & Hicks, J. (2007). Lost and found possible selves: Goals, development and well-being. *New Directions for Adult and Continuing Education, 114*(Summer), 27-37.

Markus, H., & Nurius, P. (1986). Possible selves. *American Psychologist, 41*(9), 954-969.

Smith, J., & Freund, A. M. (2002). The dynamics of possible selves in old age. *The Journals of Gerontology Series B: Psychological Sciences and Social Sciences, 57*(6), P492-P500.

Stake, R. E. (1995). *The art of case study research*. Thousand Oaks, CA: Sage.

Ann Kipling Brown, Susan R. Koff, Jeff Meiners and Charlotte Svendler Nielsen
# Dance Learning in Motion: Global Dance Education

Reports indicate that dance educators have the best intentions when offering dance experiences for young people and provide pre-service and in-service programs and professional development for those who teach dance in formal and non-formal settings. There is support of major dance and arts organizations as well as the goals of UNESCO that affirm the importance of arts education and encourage the research and practice to provide lifelong and intergenerational learning in, about and through arts education and, in this case, dance education. However, while we advocate for the inclusion of the arts and dance, there is a need to create insight into what is being taught and how young people experience this and indeed how it reflects the goals of a basic education as it is described in most core curricula at different places around the world. How does dance assist in achieving a sustainable future where the demands of the global situation requires a broader understanding of society, economics and the environment? How does dance provide those basic skills to think about different issues from different points of view, ask questions, and analyze information from various sources? What does it demand from dance educators teaching in formal as well as non-formal settings? What experiences are important to them in their teaching of young people?

People dance for example for professional, recreational and social reasons. Many dance for fun and for health and in many contexts dance is as popular as ever and participation is increasing. Recurrent dance experiences and intrinsic benefits of dance add value to people's lives, such as the growth of one's capacity to participate imaginatively and sense, perceive and judge for oneself not only in dance and the arts but also in response to social and political issues. Dance is important in education, health, human relations and social connections. And yet, there are still many young people who do not have access to dance experiences.

The authors of this chapter are initiating a study that involves several countries (Finland, Ghana, USA, Denmark, Germany, Australia, Canada, Netherlands, New Zealand, Taiwan, Brazil and Hong Kong) in ascertaining the provision of dance learning for young people in both formal and non-formal settings. The focus of this study is to present a review of existing literature in the field of dance teacher education which identifies the dance experiences that are being offered to young people. Additionally, the literature reviewed will provide the basis for further study into how young people engage in dance and how their experiences contribute to their chosen lifestyles and careers.

Susan A. O'Neill

# Engagement in the Arts

Engagement in the arts is about purposeful and meaningful learning. Engaged learners value and have a well-informed understanding of their involvement in an arts activity. They derive from their engagement a sense of relevance, purpose, and fulfillment (O'Neill, 2006; 2012). Conceptually, arts engagement is related to both student engagement and activity involvement research. Although student engagement is a relatively underdeveloped and loosely defined construct (Martin, 2007), it tends to focus on what students do when they move from being motivated to actively learning (Furrer & Skinner, 2003). It has been described as the foundation for learning and "the glue that binds it together" (Bryson & Hand, 2007, p. 60). Activity involvement research tends to focus on two components: psychological (e.g., values, meaningfulness, identity, sense of belonging), and behavioral (e.g., effort, intensity, focused concentration). It also has a dynamic nature that is moderated by individual differences and is context-dependent within interrelated personal, social, and systemic ecologies (Rose-Krasnor, 2009). Arts engagement is also embedded in sociocultural and ecological systems that combine learning with artistic creativity (Bailin, 2005) and creative expression (Csikzentmihalyi, 1988).

Not all learners are engaged in arts activities in a meaningful way. For example, music-making may refer to repetitive banging on a drum, art work may refer to scribbling, and dance may refer to minimal gestures or uncoordinated movement. According to Karkou and Glasman (2004), "this wide interpretation of what the arts stand for allows for a number of possibilities [...] to become engaged and to achieve a first level of social inclusion" (p. 61). Some youth may merely 'show up' to participate in an activity, often because it is expected of them or they want to be with their friends (Pittman, 1992). They may have little understanding of the value and importance of such activities beyond any immediate or obvious benefit they might see. Others may take on leadership roles and/or become advocates for the value of the arts for social change. They may introduce others to arts activities and gain a sense of empowerment and personal fulfillment by doing so.

For young people to be engaged meaningfully in arts activities – what Sternberg (2005) refers to as *purposeful engagement* – they need to develop a growth mindset (Dweck, 2006). A growth mindset is characterized by a passion for learning, the active seeking of challenges, a valuing of effort, and the resiliency necessary to persist in the face of obstacles or adversity (Pintrich, 2003). Larson (2000) argued that focused concentration and self-directed attention on challenging tasks is a key feature of young people's engagement in arts activities (Csikszentmihalyi et al., 1993; Larson & Kleiber, 1993). He related this to Dewey's (1913) notion of "voluntary attention" and argued that people's self-directed attention during arts activities resembles the "flow" experiences described by Csikszentmihalyi (1975). Csikszentmihalyi's (1990) concept of "flow" experience refers to engagement in a challenging activity that requires skills, as long as the quality of skills precisely matches the level of challenge. Csikszentmihalyi began thinking about engagement in arts activities when he was studying the creative process in the 1960s. He wondered why an artist would persist with a painting when it was going well, "single-mindedly, disregarding hunger, fatigue, and discomfort" (Nakamura & Csikszentmihalyi, 2002, p. 89). And yet, once it was completed the artist seemed to quickly lose interest in the artistic creation altogether. This phenomenon of intrinsically motivated activity "flow" research in the arts has continued since the 1980s.

Over the past two decades, increased attention has been focused on the decline in young people's beliefs and values in music and other arts areas. For example, my colleague Gary McPherson and I analyzed a survey of musical and artistic beliefs and values from over 24,000 elementary and secondary school students from Brazil, China, Finland, Hong Kong, Israel, Korea, Mexico, and the United States (McPherson & O'Neill, 2010). We found that learners generally hold lower expectations for becoming competent in music and visual arts and value these activities less than other subjects at school. Green (2001) and others have argued that the meaning of arts activities, the central role it plays in the emotional lives of learners, and informal learning strategies are often at odds with many formal or school arts education agendas. Further, in a climate of public accountability and demands for improved standards of performance, "it is all too easy for the 'person' of the learner and the processes and relationships of learning to be eclipsed by a 'high stakes' focus on learning outcomes" (Deakin Crick & Wilson, 2005, p. 6). In a systematic review of research from around the world on the impact of summative assessment on students' motivation for learning, researchers found that this "overfocus" on performance outcomes has a negative impact on what learners think and feel about themselves as learners, how they perceive their capacity to learn, and their energy for learning (Harlen & Deakin Crick, 2003).

Today, within the context of learner-centered educational approaches and constructivist theory based on Vygotsky (1978), engagement in the arts is viewed as a transitional, transactional and transformational process. It is transitional in the sense that learners' internal processes (e.g., thoughts, emotions, hopes, desires) come to be internalized through interactions with the environment, and are continuously modified through relational negotiations. Arts engagement is transactional because the more deeply students experience a sense of connectedness with people and larger contexts, such as those provided by schools, the more they are likely to internalize the beliefs and values and quality of relationships that will sustain their interest and engagement. Without meaningful, supportive relationships, extrinsic motivators are unlikely to be internalized or influential in promoting positive and deep arts engagement (Toshalis & Nakkula, 2012). According to Bresler (2009), connection is an essential part of all artistic activities, and yet, different arts areas achieve connection differently and need to be examined for their unique complexity and impacts on learning. Finally, engagement in the arts is transformational in that if often leads to perspective transformations (Mezirow, 1991), which in turn lead to actions or choices based on new and emergent understandings. I refer to this as *transformative arts engagement* – a learner-centred approach that fosters agency and empowers learners to be autonomous, self-directed learners. It combines a sense of connectedness and emotional engagement (Furrer & Skinner, 2003) with a capacity for reflective self-awareness (Ridley, 1991) and an impassioned spirit that recognizes "visions of still untapped possibility" (Greene, 1990, p. 67).

Transformative arts engagement may be especially important for learners in the 21$^{st}$ century who are experiencing an unprecedented amount of noise, distraction and fragmentation in their lives through fast changing advances in digital media technologies (OECD, 2012). Technology has also created an unprecedented amount of autonomy in young people's arts engagement, with identity and agency becoming more intertwined (Holland, Lachicotte, Skinner & Cain, 1998) and learning environments more participatory in "youth-only" spaces (Goldman, Booker & McDermott, 2008). We need a better understanding of how young people's artistic representations or "user created content" within the new digital media landscape make aesthetic and artistic forms of engagement part of the process of knowledge production and meaning making in their everyday lives. A recent report by the National Endowment for the Arts concluded, "the settings in which [people] choose to engage in arts activities have long expanded well beyond purpose-built arts facilities, moving into bookstores, community centers, schools, places of worship, and especially the home" (Novak-Leonard & Brown, 2011, p. 15). Future research is needed into the multiple contexts and pathways through which youth are engaged in the arts if we are to challenge narrow conceptions and optimize arts engagement across diverse learners and educational contexts around the world.

## References

Bailin, S. (2005). Artistic creativity: A cross-cultural perspective. *Childhood and Society, 1*(2), 9-26.
Bresler, L. (2009). Research education shaped by musical sensibilities. *British Journal of Music Education, 26*(1), 7-25.
Bryson, C., & Hand, L. (2007, July). *Promoting student engagement.* Higher Education Research & Development Society of Australia Conference, Adelaide.
Csikszentmihalyi, M. (1975). *Beyond boredom and anxiety: The experience of play in work and games.* San Francisco: Jossey-Bass.
Csikzentmihalyi, M. (1988). Society, culture, and person: A systems view of creativity. In R. Sternberg (Ed.), *The Nature of Creativity: Contemporary Psychological Perspectives* (pp. 325-339). Cambridge University Press.
Csikszentmihalyi, M. (1990). *Flow: The psychology of optimal experience.* New York: Harper-Collins.
Csikszentmihalyi, M., Rathunde, K., & Whalen, S. (1993). *Talented teenagers: The roots of success and failure.* Cambridge: Cambridge University Press.
Deakin Crick, R., & Wilson, K. (2005). Being a learner: A virtue for the 21$^{st}$ century. *British Journal of Educational Studies, 53*(3), 359-374.
Dewey, J. (1913). *Interest and effort in education.* Carbondale: Southern Illinois University Press.
Dweck, C. S. (2006). *Mindset: The new psychology of success.* New York: Ballantine Books.
Furrer, C., & Skinner, E. (2003). Sense of relatedness as a ractor in children's academic engagement and performance. *Journal of Educational Psychology, 95*(1), 148-162.
Goldman, S., Booker, S., & McDermott, M. (2008). Mixing the digital, social, and cultural: Learning, identity, and agency in youth participation. In D. Buckingham (Ed.), *Youth,*

*identity, and digital Media* (pp. 185-206). Cambridge, MA: The MIT Press. doi: 10.1162/dmal.9780262524834.185

Green, L. (2001). *How popular musicians learn: A way ahead for music education*. Aldershot, Hants: Ashgate.

Greene, M. (1990). The passion of the possible: Choice, multiplicity, and commitment. *Journal of Moral Education, 19*(2), 67-76.

Harlen, W., & Deakin Crick, R. (2003). Testing and motivation for learning. *Assessment in Education, 10*(2), 169-208.

Holland, D., Lachicotte, W., Skinner, D., & Cain, C. (1998). *Identity and agency in cultural worlds*. Cambridge, MA: Harvard University Press.

Karkou, V., & Glasman, J. (2004). Arts, education and society: the role of the arts in promoting the emotional wellbeing and social inclusion of young people. *Support for Learning, 19*(2), 57-65.

Larson, R. W. (2000). Toward a psychology of positive youth development. *American Psychologist, 55*(1), 170-183. doi 10.1037//0003-066X,55.1.170

Larson, R. W., & Kleiber, D. (1993). Daily experience of adolescents. In P. Tolan & B. Cohler (Eds.), *Handbook of clinical research and practice with adolescents* (pp. 125-145). New York: Wiley.

Martin, A. J. (2007). Examining a multidimensional model of student motivation and engagement using a construct validation approach. *British Journal of Educational Psychology, 77*, 413-440.

McPherson, G. E., & O'Neill, S. A. (2010). Students' motivation to study music as compared to other school subjects: A comparison of eight countries. *Research Studies in Music Education, 32*(2), 1-37.

Mezirow, J. (1991). *Transformative dimensions of adult learning*. San Francisco: Jossey-Bass.

Nakamura, J., & Csikszentmihalyi, M. (2002). The concept of flow. In C. R. Snyder & S. J. Lopez (Eds.), *Handbook of positive psychology* (pp. 89-105). New York: Oxford University Press.

Novak-Leonard, J. L., & Brown, A. S. (2011). *Beyond attendance: A multi-modal understanding of arts participation*. National Endowment for the Arts, Washington, DC. Retrieved from http://www.giarts.org/sites/default/files/beyond-attendance-multi-modal-understanding-of-arts-participation%20.pdf

O'Neill, S. A. (2006). Positive youth musical engagement. In G. McPherson (Ed.), *The child as musician: A handbook of musical development* (pp. 461-474). New York: Oxford University Press.

O'Neill, S. A. (2012). Becoming a music learner: Towards a theory of transformative music engagement. In G. E. McPherson & G. Welch (Eds.), *The Oxford handbook of music education* (Vol. 1, pp. 163-186). New York: Oxford University Press.

OECD (2012). *Connected Minds: Technology and Today's Learners*. Educational Research and Innovation, OECD Publishing. http://dx.doi.org/10.1787/9789264111011-en.

Pintrich, P. R. (2003). A motivational science perspective on the role of student motivation in learning and teaching contexts. *Journal of Educational Psychology, 95*, 667-686.

Pittman, K. J. (1992). *Defining the fourth R: Promoting youth development*. Washington, DC: Center for Youth Development and Policy Research.

Ridley, D. S. (1991). Reflective self-awareness: A basic motivational process. *Journal of Experimental Education, 60*(1) 31-48.

Rose-Krasnor, L. (2009). Future directions in youth involvement research. *Social Development, 18* (2), 497-509.

Sternberg, R. J. (2005). Intelligence, competence, and expertise. In A. Elliot and C. S. Dweck (Eds.), *The handbook of competence and motivation* (pp. 15-30). New York, NY: Guilford Press.

Toshalis, E., & Nakkula, M. J. (2012). *Motivation, engagement, and student voice: The students at the center series*. Boston, MA: Jobs for the Future.

Vygotsky, L. S. (1978). *Mind and society. The development of higher psychological processes*. Cambridge, MA: Harvard University Press.

Patricia A. González Moreno

# Creating and Fostering Partnerships to enhance Arts Education: Challenges and Opportunities

It is well known that partnerships in arts education can enhance the provision of and access to the arts for all people. In the technological area, it is also evident that information and communication technologies (ICT) facilitate the development of arts partnerships and serve as a means to advocate and develop the arts through the democratization and mobilization of knowledge and access to successful practices. This paper offers a specific example of international partnerships for professional development in the arts based on a series of webinars involving educational institutions in Canada, England, Mexico, and the United States, with diverse audiences (undergraduate and graduate students, in-service teachers, professors, and practitioners). The aim of this project was to raise the quality of arts education in higher education that it could permeate other educational levels, and to foster communication and collaboration among researchers and practitioners.

In a blended model of learning, the groups of participants gather in each institution where the simultaneous transmission takes place. After each presentation, a period of questions and answers facilitates the interaction of ideas with the speaker and among audiences. A wide range of topics on arts education has been addressed, including arts disciplines such as music, visual arts, and dance.

A research study has been conducted that aimed to examine the motivational profile of participants in the hosting institution. Based on the theoretical framework of Eccles et al. (1983), it investigated the participants' expectations (perceptions of competence, confidence, and difficulty) and values attributed to participating in the program (interest, importance, usefulness, cost), through questionnaires, observations, and interviews. Preliminary results (González-Moreno, 2012) showed that participants held overall high perceptions of value. Among the environmental factors that positively influenced their experience in the program are the relevance of the topic, expected quality, and speakers' expertise. However, participants' response was less strongly determined by external encouragement to attend (i.e., by educational authorities and job supervisors). Environmental factors that negatively affected their continuous participation included job and academic responsibilities, lack of information and provision of additional programs for professional development, and lack of external incentives for participation. However, when asked about their experience with this type of blended model of learning, the participants attributed a lower cost to participate than traditional models of learning.

Results from the study suggest the expanding possibilities in the use of ICT to increase access to current research-based knowledge, but participation and engagement are still highly dependent on the support of educational authorities and other agents. It was also evident that personal efforts need to be made to strengthen collaboration and support among colleagues within and across arts disciplines in order to reduce teacher resistance.

The use of ICT also implies challenges and limitations (e.g., time constraints, technical flaws, and limited interaction). Nonetheless, the positive outcomes overcome those challenges. ICT increases the opportunities to enhance communication, knowledge exchange, cultural understanding, and critical thinking, as well as national and international collaboration among researchers and practitioners, with reduced costs for researchers, participants, and organizers.

## References

Eccles (Parsons), J., Adlre, T. F., Futterman, R., Goff, S. B., Kaczala, C. M., Meece, J. L., et al. (1983). Expectancies, values, and academic behaviors. In J. T. Spence (Ed.), *Achievement and achievement motivation: Psychological and sociological approaches* (pp. 75-146). San Francisco, CA: W. H. Freeman.

González-Moreno, P. A. (2012). *Impact of a technology-based program for professional development in music and music education.* Paper presented at the Twenty-Fourth International Seminar of Research in Music Education of the International Society for Music Education, Thessaloniki, Greece.

Sergio Figueiredo

# Why Advocacy? Music and Arts Education in the Brazilian Context

This text presents a discussion of advocacy in the Brazilian context, including the need for a broader view of advocacy and its role in preparing arts and music teachers.

## Why Advocacy?

Music is unquestionably a trait of the human experience. A growing body of literature argues in favor of music and arts in the formation of individuals. However, there still is need for more thorough discussion regarding the value of music and arts in education.

Although the ubiquitous presence of the arts in human lives could be an argument against the need for arts in education, Reimer (2005) reminds us, with respect to music, that a number of philosophers and scholars have affirmed that

> music is so basic to the human condition, so foundational for a life well lived, so humanizing in its powers to deepen and widen what people can experience, as to be not only worthy of inclusion as a basic school subject but essential if all people, including youngsters, are to realize the potentials their humanity affords. (p. 1)

If music is basic to the human condition, why do so many people still lack access to music education and how can the situation be remedied? Advocacy could be a powerful tool to help build a worthy space for music in the formation of human beings, whether in schools or in other non-formal environments.

Mota and Figueiredo (2012) discuss and consider the need to 'reframe' the concepts of advocacy. They suggest three different domains for discussion. In the first domain, "advocacy appears as a logical form of lobbying, a professional activity that should be performed by those who are in the best position to tell and persuade politicians why music education is essential" (Mota & Figueiredo, 2012, p. 189). In political action advocacy, the need is to convince administrators that music and arts education have an important place in preparing citizens.

In the second domain, scholars bring findings from the cognitive neurosciences to support the importance of music education. Neuroscience research has shown that music and arts education have a positive impact on human cognition. According to Gruhn, music "stimulates the growth of brain structures and connects many activated brain areas" (2005, p. 100). Peretz reinforces this finding: "Music is unique. Musical abilities flourish independently, without much assistance from other cognitive and affective systems" (2005, p. 104). Thus, advocates can point to a number of benefits of music education which have been established scientifically.

In the third domain, Mota and Figueiredo focus on Bowman's ideas of advocacy as a tool. Bowman explains: "like all tools, it [advocacy] may be useful. But like all tools it has its limitations and potential dangers, its proper and improper uses" (2009, p. 1). Specifically, Bowman cautions the "passion for advocacy" could supplant other tools that are important "to the future of our profession". In particular, advocacy should not become a substitute for philosophical inquiry, which Bowman considers a powerful and relevant tool for exploring the value of music education. In addition, Bowman argues, "involvement in music does not automatically lead to desirable educational outcomes" (p. 2). Bowman (2009) reinforces that "advocacy is a useful and sometimes an important tool. It is no substitute, however, for philosophical inquiry or for professional decision making based on local needs and circumstances" (p. 9).

## The Brazilian Context

The status of music and arts education in Brazil, in schools and other educational contexts, exemplifies the need for balance between advocacy and philosophical inquiry.

Brazil is a huge country characterized by tremendous cultural diversity. To think about music education in Brazil is to acknowledge a multitude of perspectives, which raises a crucial question: What kind of music education serves in the Brazilian context? Coupled with this question is the issue of investing in music teacher preparation, which assumes a national commitment to music education in and out of schools.

The preparation of music teachers in Brazil is currently a major challenge. Ongoing research has shown that less than 30% of students in undergraduate courses for music educators intend to teach in regular public schools (Figueiredo & Soares, 2012). On one hand, we are advocating for music in schools, while, on the other hand, we do not have enough professional music teachers to offer music education in schools.

In 1971, a Brazilian law established that *Educação Artística* – Artistic Education – was a required subject in school curriculums. However, one teacher was responsible for teaching all artistic disciplines. As a result, the quality of arts education decreased and many music educators decided to deliver private lessons or work in specialized schools. From that period, music became one of the least offered arts activities in regular schools, especially in public educational systems.

In 1996, a new law changed *Educação Artística* to *Arte* (Arts), without defining what areas should be taught. In 2008, as a result of a national movement championing music in schools, a new law (11769) established music as a compulsory content in school curriculums. Advocacy was a powerful tool in the process of forming and passing this law.

The 2008 law made music education compulsory, but further advocacy is required in order to convince local administrators to implement music education in schools. Many administrators continue the old-fashioned tradition of having one teacher to teach all the arts.

Our advocacy is now focused on the quality of music education practices we would like to see in schools. Here, I remember Bowman's arguments regarding the need for philosophical inquiry beyond advocacy. Convincing politicians and administrators of the importance of music in schools is one part of the process, but the quality of music education depends on other factors beyond political action. As we advocate for the arts to have a place in the school curriculum, we need to be conscious of our responsibility regarding the consistency of this teaching.

To summarize our main points:
1. We need advocacy to convince politicians and educational administrators that music and arts education are essential, which implies changing the official orientation to the arts and how they should be taught in different contexts;
2. we need suitable equipment to develop significant experiences with the students;
3. and, primarily, we need teachers in the diverse arts disciplines who are committed to developing significant experiences for all students.

In meeting these three needs, advocacy and critical thinking are equally necessary. Our first responsibility is to argue, convince, and guarantee that arts education is part of the school curriculum for all students, including offering students opportunities to learn how the arts have historically contributed to human experiences everywhere. Our second, but no less important, responsibility is to ensure that high quality arts education experiences are offered in schools, and this requires professional teachers who are very well prepared for the continuing challenges of basic education in a changing world.

## Final Thoughts

Advocacy and critical thinking are intertwined. In advocating for significant arts education and seeking to convince people, we need to understand the importance of arts in education. As Bowman points out, putting ideas into practice requires the critical assessment of specific circumstances and contextual variables (2007, 2009).

Connecting advocacy to philosophical praxis is essential to deepen our discernment of what kind of music and arts education are appropriate in specific contexts. In Brazil, we are facing a lot of challenges, but, beyond the difficulties, a number of successful experiences in different parts of the country offer encouragement. Such positive experiences move us forward. In other words, a democratic music education is possible when we have a collective endeavor to make a better world, in which music and arts education are accessible to every person in our country.

# References

Bowman, W. (2007). Who is the 'We'? Rethinking professionalism in music education. *Action, Criticism, and Theory for Music Education, 6*(4), 109–131.

Bowman, W. (2009). *Music & Music Education Advocacy from Critical Perspective. IMC World Forum on Music, Tunis, Tunisia* (pp. 1-10). Retrieved from: http://www.gregsandow.com/BookBlog/Wayne_Bowman_Tunis.pdf

Figueiredo, S. L. F. & Soares, J. (2012). Music teacher's experiences of initial teacher preparation in Brazil: a broad perspective. Thessaloniki, Greece: ISME. *Conference Proceedings of the 30th ISME World Conference* (pp. 339-343).

Gruhn, W. (2005). Children need music. *International Journal of Music Education, 23*(2), 99-101.

Mota, G. & Figueiredo, S. (2012). Initiating Music Programs in New Contexts: In *Search of a Democratic Music Education. The Oxford Handbook of Music Education.* Oxford: Oxford University Press (pp. 59-70).

Peretz, I. (2005). The nature of music. *International Journal of Music Education, 23*(2), 103-105.

Reimer, B. (2005). The danger of music education advocacy. *International Journal of Music Education, 23*(2), 139-142.

Samia ElSheikh and Mai Nour

# Curriculum Development and Change are a Need to the Community in Egypt

Egyptian curriculum development and change over the past thirty years were affected by the community needs. Thirty years ago, art education was obsolete and categorized as a non-important subject in school programs. The community gave more importance to science, math, language, and social studies. This was due to the Egyptian education system's practice of distributing higher score students to science-related colleges (a process of distributing graduates in Egypt according to their scores in high school).

With time, people came to believe that a higher score was the only way to reach the top colleges and is the final objective for their children. Building up the students' personality was not a goal. So, schools neglected all arts activities such as art, music and sports classes. They replaced those classes with more important subjects as they believed. Arts teachers started to abandon teaching and look for other jobs.

In the '90s the community began to become dissatisfied with general education and people started to look for private schools. Private schools concentrated on an ideal education and followed an international curriculum. It took time for private schools to be approved by society and general education authorities. People observed that private school students became more independent and developed a better personality and character. Arts education became important again.

The community influenced education providers and in the last few years art teachers began to open art centers outside school systems. Private art centers now present art workshops in all art fields such as painting, printmaking and hand crafts. But they are not aware of their educational role. Art education is not merely a series of workshops teaching art techniques. It is a body of knowledge and techniques aimed at developing awareness. Now, the general education system needs to improve its curricula and put art education back "on the map" of a comprehensive education. An important step towards achieving this goal is the linking of schools and community through conferences. In 2013 there was a conference: Arts and Education in the Third Millennium. Researchers agreed on the following recommendations:
- Curricula and programs should include arts education with good attention to the development of creative thinking skills as a requirement for the development of society.
- Reconsidering the return of art education as an fundamental subject compared to other scientific subjects.
- Activating art activities to foster self-confidence and creativity.

- The establishment of an annual art competition on behalf of the Faculty of Art Education, where General school students compete for a cash prize and earn a certificate of appreciation.
- The establishment of courses and workshops to develop the skills of teachers and supervisors of art education and activating the role of art education in rehabilitation to cope with variables and requirements of the society.

It is important to work hard to support art education and return it to a central place in a comprehensive education.

Galyna P. Shevchenko

# Improving the Quality of Artistic Education through Interaction of Different Kinds of Art: The Experience of Ukraine

Interconnection of different art forms is one of the most effective ways to improve quality in arts education. Pedagogical science and practice in Ukraine have stored versatile experience of the use of this interconnection for the purpose to develop students' aesthetic attitude towards art and reality, their aesthetic feelings, aesthetic experiences, interest in different art forms, imagination, aesthetic perception and aesthetic tastes. When art education involves the integration of many types of art, artistry and aesthetics are developed. Furthermore, the interaction of different art forms is both a cultural and historic phenomenon reflecting complex processes of cultural development in human society, along with connections and relationships within human consciousness, a variety of human practice and specific regularities of artistic activity.

This paper will first explore theories of arts integration and then list specific applications found in art education pedagogy. In the paper the kinds of connections of arts according to correlation and integration types are defined; genetic, morphological and functional interconnections of different kinds of art in which organic interconnection of arts in pedagogical processes is shown are revealed; principles and types of interconnections of arts are presented.

A perfect style of art is achieved through the interconnection of different kinds of art, overcoming specific boundaries of art without destroying its specific advantages (F. Schiller). While each kind of art does have its own boundaries defined by the specifics of artistic image creation, each simultaneously possesses the opportunity to enter into other kinds of art, enriching and enlarging their imagery and figurative means with the help of direct and indirect reflection as well as straight or mediated depiction. The arts synthesis concept of R. Wagner known as "*Gesamtkunstwerk*" was introduced into science as the principle of cultural integrity. Boundaries of each kind of art are flexible due to the ability of human thinking to make associations. These associations can create the possibilities that one art form can borrow their specific means of imagery from adjacent kinds of art: the ability of music and literature to 'depict' and the ability of fine arts to 'sound, speak'.

There are particular types of connections between separate parts making the whole. The most remarkable connections are those involving *correlation* and/or *integration*. Correlative connection is a combination of art forms where one type can be easily replaced with the other one. Integrative connection is a deeper one, where each kind of art participates in interaction submitting to the whole integrity, the general idea.

Quality composition and imagery integrity unites different kinds of art into artistic synthesis. Quality distinctness is the basis of all kinds of art interaction. Interconnection of "expressiveness" and "pictorial depiction" is the basis for imaginary start of kinds of art interaction. Quality distinctness of each art, interaction of "pictorial depiction" and "expressiveness" are characteristic of artistic integrity.

Interaction of arts as universal regularity of arts culture development is realized at different levels:
- inside a separate art that is 'synesthesiality',
- between different arts and their genres,
- between arts and social existence.

Interaction of arts is stipulated by the nature of organs of sense and feeling interacting in the process of general aesthetic sensuality. Interaction of arts as an integral system that is 'the unity of diverse' excludes mechanical combination of any kinds as it is always subdued to inner artistic logic, harmony based on the unity of similar and different in the means of life depiction.

As with any integral system, interaction of arts transforms each art that interacts with some other one and forms a qualitatively new artistic integrity that has such a complex pedagogical impact on the personality that can hardly be made by any separate art. Natural interaction of arts in pedagogical process is seen in finding out and activating genetic, morphological and functional interconnection of arts.

Genetic interconnection is stipulated by the unity of arts origin, syncretism, unity of social and aesthetic essence, unity of general and specific in each art. Morphologic connections show the artistic and aesthetic construction of art itself: the essence of a piece of art, artistic image, the peculiarities of artistic depiction in different arts, the unity of contents and form.

Functional connections help teenagers to form the understanding of various functions characteristic of all arts: cognitive, educational, hedonistic, communicative, and others. The complexity of educational influences lies in functional connections of arts.

The principles of arts interaction are as follows:
- the principle of taking into consideration general and special in art;
- the principle of associative nature of artistic impact;
- the principle of interconnection of sensual and logic;
- the principle of taking into consideration the peculiarities of different arts influence on personality; and
- the principle of creative activity.

Interaction of arts will promote general cultural development only when all the arts participating in interconnection are treated as the most concentrated expression of aesthetics.

Types of interaction:
- connecting, in didactics it is identical to the notion of interdisciplinary connection;
- integrative, unites several kinds of art on the basis of qualitative compositional and imagery unity into unique artistic synthesis according to the character of its emotional and aesthetic influence;
- correlative type of interaction unites kinds of art according to the principle 'dominating – subordinate' and presupposes hierarchy of using different arts when subduing them to a particular artistic dominant;
- integrative and correlative type of interaction, when elements of both integrative and correlative connections of different kinds of art are simultaneously used in pedagogical process; and
- creatively transforming type of interaction based on versatile creative artistic and aesthetic activity of learners.

Art integrates according to several characteristics:
- stylistic commonness;
- thematic similarity;
- commonness of emotional contents and spirit;
- principle of analogy; and
- principle of contrast.

The nature of art is aesthetic. Artistic value is some kind of aesthetic value. Aesthetic relation with art is always ideological being a unique communicative interaction. It is a visible image of culture.

Teresa Torres de Eça

# Comparangoleiros: A Transnational Arts Education Project

Comparangoleiros was a transnational arts education project coordinated by the Portuguese art teachers association APECV and conducted during 2011 and 2012 in schools from Portugal, Brazil, Latvia and Timor Lorosai. The 500 participants of the project experienced collaborative and embodied learning through performances inspired in knowledge of local cultures. Through collaborative actions based on contemporary arts students from different regions of the globe they were able to acquire personal, social and cultural skills.

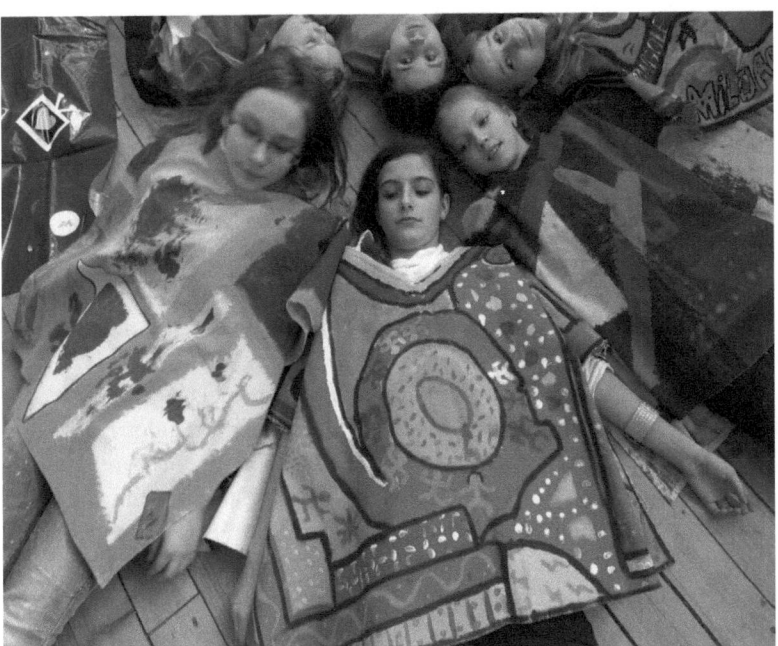

Figure 1: Students from Pardaugavas Music School in Riga, Latvia, wearing Parangolés made by students from EMEF Prestes Maia School in S. Paulo, Brazil

APECV, founded in 1988, is a Portuguese association of professionals in visual arts education. The interest of the association in developing intercultural projects is essentially centred on experimentation of new strategies for arts educators through a dialogic learning environment. APECV intercultural projects seek new strategies to promote the arts as means to integrate "Peace Education" and "Education for Sustainable Development"

Figure 2: Students and teachers from Portugal during a performance in a public space in Lisboa, wearing parangolés done by Latvian, Portuguese and Brazilian students.

through the arts in educational practices. Comparangoleiros was one of the intercultural projects promoted by APECV during the period 2009-2012.

The Comparangoleiros idea started during an intercultural project with the teachers Dace Paeglite from Latvia, Ariclaudio Francisco da Silva from S. Paulo, Brazil and teachers from APECV in Portugal. They were conducting an interchange where students aged 5-15 years old had an opportunity to learn about the work of artists from the other countries: Boris Berzins (Latvian), Angelo de Souza and Graça Morais (Portuguese) and Helio Oiticica (Brazilian). Teachers during this first experience in 2009 realised the great potential of the ideas of the artist Helio Oiticica for education, especially with his *Parangolé* series. Oiticica defined *Parangolés* as capes, flags, banners and tents made from layers of painted fabric, plastics, mats, screens, ropes and other materials. Literally habitable paintings, they were designed to be worn or carried while dancing to the rhythm of samba. The idea of habitable works of art and the possibility of using the paintings as living sculptures was soon adopted for the next interchange, and in 2010, more teachers from Brazil, Timor and Portugal joined the group. They named the project 'Comparangoleiros', referencing the Oiticica source and the concept of companionship that was inherent to the way the group was working together. Teachers used the social network Facebook page called 'Comparangoleiros', created by a Portuguese student for the project, as the main platform for sharing the experiences between participants. During 2010-2011 teachers helped students to create large paintings that were later used in group performances so the art work was not only visual but also dealt with sound and movement as a living experience. Through such living experiences students were able to express their culture in visual stories through painting and collages in the parangolés. The parangolés were inhabited in group performances exploring notions of colour, space and rhythm to create stories with the movement of their bodies. Parangolés travelled from country to country so others students could not only see but also wear and inhabit the work done by others and make new choreographies in a remix process. Teachers recorded the project in images, written reflections and video clips to be shared by the community in the Facebook group. In 2011-2012 the project gained more participants from non formal contexts and was also extended experimentally to adults in community settings.

During the evaluation of the project, teachers reported that through the project participants developed creativity and imagination, critical thinking and problem solving skills. By searching their cultures and the cultures of others they acquired knowledge in many fields. By producing the works they acquired design and visual media knowledge. By interchanging the visual works and performances and by engaging in oral and visual conversations with students from other countries they developed communication tools through collaborative work. They increased their knowledge about their own cultures so that they could explain themselves to the others and they became aware about others' cultures through the interchange of images, videos and art works. Students also acquired more awareness about their personal and social responsibilities. They acquired self-esteem in the process because their works were appreciated by students from other countries. In sum, students acquired important cognitive and meta-cognitive skills: skills for life.

# An Artist Reflects

Judith Marcuse

# An Artist's Odyssey: Adventures in Art and Education

*The Social Sciences and Humanities Research Council of Canada has recently awarded a $2.5 million grant to the Vancouver-based International Centre of Art for Social Change for a five-year research project in teaching, evaluation and capacity-building in the area of art for social change. The Centre is a partnership between Judith Marcuse Projects and Simon Fraser University and the first of its kind in North America.*

## Starting Out

There was never a decision; I always knew I'd be a dancer. Now, reflecting on over 50 years of life in the arts, I begin to understand more fully how education and opportunity, along with my own passions and hungers, have fuelled the many directions this journey has taken. Perhaps you will recognize elements of your own experience in my unpredictable odyssey; perhaps we share some of the challenges, delights and lessons learned.

I am what some people call a red diaper baby. The oldest of four children, I grew up in a Montreal middle-class household where my parents – my mother a pianist and dance accompanist and my father an engineer – were actively engaged in progressive causes. I remember listening in on lively meetings and hearing my mother typing what seemed the endless minutes of those dialogues. Family dinners consisted of food for both our bodies and minds; we discussed the news, talked about politics and social justice and I began to develop critical perspectives. I never felt that my own voice was unimportant.

There was a lot of music in our lives; we sang in the car, listened to classical music and jazz, to Pete Seeger, the Weavers and Paul Robeson and, of course, my mother on the piano in our living room. We lived with the art of Kollwitz, Orozco and Rivera on our walls. I was taken to concerts, dance performances (I have strong memories of the Kirov Ballet and the Moiseyev dancing on a stage built over the ice in the Montreal Forum hockey arena) and to what little English theatre was available in Montreal in those days. The Quebec francophone cultural/political revolution had yet to take place and we lived an entirely Anglophone existence. Throughout my childhood, I heard French only on the street and in badly-taught lessons at school. We lived a privileged and peaceful life.

In retrospect, school played a far less influential role in my early development than my life at home and in the dance studio. I started taking dance lessons at age four with my aunt, still my major teacher 20 years after her death. Elsie Salomons had trained with a Russian émigré ballet teacher and with the socially-engaged choreographer, Kurt Jooss, in England. What set her apart from most traditional teachers was that she believed in, and vigorously nurtured, the creativity of every student, children and adults alike. Every class included the challenge of collectively creating short dances with themes we chose together and with music that my mother and other accompanists improvised according to our directions. Classes were adventures in imagination; Elsie was dramatic, enthusiastic and beloved. I learned that technique was important, but not the centre of creativity, that risk was exciting and welcomed, and that group collaboration could be both challenging and fun. I also learned that making dances was different from watching but just as satisfying. By age 10, I was taking dance lessons almost every day of the week and was performing in a variety of settings in and around Montreal. As Leonard Cohen says about becoming a poet, my future as an artist was a verdict, not a decision.

In 1962, at the age of 15, I left Montreal to attend the Royal Ballet School in London. I knew that the cost of my training, even with a welcome provincial scholarship, was a stretch for my parents. Even then, I was very aware of my privilege. (I have continued to depend, in some major part, on various forms of public and private sector support throughout my whole career, and for that reason alone count myself lucky to live in Canada.)

The Royal Ballet School was a Victorian enclave in a vibrant London that was Carnaby Street, the Beatles, impenetrable smog, damp cold and chilblains, my introduction to a pervasive and visible class system and challenging food: cheap "greens" (the tops of vegetables), liver sausage and fried everything. Here, too, were the first visits of the Martha Graham and Paul Taylor dance companies, great theatre and music of all genres, fabulous museums and galleries, dance and music performances from India and Africa at the Commonwealth Institute, long Sundays wandering new parts of the city and the delights of relative independence.

In some respects, I led a double life. The rigours and hierarchies of the School, where I was a year younger than most, as well as a small fish in a very big pond, were daunting. In those days, especially in the case of the foreign students (most of us from "the colonies"), the theory was that our technique was to be broken down and reconstructed according to the aesthetics of the School.

My own creativity was set aside; many of the pure joys of moving and of personal expression were to be delayed gratifications. But my technique improved and was rewarded with opportunities to join the professionals as an extra on stage at Covent Garden where, while holding a spear or sitting at the foot of a throne, I watched some of the world's greatest dancers and opera singers perform: Fonteyn, Beriosova, Bruhn, Nureyev and many, many others. I often attended performances several nights a week, either on stage or in the audience. I ate backstage in the Covent Garden canteen with real members of the Royal Ballet – who rarely, if ever, deigned to speak with a student. I stood at the back the stalls at the Garden, smelling the perfumes of rich patrons who frequently left after the first intermission, their vacated seats a welcome respite for aching legs. What an education!

After nearly three years of diverse and very rich experiences in London and a foot injury that eventually sent me home for treatment, I had learned many lessons – about discipline, technical excellence, brutal competition, large-scale "high" art and its own internal cultures, new-form arts and their relevance (or lack of it) for the general population. I was no longer interested in joining the Royal Ballet, but knew that I needed to dance. I was 17 and getting back into shape when I received an invitation to join Les Grands Ballets Canadiens. This launched 25 years of work in repertory dance companies based in Canada, the US and in London, Europe and the Middle East.

## On the Road

I worked with dozens of diverse choreographers, some of them very inspiring and many challenging. My favourite times in the studio were in new creation periods. I performed and travelled the world, performing in an astonishing variety of settings – from an outdoor amphitheatre outside of Rangoon where we were among the first visitors to be allowed into the country in 10 years, to some of the great theatres of Europe, such as the Fenice in Venice. I saw slums in Manila, side by side with great wealth. I was warned to be careful about subjects for conversation during receptions in Ceausescu's Romania where armed soldiers stood at the sides of the stage and where all our makeup was stolen from the dressing rooms. Audiences ranged from bejewelled elites, when we became diplomatic "ambassadors", to performances for packed audiences of school children in the UK. In Seoul, Korea, after the shows and past curfew, we were escorted back to the hotel in bulletproof vehicles. A challenge on tour was to experience more of where we were, to circumvent the hotel/theatre/hotel/bus/airport routine whenever possible, but we often existed in a bubble. I began to think more about the relevance of the work I was performing for different audiences.

Working conditions varied. Early touring could be a nightmare; one truly brutal three months of one-night stands, travelling in a bus, galvanized a small group of us to piece together a 48-page basic agreement (my mother typed it!) for presentation to the local union but, at that time, we were too unimportant for them. In another company, the female dancers challenged management when we learned that the men in the company had long-received larger salaries than the women. Before long, our rights were acknowledged and we won parity. Victory was possible!

In some settings, the working conditions of dancers have improved substantially, but the profession continues to be very demanding: life is financially challenging and typically our careers are short. Why did professional sports have it so much better? I began to ask more questions about the arts and their place in our lives.

I met my husband-to-be, a social anthropologist and another Canadian, in 1971 when we were both working in Israel. At that time, one could easily travel to the Occupied Territories – which we did. But, looking back, I'm shocked to realize now that the company, a leading ensemble based in Tel Aviv, never worked with a Palestinian artist, nor did we ever perform in the Occupied Territories … and this was never questioned. How easy it is not to question. Ironically, my first "professional" choreography was a bumblebee dance for a children's program on Israel's Arabic language network.

By 1974, I decided to take a break as my husband prepared for his doctoral exams. Berkeley, California, was an exciting and vital place to be, but without a visa, I clandestinely cleaned houses, sold cosmetics door-to-door (for one week!), baked bread and took time to reflect on what was next. Six months later, now with a visa, I was back in the studio, choreographing for a large company in Oakland. The Vietnam War was still very present; I borrowed a huge Asian gong from our neighbour, an already-famous war photographer, to use as part of my first sound collage to accompany my choreography, a circus-like piece about conflict. I never saw it in performance as a call from London took me back to the UK and to the most influential company experience of my career.

Ballet Rambert, as it was called in those days (today it's simply Rambert) is the oldest dance company in England. Since its founding in 1926, it has been home to some of the world's great choreographers. Its emphasis on creation from a wide variety of contemporary choreographers and the egalitarian culture of the ensemble of 15 very strong, individualistic dancers ("a company of soloists") plus intense performing and touring schedules (often eight shows a week) were just what I needed ... and wanted.

We moved to London and it was with Rambert, after the creation of two pieces for the company, that I decided that choreography was now a necessary part of my life. The first piece for the company was about the working lives of women, inspired by Studs Terkel's book, *Working*. The second was an exploration of female archetypes and stereotypes. This was a time when feminism was yet to enter the mainstream in the UK, and some of the men in the company initially objected to performing my portrayal of male stereotypes. The women were enthusiastic from the start. It was a lesson in looking inward to our *own lives* rather than commenting on the lives of others, though I'm now sure we and the work would have profited from more dialogue about our feelings and attitudes.

Although I was offered an annual commission by Rambert, I wanted to choreograph more. I had just received a national choreographic prize in Canada. In 1976 I left Rambert, and we returned to Canada settling in Vancouver, where I began eight years of freelance work with ballet and contemporary companies, in opera, theatre, film and television – including a large-scale, multi-disciplinary production that included Ronnie Gilbert, one of the original Weavers, as one of the musicians. Back to roots!

The next 15 years, under the umbrella of our organization, Judith Marcuse Projects (JMP), saw the creation of a national/international touring repertory dance company that commissioned and presented my work and that of a wide range of other creators. We toured extensively and our programming included special participatory work for children. At that time, arts education had been severely cut across Canada and dance, particularly more contemporary forms, were often foreign languages. We created community residencies, often introducing the local arts council to the school board – an early encounter with the institutional, structural silos within which so many of us often work – and I began to talk to our audiences from the stage about the dances we performed. We produced six annual *KISS Projects*, popular month-long, multi-arts festivals that commissioned new work and brought theatre, dance and visual artists and audiences together. We were successful, but something was missing for me.

## A Change of Course

Our daughter was an about-to-be teenager and a week of performances for children in an inner city high school theatre made it clear that here was a very different youth culture from the one I had experienced. Teachers and the policeman on staff recounted stories of inter-cultural tensions and violence in the school. As an artist and mother, I found this very rich territory for exploration, and it set our organization on an exciting new trajectory of long-term, large-scale youth-centred initiatives dealing with issues that were central to the concerns of young people.

Over the next 18 years, JMP produced three of these initiatives, each over a five to six-year period. The *ICE Project* explored issues that can lead to teen suicide; the *FIRE Project* looked at how young people experience violence in their lives; the *EARTH Project* was about environmental and social justice. Each initiative involved hundreds of 15- to 18-year-old youth in several years of diverse arts workshops designed to explore their thoughts and feelings about these specific issues in their lives. The materials that came out of this process were translated into live professional dance/theatre productions that toured Canada and were adapted for network television and classroom use, along with youth-created support materials, post-show facilitated dialogues and partnerships with social service and educational institutions across the country. We performed in mall atria after shopping hours, in theatres and in arenas.

We worked hard to respect and nurture the voices of the young participants who were hungry to share their stories, often surprised that others were truly interested. Different forms of dialogue were integrated into virtually every aspect of our work on these projects. Public reaction was positive and sometimes overwhelming, for example, when we received emails from youth informing us that seeing the *ICE: beyond cool* production kept them from attempting suicide. Despite the huge challenges of funding these projects, we knew they were important and effective. I learned to "read the room" in a much deeper way and was often stunned by the power of the images and words created by our young participants, as well as by the depth of dialogue enabled by these metaphors.

The larger worlds of art for social change had opened up; I relied on the collaboration of more experienced community-based artists as I further developed my own methodologies. My activist background and artistic practice had come together in new ways.

One thing I soon realized was that people doing work like ours rarely connected with each other. We convened two international large-scale gatherings, the first, a UNESCO-sponsored five-day event during which 300 young activists and community-based artists from 26 countries shared their work and the second, a multi-faceted international arts festival that attracted 20,000 visitors during the United Nations Environmental Program's *World Urban Forum* held in Vancouver. We produced a research document of 48 case studies and analyses of organizations doing these forms of socially-engaged work. (This study, *Toward Training: The Meanings and Practices of Social Change Work in the Arts*, written by Dr. Yael Harlip, is available, along with much additional material, on our website at www.icasc.ca.) I learned how different forms of arts practice were implemented in all kinds of change agendas around the world. The field was growing at a huge rate, but was (and still is) largely under the radar.

An honorary doctorate (I am a high school dropout with a few "O" levels), brought me into contact with Vancouver's Simon Fraser University (SFU). I began to teach about the work I called art for social change (ASC) in academic and community settings, developing hands-on experiential learning approaches as an essential part of the curricula, often bringing community-based, non-credit learners together with for-credit students. Working with colleagues, I developed new pedagogical, dialogic and other communications/facilitation skills.

I learned about how others were doing community-engaged activist work in Canada and began to travel around the globe, teaching, speaking, consulting and watching others working *in situ* to better understand their approaches – in Pakistan and India, Japan and Senegal, from The Hague and Helsinki to California and Ecuador. The variety and excellence of much of this work, often in very challenging contexts, was, and continues to be, energizing and inspiring.

In 2008, with colleagues at SFU, and in partnership with Judith Marcuse Projects, we created the International Centre of Art for Social Change. ICASC is designed to nurture ASC in Canada and abroad by providing an array of resources, including research, learning opportunities, events and networking. The Centre continues to develop its initiatives, the most recent, a major, five-year national study on art for social change, the first of its kind in Canada.

## Some Reflections on ASC

I like the term "art for social change" because it implies *action* for change, but there are many names for the diverse forms of community-engaged arts practices taking place around the world, each with its own nuanced meaning, goals and methods. Despite the range of approaches, many of us share basic principles; one of the most important is the notion that *we are all the experts of our own lives and that, once inside these art-making spaces, we have equal voice.* Making art together becomes a form of cultural democracy in which dialogue, rooted in the use of metaphor, can produce new ideas and energy for positive change.

Storytelling, theatre, movement, music, visual and other art forms enable us to question relationships between personal and public realities. In this process, the artist/facilitator becomes a catalyst, in service to the process and people involved in arts-based exploration. Facilitated, collective art-making can reveal deep and nuanced truths for participants, while also providing opportunities for dialogue across silos of difference. Partnerships with organizations in a wide variety of sectors increase the work's impact and sustainability. These engaged forms create new understanding, knowledge and empathy, reducing isolation, and nurturing, as the writer and arts-activist Arlene Goldbard puts it, a "culture of possibility." We can investigate the lives we lead and work more effectively for the changes we want to make.

Over and over, I have seen the remarkable transformation of thought and feeling that happens, often very quickly, when head, heart and hands get the chance to speak, to connect with each other. Of course, as a dance person, I am most enthralled with practices that engage our bodies.

Education – the teaching and learning of specific skills and approaches – is essential if the work is to be ethical, safe and effective. Expertise in facilitation and other communication skills are central, as is the capacity to create partnerships between artists and non-arts organizations. Evaluation of the work's impact (how does one measure a smile?) is a major issue worldwide. Documentation provides important resources for others. I also believe that experiential learning – working alongside professional artists – is one of the best ways for individuals to gain a deeper understanding of these multi-layered processes.

We now see ASC work in an extraordinary range of sectors around the world: in health promotion and policy creation, medical training, environmental policy creation, education and advocacy, in work for human and economic rights, within justice systems, in conflict mediation, support work with immigrant populations, youth and elders, as expressions/translations of research results … to name just a few. Often, the *process* of art-making is more important than the product that is created. And not all of this work is directly issue-based – the work can be a celebration of a community's history or a teenager's story simply about what it's like to be *me*.

Culture is at the heart of how we perceive ourselves and the world around us – and most art forms can potentially lead to social change. Many of us, however, live in a vortex of corporate, profit-driven culture where art is consumed, not made. Our own stories often go unexpressed and unheard; even in places where traditional culture survives, it is often under siege. (In terms of international law, the passing of UNESCO's Convention on the Protection and Promotion of the Diversity of Cultural Expression was a positive step in the right direction, as was the non-binding Universal Declaration on Cultural Diversity.)

As we begin to realize the limits of technology to solve complex and urgent issues, values-based, creative and candid "conversations" within and across ideological, professional and cultural silos become essential. ASC provides rich contexts for unorthodox forms of dialogue, while also providing opportunities for sustainable collaboration. Innovation becomes more effective when the right brain is engaged!

In some settings, arts and academic communities have created a hierarchy of values in the arts, viewing community-based change work and arts education as somehow less important than "pure" art creation. There are lingering debates about the legitimacy of the arts as instrumental vehicles, as opposed to their significance as an organic part of an arts ecology in which each form, each approach, is equally valid and able to nurture the whole. I see this segmentation largely as a consequence of limited support for arts and cultural practices and argue for a "wide shot" of our ecology rather than a narrow, close-up view that emphasizes a narrow, sometimes rigid, definition of artistic excellence.

## The New Five-Year ASC! Research Project, Supported by the Social Sciences and Humanities Research Council of Canada

Our premise is that there are two major forms of ASC:
1. art that is made by artists wherein social commentary is embedded in their creations; and
2. art that is made by groups of people, facilitated by an artist or group of artists.

Our research explores the second of these forms. The team assembled for this work is composed of artists, scholars and research assistants based in six Canadian universities who are working collaboratively with 15 partnering community-based organizations. Divided into research "pods", the work has three main, interconnected focuses:
1. teaching and learning in community and educational settings;
2. evaluation of ASC work; and
3. building capacity for partnerships in both the private and public sectors.

We plan to nurture the development of networks and knowledge-exchange as well as provide accessible and useful resources for the field. We will host virtual and in-person events, create and examine field studies across the country, offer a moveable Summer Institute and support a new cohort of scholars and artist/practitioners. At the end of the five years, we intend to deliver Canada's first open source, online ASC textbook. It's an ambitious agenda!

## Linking the Past with the Present

It has been a circuitous and unpredictable journey, but one that, perhaps, has a certain inherent logic. As I look back, it becomes clear that much of what I have learned was through the wisdom and generosity of others. Curiosity, restlessness and a profound belief in the transformative power of the arts have propelled me into unknown territories. Privilege, including opportunities to make choices, has helped make this possible. The odyssey continues. Where will this new process of collaborative and creative exploration lead? My one certainty is that our collective, creative energy has the capacity to change the world.

## Contributors

*Anne Bamford* is Director of the Education Commission and Director of the International Research Agency and Director of the Education Commission. Anne has been recognized nationally and internationally for her research in arts education, emerging literacies and visual communication. She is an expert in the international dimension of arts and cultural education and through her research, she has pursued issues of innovation, social impact and equity and diversity. A world scholar for UNESCO, Anne has conducted major national impact and evaluation studies for the governments of Denmark, The Netherlands, Belgium, Iceland, Hong Kong, Ireland and Norway. Amongst her numerous articles and book chapters, Anne is author of the "Wow Factor: Global research compendium on the impact of the arts in education" which has been published in five languages and distributed in more than 40 countries. Anne is a former Professor at the University of the Arts London and a Professor at St Mary's University College, London and the Institute of Education, Hong Kong.

*Ralph Buck*, Head of Dance Studies, University of Auckland has been recognised with several teaching and leadership awards. His research and teaching has been presented around the world and in leading research journals and books. His work with the World Alliance for Arts Education and UNESCO draws attention to potential roles of dance as a dynamic agent for change within security, health and education concerns. r.buck@auckland.ac.nz

*Lily Chen-Hafteck*, Ph.D. is currently a professor of music education at University of California, Los Angeles (UCLA), USA. Before that, she has worked at Kean University, NJ, USA, University of Pretoria, South Africa, University of Surrey Roehampton, U.K. and Hong Kong Baptist University, Hong Kong. Her research interests include early childhood music and multicultural music education. She is the founder and director of the *Educating the Creative Mind* project, funded by National Endowment for the Arts; and a co-investigator of *Advancing Interdisciplinary Research in Singing* (AIRS) project, funded by the Social Sciences and Humanities Research Council (SSHRC) of Canada.

*Cynthia Cohen* is Director of the program Peacebuilding and the Arts at Brandeis University, where she leads action/reflection research projects, and writes and teaches about work at the nexus of the arts, culture, justice and peace. She directed the Brandeis/Theatre Without Borders collaboration "Acting Together on the World Stage", co-edited the Acting Together anthologies and co-created the documentary and toolkit (www.actingtogether.org). She directs ReCAST, Inc., a non-profit organization partnering with Brandeis and New Village Press on the dissemination of Acting Together resources. Dr. Cohen has written extensively on the aesthetic and ethical dimensions of peacebuilding. In addition, Dr. Cohen has worked as a dialogue facilitator, with communities in the Middle East, Sri Lanka, Central America and the United States. Prior to her tenure at Brandeis, she directed a community-based, anti-racist oral history center in the Boston area.

*Andrea Creech* is Reader in Education at the Institute of Education, London, where she leads a programme of professional training for Conservatoire teachers. Following an international orchestral career Andrea was director of a Community Music School, developing programmes for learners of all ages. Since completing her PhD in Psychology in Music Education (focusing on interpersonal dynamics in teaching and learning), Andrea has led several funded research projects relating to musical engagement across the lifespan. Andrea has presented at international conferences and published widely on issues relating to musical development and music education across the lifespan.

*Mousumi De* is an independent artist and researcher, working with visual arts, media and new media for peacebuilding, peace education, conflict transformation and social development projects in India and other countries. She is an Associate Instructor at Indiana University, Bloomington, USA, teaching pre-service elementary and generalist teachers and completing a PhD in Curriculum and Instruction that explores emotional and social development through the arts. She is co-founder of the Asian Society for Education through the Arts and Media (India), Honorary Research Fellow with Indian Institute of Sustainable Development (IISD), New Delhi, and Editor of Newsletter for International Society for Education through Art (InSEA).

*Wolfgang Dietrich* holds the UNESCO Chair for Peace Studies at the University of Innsbruck/Austria. He is program director of the MA Program for Peace, Development, Security and International Conflict Transformation at the same University. He is member of the Austrian UNESCO Commission. His more than 200 academic writings have been published in many languages. He has taught in departments for peace and conflict studies, political science, history, arts and law at universities all over the world. He holds Doctorates in History, Literature and Law and is promoted to the degree of "Universitätsdozent" in Political Science.

*Teresa Torres de Eça* is President of the Portuguese Art Teachers Association APECV and Vice President of the International Society for Education Through Art – InSEA. Currently she collaborates with the Research Institute in Art, Design and Society, FBAUP, Porto, Portugal. She earned her Ph.D. at the University of Surrey-Roehampton, UK (2004), a Master in Art Craft and Design Education at University of Surrey-Roehampton, UK (1999), and Bachelor of Fine Arts degree from Fine Arts School in University of Porto, Portugal (1985).

*Samia ElSheikh* is a Professor of Art Education, teaching hand weaving at the Faculty of Art Education, Helwan University, Egypt. She received her Ph.D. through a channel program between University of Helwan and New York in 1993. She is a member in national and international organizations and her research interests have spanned in-service arts education and fiber arts issues. She has been showing her art works in solo and group exhibitions. She participated in many conferences. She helped with the launching of "AmSea" Africa & Middle East organization for Education through Arts in Cairo.

*Eugène van Erven* is Senior Lecturer in Theatre at Utrecht University, where he teaches community art and coordinates the Creative Cities Minor. He holds a Ph.D. in Comparative Literature from Vanderbilt University in the US (1985). Besides his academic work he is also professionally active in the cultural field as artistic director of the International Community Arts Festival (ICAF) in Rotterdam. He is the author of many peer reviewed articles and the following books: *Radical People's Theatre* (Indiana University Press 1988), *The Playful Revolution: Theatre and Liberation in Asia* (Indiana 1992), *Community Theatre: Global Perspectives* (Routledge 2001, including a companion video), and *Community Arts Dialogues* (Treaty of Utrecht 2013, including a companion video). He also serves on the editorial board of *Research in Drama Education*.

*Naomi Faik-Simet* is a dance researcher with the Institute of Papua New Guinea Studies. Her research focuses on dance education which investigates the processes of the transmission of cultural knowledge in indigenous Papua New Guinean performances. She has worked with a number of schools in the country promoting cultural education through dance. Her present work includes the development of the arts syllabus with a focus on the implementation of dance as a subject of knowledge in schools.

*Tatiana Fedorova*, Head of the Department of Expert and Analytical Resources on Cultural Policy, Culture and Arts Studies, InformKultura Research and Information Centre of the Russian State Library. She took part in the exercise of complying the National Reports on Cultural Policy in the Russian Federation (1996, 2013), the analytical report "Arts Education in the Russian Federation: Building Creative Capacities in the 21st Century"; since 2001 she contributes to the Russian profile of the "Compendium of Cultur-

al Policies and Trends in Europe", which is the joint Council of Europe/ERICarts online project.

*Sergio Figueiredo* (Bachelor in Conducting and Composition; Master and Ph.D. in Music Education) is Associate Professor at the Music Department of the State University of *Santa Catarina*, UDESC, Brazil. His research interests include school music education, foundations of music education, initial and continuing teacher education, educational policies and choral music education. He was president of the Brazilian Association of Music Education – ABEM, between 2005 and 2009. Currently he is a member of the Directory of ANPPOM – The Brazilian Association for Research in Music; co-chair of the ISME Research Commission (2012-2014) and a member of the ISME Board (2012-2014).

*Thalia R. Goldstein* is an Assistant Professor of Psychology at Pace University in New York City. Her research interests lie at the intersection of social cognition and imagination. She studies how actors participate in and create fictional worlds onstage, the effects of role play and pretend play on social cognitive abilities, and how young children understand and react to watching fictional worlds. Her work has been supported by The John Templeton Foundation, NSF, APF, and the DHS and she has won awards from SRCD, APA Division 10, and IGEL. Thalia earned her B.A. from Cornell University in Theatre and Psychology, her Ph.D. from Boston College and completed a postdoctoral fellowship at Yale University. She spent several years as a professional actress and dancer in New York City.

*Patricia A. González-Moreno* is Professor of Music Education at the Faculty of Arts, Autonomous University of Chihuahua, Mexico, where she teaches courses in music, music education, educational psychology, and art philosophy. Her research interests include music psychology, music teacher education, and professional development in music and the arts. Before earning her Ph.D. in Music Education from the University of Illinois, she taught general music in basic education for seven years. She is a Board Member of the International Society for Music Education and chair of the ISME Advocacy Standing Committee (2012-2014).

*Peter Harris* is head of Educational and Community Theatre at Western Galilee academic college and a lecturer at Tel Aviv University Theatre Arts department. Harris is also a theatre director and CBT practitioner. He has set up and run innovative applied theatre projects in Israel and has conducted a variety of workshops globally including: USA, Thailand, Philippines, Singapore, Australia and Taiwan. Present research focuses on the potential of the dramatic space for advancing dialogue and understanding in a "multi-vocal" society improving "re-entry" into society of offenders, substance abusers and street women.

*Benedicte Helvad* has been head of the secretariat of The Network for Children and Culture. The network is the advisory body for the Minister and the Ministry of Culture in Denmark. Benedicte is a fully qualified educator, has been nursery school head and teacher of nursery school heads. She has worked as an education consultant and consultant for the politicians in the municipalities. She has been elected chairman of the union of education consultants and later senior advisor in the Danish Agency of Culture.

*Barend van Heusden* holds the chair of Culture and Cognition, with special reference to the Arts, in the Department of Arts, Culture and Media Studies at the University of Groningen in the Netherlands. He has published articles and books in the fields of literary and culture theory, semiotics and cognition, as well as arts and culture education. Since 2009, he supervises the national project 'Culture in the Mirror: toward a curriculum for culture education'. In this project, culture education is approached from a cognitive-semiotic perspective. A framework is developed that allows schools and teachers to design a culture curriculum tailored to the pupils' development and culture. Personal homepage: http://www.rug.nl/staff/b.p.van.heusden/index; homepage of the 'Culture in the Mirror'-project: http://www.cultuurindespiegel.nl

*Yeon-hee Jung* is a director general of Korea Arts & Culture Education Service (KACES). Formerly a secondary visual arts school teacher, she waged a movement on arts education advocacy until 2005, and obtained her Ph.D. at Korea National University of Education in 2007. She had planned the 2nd UNESCO World Conference on Arts Education (Seoul, Korea, 2010) and coordinated the academic programs, and particularly played an important role in preparing the "Seoul Agenda: Goals for the Development of Arts Education". Her research interests include practical competences to promote social values of arts and cultural education and cultural policies. She has published in the Art Education Research Review, Korean Society for Education through Art and other arts-related journals. Her recent dissertation topics are: "Expansions of Sustainable Thinking through Arts Education, 2011" and "Revisiting the Legitimacy of Arts and Cultural Education Policy, 2013".

*Susanne Keuchel* is Director of Remscheid academy for arts education. Before that she was Executive Director of the Centre for Cultural Research. She was trained in musicology (major), German studies and sociology at the University of Bonn and the Berlin University of Technology. She is honorary professor at the Institute of Cultural Policy of Hildesheim University and lecturer at the Hamburg Academy of Music and Drama.

# Contributors

*Ann Kipling Brown*, Ph.D. is Associate Professor Emerita of the University of Regina, Canada. She works extensively in dance and dance education with children, youth and adults and leads classes in technique, composition, and notation. Her research and publications focus on dance pedagogy, the integration of notation in dance programs, the application of technology in dance education, and the role of dance in the child's and adult's lived world.

*Jan Jaap Knol* (1963) directs the Fund for Cultural Participation, based in Utrecht, the Netherlands (www.cultuurparticipatie.nl). As its name implies, the Fund promotes participation in culture, especially by encouraging people to engage in the arts and culture themselves. Cultural Education is a high priority for the Fund. Jan Jaap Knol studied Dutch Language and Literature at Rijksuniversiteit Groningen. Previously he worked as Head of the Program Culture and School of the Dutch Ministry of Education and Culture.

*Susan R. Koff* is a clinical associate professor and director of the Dance Education Program in the Steinhardt School at New York University. She previously was at Teachers College, Columbia University, Louisiana State University in Baton Rouge, University of Denver, Pennsylvania State University, and the Jerusalem Rubin Academy of Music and Dance in Israel. Dr. Koff's academic and service activities are in the area of dance education, within the United States and in an international arena. She currently serves as the secretary of the board for Dance and the Child International (daCi).

*Fianne Konings* is an independent researcher, doing her Ph.D.-research at the University of Groningen (department of Arts, Culture and Media). Her Ph.D.-research under supervision of Barend van Heusden is about the contribution of cultural institutions to a curriculum for cultural education. Konings graduated as a primary school teacher and has a master in Art and Culture Studies (Erasmus University Rotterdam). She was a schoolteacher and worked as educator in cultural institutions. Currently she also teaches art education at the Master of Education in Arts of ArtEZ Institute of the Arts. Personal homepage: www.bureaukoningskunst.nl

*Samuel Leong* (Ph.D.) is Associate Dean, Faculty of Liberal Arts and Social Sciences and Head of Department of Cultural and Creative Arts at the Hong Kong Institute of Education. He is also Director of UNESCO Observatory for Research in Local Cultures and Creativity in Education.

Contributors | 239

*Eckart Liebau*, 1967–1974 academic studies of pedagogy, sociology, political science and history at Goettingen and Munich. 1974–1987 diverse scientific pedagogical projects (Universities of Goettingen, Kassel, Hamburg, Tuebingen). 1979 promotion/doctorate (Goettingen) in pedagogy. 1987 habilitation/state doctorate (Hamburg) in Pedagogy. 1988–1992 Heisenberg-Scholarship of the DFG (Award of the German Research Foundation) (University of Tuebingen). 1992 chair of pedagogy at the Institute of Education, University of Erlangen-Nuremberg. 2010 UNESCO-Chair in Arts and Culture in Education, University of Erlangen-Nuremberg. 2013 Chairman of the Council for Cultural Education (initiated by Stiftung Mercator, in cooperation with six German foundations).

*John Lievens* is associate professor at the Department of Sociology of Ghent University (Belgium). He teaches several courses in statistics and demography. His research focuses on culture and art participation/consumption, amateur art participation, perception of culture, lifestyles, sexual behavior, and partner choice in ethnic minorities.

*Christian Manhart*, art historian and archaeologist. Joined UNESCO in 1987 and worked for the conservation of heritage sites, in Africa later in Asia, in particular in Afghanistan. For several years responsible for partnerships and communication of the World Heritage Centre. Later he was in charge of the international conventions for the protection of cultural heritage in the event of armed conflict, the underwater heritage, the fight against illicit traffic of cultural property and its restitution. At present he is responsible for the UNESCO programmes for museums and creativity, including arts education.

*Judith Marcuse*, LL.D. (Hon.). Judith Marcuse's career spans over 40 years of professional work as a dancer, choreographer, director, producer, teacher, writer, consultant and lecturer in Canada and abroad. She has created over 100 original works for live performance by dance, theatre and opera companies as well as for film and television and has produced seven large-scale, international arts festivals. Her repertory contemporary dance company toured extensively in Canada and abroad for 15 years, while also producing community residencies and programs designed for youth. Among many initiatives, her youth-focused, five-year, issue-based *ICE*, *FIRE* and *EARTH* projects involved thousands of youth in workshops, national touring, television production and community collaborations. Founder and Co-Director of the International Centre of Art for Social Change (www.icasc.ca), a partnership with Simon Fraser University, she is a Senior Fellow of Ashoka International. Among many honours, she has received the Lee and Chalmers Canadian choreographic awards and an honorary doctorate. She is an Adjunct Professor and Artist in Residence at Vancouver's Simon Fraser University and is leading the *ASC! Project*, a five-year SSHRC-funded national research initiative on art for social change.

*Jeff Meiners* works at the University of South Australia. He has taught extensively in schools, universities, as leader of a dance education team in London, and with Ausdance to support dance development. Jeff works with the National Advocates for Arts Education, government and education departments plus overseas projects and as movement director for children's theatre. Jeff was the Australia Council Dance Board's Community Representative (2002-2007), 2009 Australian Dance Award winner for Outstanding Services to Dance Education and dance writer for the new Australian national curriculum's Arts Shape paper. Jeff's doctoral research focuses on dance in the primary school curriculum.

*Gerd Michelsen*, Prof. Dr., born 1948, he studied economics in Freiburg i.Br. (Germany); Ph.D. in economics and 'venia legendi' in adult education. From June 1995 to October 2013 Professor for Ecology, esp. Sustainability and Environmental Communication at Leuphana University Lüneburg, Institute for Sustainability and Environmental Communication; since November 2014 Senior-Professor for Sustainability Science. 1998 B.A.U.M. Scientific Award; UNESCO Chair "Higher Education for Sustainable Development"; member of the German National Committee "World Decade for Education for Sustainable Development"; research and publications in (higher) education for sustainable development, sustainability and environmental communication, sustainable consumption.

*Liubava Moreva*, Program Specialist for Culture at the UNESCO Office in Moscow for Armenia, Azerbaijan, Belarus, the Republic of Moldova and the Russian Federation (since May 2004 until present); Professor of Philosophy (Ph.D. in Philosophy and Cultural studies). Before joining UNESCO she acted as the Director of the St. Petersburg Branch of the Russian Institute for Cultural Research (1997-2004); Founder and Honorary Professor of the UNESCO Chair on Comparative Studies of Spiritual Traditions, their Specific Cultures and Interreligious Dialogue; Founder and Editor-in-Chief of the transdisciplinary journal «International Readings on Theory, History and Philosophy of Culture» (1993-2004); Academic Director of the Philosophical and Cultural Research Center «EIDOS» at the St. Petersburg Association of Scientists and Scholars (1991-2004). Her primary areas of research include Philosophy of Culture and Arts, Religious Studies, Hermeneutics and Phenomenology.

*Charlotte Svendler Nielsen*, Ph.D., assistant professor, University of Copenhagen. Research focuses on embodiment of learning and teaching and teaching areas are dance and educational science of movement. 2013-2014 contracted as researcher for the Danish Ministry of Education's research project "Learning in Movement". Co-editor of *Dance Education around the World* (Routledge, forthcoming 2015) and of the *Nordic Journal of Dance*. Executive board member (research officer) of Dance and the Child International (daCi), chair of the research committee of the daCi & World Dance Alliance Global Summit 2012 and program chair of daCi 2015 to be held in Copenhagen.

*Mai Abdul monem Atta Nour*, Associate professor of Curricula and methods of teaching art education at the faculty of art education, Helwan University. 2001: Ph.D. titled "Designing a program to discover and nurturing talented students in visual arts in Egypt". 2011: Head of measurement and evaluation unit of the Faculty of Art Education. 2008/2009: Participated with others to design the levels of standard content of art education, National Authority to ensure the quality of education and accreditation.

*Larry O'Farrell* is Professor Emeritus and holder of the UNESCO Chair in Arts and Learning, Faculty of Education, Queen's University, Canada. He is Chair, Board of Directors, Canadian Network for Arts and Learning and Chair, Steering Committee, International Network for Research in Arts Education. Larry served two terms as President of the International Drama/Theatre and Education Association (IDEA). As a member of the international advisory committee and General Rapporteur for the 2nd UNESCO World Conference on Arts Education (Seoul, Korea, 2010) he was instrumental in preparing *The Seoul Agenda: Goals for the Development of Arts Education*. His research includes participation in international studies on creativity in drama/theatre and arts education, singing, and monitoring the Seoul Agenda. Larry is Honorary Professor at the Hong Kong Institute of Education. In 2011 he received the Campton Bell Lifetime Achievement Award presented by the American Alliance for Theatre and Education.

*Susan O'Neill* is Associate Professor in the Faculty of Education at Simon Fraser University and Director of MODAL Research Group. She is Senior Editor of the Canadian Music Educators' Biennial Book Series, *Research to Practice*. She has been a Visiting Fellow at the University of Michigan, USA (2001-2003) and the University of Melbourne (2012). Her international collaborative projects explore young people's musical and artistic engagement in ways that contribute to expansive and equitable learning opportunities, positive values, self-identities, motivation, wellbeing, intergenerational learning relationships and intercultural understandings.

*Vedat Özsoy* is a Professor of Art Education and the Dean of Faculty of Fine Arts, Design and Architecture at the TOBB University of Economics and Technology, Ankara, Turkey. He is founder of the Turkish Visual Arts Education Association (GÖRSED). He is InSEA World Councilor (2008-2014). He organized InSEA 7th European Regional Congress 2004, in Istanbul. His research involves qualitative inquiries in art and design education, art teacher education, curriculum studies and museum education. He participated in 15 Painting Exhibitions. His 31 articles and 3 books have been published. He is the editor of 4 books.

*Robin Pascoe* is Senior Lecturer in Arts and Drama Education, School of Education, Murdoch University, Perth, Western Australia. He teaches curriculum units on Arts Education in Primary schools and Teaching Drama in Secondary Schools and is Academic Chair of Secondary courses. Before joining the University, Robin held a range of curriculum positions in Western Australia including Superintendent for the Arts. He was writer of the Arts in the Western Australian *Curriculum Framework* (1998). Robin was a co-director of the Australian Government National Review of School Music (2005) and a team member of the National Review of Visual Education (2006). Robin was an advisor and writer for the Australian Curriculum, Assessment and Reporting Authority (ACARA) developing the *Australian Curriculum: The Arts* (2009-2014). Robin is the President of IDEA, the International Drama/Theatre and Education Association, and a former President of Drama Australia.

*Nicole Pereira* has recently completed her Bachelor of Dance Studies Honours degree and is currently a Ph.D. student in dance at The University of Auckland. Nicole has won several academic scholarships, performed at international and national dance festivals and taught workshops in various international forums. Nicole's recent research has included investigating the links between global and local Arts Education policies. Additional research projects include approaches to dance education in tertiary dance courses. Nicole is passionate about community dance and dance education and endeavors to continue her research in this field.

*Matt Qvortrup* is a Senior Lecturer at Cranfield University and a visiting fellow at Kings College London. The winner of the Political Studies Association (PSA) Award 2013 he has published extensively in the fields of philosophy and political science. His most recent book is *Referendums and Ethnic Conflict* (University of Pennsylvania Press, 2014).

*Nicholas Rowe* holds a Ph.D. in Dance Studies from the University of Kent at Canterbury, and is currently an Associate Professor in Dance Studies at the University of Auckland. His books include *Art, During Siege* (2004), *Raising Dust: a cultural history of dance in Palestine* (2010), and *Talking Dance: contemporary histories from the Southern Mediterranean* (2014).

*Diederik Schönau*, psychologist and art historian, works at Cito, the Dutch institute for educational measurement since 1981. He is currently senior consultant at Cito International. He has been Professor of Arts Education at ArtEZ Institute for the Arts in Zwolle (2007-2010) and President of InSEA (1999-2002). He has published extensively in national and international journals on issues in art education. His main interests are in student developmental self-assessment in the arts, and in issues related to the psychological function of art in education.
E-mail: dwschonau@gmail.com; LinkedIn: nl.linkedin.com/pub/diederik-schönau/b/b1b/4b6

Contributors | 243

*Shifra Schonmann* is Professor Emerita, holder of the Bar-Netzer Chair of Education and Society at the University of Haifa, Israel. Her areas of research are aesthetics, theatre/drama education, and theatre for young people, curriculum, and teacher education. She has published numerous articles and books, has been a visiting professor at leading universities and an invited speaker in international conferences.

*Galyna Shevchenko* is head of the UNESCO Chair "Spiritual Cultural Values of Upbringing and Education", director of the Scientific Research Institute of Spiritual Development of Man, head of the Chair of Pedagogics, corresponding member of the National Academy of Pedagogical Sciences of Ukraine, doctor of Pedagogical Sciences, professor, honorable professor of the Volodymyr Dahl East-Ukrainian National University, honored science and technique worker of Ukraine and member of the National Committee of Ukraine in the line of UNESCO. Present research focuses on arts education, the problem of spirituality of a personality, interaction of kinds of art, aesthetics education of youth by means of complex of arts.

*Dr. Jessy Siongers* (1972) is affiliated with the Research group CuDOS and is coordinator of the Cultural Policy Research Centre at the Department of Sociology of Ghent University. Her main research interests are situated within the domains of cultural sociology, sociology of education and sociology of youth. In the past she conducted research and published on the cultural preferences and values of adolescents, cultural participation, the link between cultural preferences and social attitudes, amateur arts, values education, cultural education and cultural profiles of teachers.

*Dries Vanherwegen* (1985) holds a Master's Degree in Sociology of Culture and Education (KULeuven) and works at Ghent University since 2008. He is currently working as a researcher at the Cultural Policy Research Centre related to the research group CuDOS at the Sociology Department. His research focuses on active arts participation, cultural capital, social reproduction and cultural mobility, and art education. He is currently finalizing a Ph.D. on inequalities in participation in art education, the role of school characteristics, and the effects of art education on cultural participation, cultural perceptions and school performance.

*Lode Vermeersch* is a senior research associate at *HIVA – Research Institute for Work and Society*, a multidisciplinary research institute associated with the University of Leuven (KU Leuven, Belgium). Lode is also a senior research associate at the Department of Educational Sciences at the university of Brussels (Vrije Universiteit Brussel, Belgium). Lode holds a master's degree in Educational Sciences and an advanced mas-

ter's degree in Cultural Studies. His research interests lie in the field of arts and cultural education, (visual) literacy, low literacy, cultural policies and lifelong learning.

*Stéphan Vincent-Lancrin* is a Senior Analyst and Project Leader at the Organisation for Economic Co-operation and Development (OECD), Directorate for Education and Skills. His current interests cover: the nature and level of education and skills that matter in innovation and knowledge societies; the innovation ecology in the education sector; the measurement of innovation in education. His interest in arts education relates to his research on the impact of various curricula and pedagogies on individual skills. Stéphan also works extensively on higher education, covering many dimensions (internationalisation and trade in higher education, the role of technology, the impact of different pedagogies, research, equity, etc.). He has authored many articles and book chapters and edited several books. His most recent book, co-authored with Ellen Winner and Thalia Goldstein, is *Art for Art's Sake. The impact of arts education* (OECD Publishing).

*Ernst Wagner* studied visual arts at the Academy of Fine Arts Munich, exhibited works of art in Germany and the United States, worked as a teacher for visual arts, studied art history and philosophy at the University of Munich, graduated with a Ph.D. in art history. Currently employed at the Institute for School Quality and Research in Education in Munich (since 2006) and at the UNESCO-Chair in Arts and Culture in Education at the University of Erlangen-Nuremberg as a lecturer and executive coordinator (since 2008).

*Michael Wimmer* was Director of the Austrian Culture Service from 1987–2003 and is director of EDUCULT – Institute for Cultural Policy and Cultural Management since 2003. He is lecturer on cultural policy issues at the University of Vienna and University of Applied Arts and adviser for the Austrian Minister for Education, Arts and Culture, the Council of Europe, UNESCO, the European Commission and the European Parliament.

© www.lukasbeck.com

*Ellen Winner* is Professor and Chair of Psychology at Boston College, and Senior Research Associate at Project Zero, Harvard Graduate School of Education. She directs the Arts and Mind Lab, which focuses on cognition in the arts in typical and gifted children. She is the author of over 100 articles and four books: Invented Worlds: The Psychology of the Arts, The Point of Words: Children's Understanding of Metaphor and Irony, Gifted Children: Myths and Realities, and co-author of Studio Thinking: The Real Benefits of Visual Arts Education.